Jesus and the Demise of Death

Resurrection, Afterlife,
and the Fate of the Christian

Matthew Levering

BAYLOR UNIVERSITY PRESS

© 2012 by Baylor University Press
Waco, Texas 76798-7363

Scripture quotations are from the New Revised Standard Version Bible Catholic Edition, copyright 1965, published by Thomas Nelson Publishers. Used by permission. All rights reserved.

Cover Design by Dean Bornstein
Cover Image: "The Resurrection," c.1380 (tempera on panel) by Master of the Trebon Altarpiece (fl.1380). Narodni Galerie, Prague, Czech Republic/ Giraudon/ The Bridgeman Art Library

Library of Congress Cataloging-in-Publication Data

Levering, Matthew, 1971-
  Jesus and the demise of death : resurrection, afterlife, and the fate of the Christian / Matthew Levering.
  238 p. cm.
  Includes bibliographical references (p. 193) and index.
  ISBN 978-1-60258-447-1 (pbk. : alk. paper)
  1. Eschatology. 2. Catholic Church--Doctrines. I. Title.
  BT821.3.L48 2012
  236--dc23
                                    2011032295

BAYLOR
UNIVERSITY

Printed in the United States of America on acid-free paper with a minimum of 30% PCW recycled content.

Jesus and the Demise of Death

Given the uncertainty of which we are so certain concerning eternity, perhaps only a post-postmodern turn can save us from being overwhelmed by our impending doom, our terminal temporality.

—Carlos Eire, *A Very Brief History of Eternity*

To Ralph and Patty Levering

Contents

Acknowledgments

 ⌒·⌒

Like many people, I have often wondered what there is for me and my loved ones after death: what happens to us? Should even a theologian preserve a discreet silence? As Christians, however, we have much to hope for and much reason for hope. Holding "fast the word of life" (Phil 2:12), I wish to speak about this hope through Scripture and through the doctrinal and theological tradition of the Church, which benefited from Greek philosophical culture.

Many wonderful people helped me with this project. As will be clear in the pages that follow, I owe a special debt to N. T. Wright, without, however, ever having conversed with him. Although at times I disagree with him, I do so from a position of broad agreement with and strong admiration for what he has contributed to biblical studies. When the Dominicans of the Aquinas Institute of Theology in St. Louis invited me to deliver their Aquinas Lecture in January 2010, I presented an early draft of chapter 1. The Dominican community in St. Louis showed me gracious hospitality, and I owe particular thanks to Dominic Holtz, O.P. Michael Drever invited me to lecture on God and Greek philosophy at the Society of Biblical Literature, and the resulting conversations benefited me in preparing this book. Timothy

Gray and Jared Staudt of the Augustine Institute invited me to speak at the first Nova et Vetera Conference in Denver, where I presented a draft of chapter 5, later published as "Eternal Life: A Merited Free Gift?" in *Nova et Vetera* 9 (2011): 149–62. I thank Tim and Jared for their wonderful hospitality, and I also gained from conversations at the conference with Ted Sri, Gary Anderson, Reinhard Hütter, Bruce Marshall, Thomas Joseph White, O.P., Romanus Cessario, O.P., Charles Morerod, O.P., and Jeremy Holmes.

Matthew Archer helped me assemble the secondary literature for this project, as did, at a later stage, Alan Mostrom, who also skillfully compiled the bibliography. The Index was generously prepared by Jason Heron. It has been a privilege to work with these three promising doctoral students. After I wrote a first draft of the chapters, Jörgen Vijgen persuaded me that the project was not hopeless. The long work of revision was enriched by the generosity of those who read and criticized the drafts: Reginald Lynch, O.P., Sean Fagan, Chad Raith, and Jared Staudt. I could not have proceeded without their help. Carey Newman of Baylor University Press deserves special thanks. With his wit, encouragement, guidance, and criticisms, he made the whole process far more enjoyable and fruitful than it otherwise would have been.

Let me gratefully acknowledge the friendship of Michael Vanderburgh: "I was a stranger and you welcomed me" (Matt 25:35). For the welcome you gave me and my family in Dayton, may God reward you as Jesus has promised: "Come, O blessed of my Father, inherit the kingdom prepared for you from the foundation of the world" (Matt 25:34). While working on this book, I have had my family as a constant source of fun. My beautiful wife, Joy, is God's blessing to me. I am amazed by watching my children get older, and I'm so glad to share in their lives. My parents and Joy's parents helped us in a difficult financial situation when we were renting a house in Dayton. And it is to my beloved father and mother, Ralph and Patty Levering, with gratitude and love, that I dedicate this book.

Introduction

༐

The eminent biblical scholar Richard B. Hays calls upon contemporary theologians to "press forward to a robust recovery of apocalyptic teaching and preaching."[1] By "apocalyptic," he has in view the Church's traditional teaching about "the ultimate glorification of Jesus Christ as Lord over all creation, the resurrection of the body, God's final judgment of all humanity, and 'the life of the world to come' in true justice and peace."[2] When it comes to theological discussion of these themes, however, the past century has been a tumultuous one. The Church's traditional eschatology has fallen out of favor.[3] For many theologians and biblical scholars, significant portions of the Church's traditional eschatology reflect an outdated worldview.[4]

Taking up Hays' challenge, I seek to contribute to the "robust recovery of apocalyptic teaching and preaching" by setting forth a theology of resurrection and eternal life (Christ's and ours). By means of a constructive retrieval of Thomas Aquinas' theology of resurrection and eternal life, I argue that the Church's traditional eschatology has a biblical perspicacity that has been missed by its critics.[5] Since we learn about resurrection and eternal life from Scripture, I also examine in some detail the

1

approaches of biblical scholars to these topics.[6] This exegetical engagement provides the basis for appropriating Aquinas' theological insights in a contemporary fashion. In this regard I agree with Joseph Ratzinger that theological insights "must be capable of holding up in biblical terms, but it would be false to treat them as exegetical conclusions because the way we have decided in their favor is that appropriate to systematic thought."[7] A Thomistic theology of resurrection and eternal life should accord with Scripture without claiming to derive "exegetical conclusions" in a strict sense.

In preparing this book, I was inspired by Alexander Schmemann's remark that "it is our whole faith that by His own death Christ changed the very nature of death, made it a *passage*—a 'passover,' a 'Pascha'—into the Kingdom of God."[8] Since Jesus' redemptive death has enabled our death to be a "passage" into the kingdom of God, the book has two sections, one on Jesus' passage (his descent into hell, resurrection, and ascension), and one on the Church's passage.[9] It may seem unusual that I do not include a chapter on the cross, given that eschatological communion with the Trinity is attained in and through Christ's cross.[10] In this book, however, my fundamental concern is what happens after death to Jesus and to those who follow him,[11] a concern that is inseparable, of course, from how the Church participates in Jesus' paschal mystery here and now.

The book's first section, comprising three chapters, explores Jesus Christ as the one "who discloses to us what 'existence in transition' means."[12] Chapter 1 asks whether, in accord with the Apostles' Creed, contemporary Christians should affirm that Jesus descended into hell when he died, and if so, how to understand this affirmation. Agreeing with N. T. Wright that an intermediate state exists (after death but prior to resurrection), I argue that the dead Jesus joined the holy people who preceded him, and that his sojourning with them was a joyful one because he was present as the conqueror of sin. Chapter 2 treats Jesus' glorious resurrection from the dead "in accordance with the scriptures" of Israel (1 Cor 15:4). In light of the historical reflection on resurrection faith (Jewish and Christian) provided by Jon Levenson, N. T. Wright, Dale Allison, and James Dunn, I inquire into whether theology has anything to add, particularly as regards the relationship of Jesus' resurrection to Israel and the Church. Chapter 3 studies Jesus' ascension in his flesh to the right hand of the Father, from whence he pours forth the Holy Spirit, who "is love drawing us up to heavenly things."[13] I seek to distinguish Jesus' humanity and divinity in the glorification of Jesus and in the sending of the Spirit, and I inquire into the meaning of the Father's "right hand." These chapters emphasize that at every step of Jesus' passage we are included: Jesus rejoices with the believing dead in the intermediate state; his glorious resurrection is in various ways the cause of ours; and his ascension to the right hand of the Father enables him to glorify us. As Douglas Farrow says, "our destiny is bound up with that of Jesus."[14]

The second section, on our passage, occupies the final four chapters. Chapter 4 examines the eschatological community that even now participates in Christ's resurrection and that awaits his return in glory and the consummation of history. Taking my bearings largely from the Book of Acts, I explore how faith, eucharistic worship, and charitable almsgiving relate us to Jesus. I ask whether Aquinas' portrait of these realities obscures the eschatological orientation that they have in the New Testament. The fifth and sixth chapters address topics that are fundamental for conceiving of the world to come in relation to this world: whether God enables our actions to merit eternal life, and whether God has created us with a spiritual soul. Lastly, chapter 7 asks how the life of the world to come—beatific vision, bodily resurrection, the new creation—fulfills the passage on which the church is already embarked (as sketched in chapter 4). I agree here with Richard Bauckham and Trevor Hart: "Humans have been created to find our eternal fulfilment and joy in the vision of God. Creatures can have no completion or perfection in themselves alone, and human creatures will find their faculties of love, knowledge and enjoyment of beauty fully satisfied only in relation to God."[15] As Bauckham and Hart point out, the vision of God does not compete with our knowledge and love for creatures, as it would if God were a reality *alongside* creatures rather than the transcendent Creator in whom all creatures have their being. The portrait of our eternal life in the Trinity that I offer in this final chapter requires, in Hays' evocative phrase, "the conversion of the imagination."[16]

SCRIPTURE, THE SOUL OF ESCHATOLOGY?

How can theologians claim to know so much about resurrection and eternal life? At the 2008 Synod of Bishops, devoted to the topic of Sacred Scripture, Pope Benedict XVI stated that "where exegesis is not theology, Scripture cannot be the soul of theology, and conversely, where theology is not essentially the interpretation of the Church's Scripture, such a theology no longer has a foundation."[17] The status of Scripture as the "soul of theology" is affirmed by the Second Vatican Council's Dogmatic Constitution on Divine Revelation, *Dei Verbum* (§24), and is also underscored by Benedict XVI's recent Apostolic Exhortation *Verbum Domini*. Indeed, in *Verbum Domini* he urges, "It is my hope that, in fidelity to the teaching of the Second Vatican Council, the study of sacred Scripture, read within the communion of the universal Church, will truly be the soul of theological studies."[18]

But has this been the case for traditional Christian eschatology? Consider, for example, the events that followed upon Jesus' death. According to the Apostles' Creed, Jesus Christ "descended into hell."[19] The *Catechism of the Catholic Church* interprets Jesus' descent into hell in the following manner: "In his human soul united to his divine person, the dead Christ went down to the realm of the dead. He opened heaven's gates for the just who had gone before him" (§637). How does the Catechism know this? In accord with its rightful emphasis on doctrinal continuity, the Catechism here cites the *Roman Catechism* published in the wake of the Council of Trent. But does Scripture, as the "soul of theological studies," suggest any grounds for the interpretation of the Apostles' Creed that is offered by the two Catechisms?[20] It might seem that a more biblically rooted theology would move away from the claim that the dead Christ "opened heaven's gates for the just who had gone before him."

Similarly, regarding Jesus' resurrection, the Catechism affirms that "the hypothesis that the Resurrection was produced by the apostles' faith (or credulity) will not hold up. On the contrary, their faith in the Resurrection was born, under the action of divine grace, from their direct experience of the reality of the risen Jesus" (§644). Here there is much more biblical evidence than in the case of Christ's descent into hell. Nonetheless, it is notable that biblical scholars themselves debate whether the first Christians' faith in Jesus' resurrection was the result of the disciples' wishful thinking or perhaps the result of apparitions of an exalted Jesus (similar to later Marian apparitions). The Catechism's insistence that "the hypothesis that the Resurrection was produced by the apostles' faith (or credulity) will not hold up" suggests that this hypothesis "will not hold up" precisely as a matter of biblical scholarship. Even if so, the question is what theologians can contribute to the discussion.

In accord with John 20:17 and especially Acts 1:9, the Apostles' Creed confesses that after his resurrection Jesus "ascended into heaven." Numerous biblical texts depict the ascended Jesus sitting at the right hand of the Father. With regard to the meaning of Jesus' ascension to the right hand of the Father, the Catechism quotes three texts from the Letter to the Hebrews, along with a passage from John Damascene. Damascene rules out the notion of a bodily God, but many biblical scholars today consider that Psalm 110:1—"The Lord says to my lord: 'Sit at my right hand, till I make your enemies your footstool'"—envisions a bodily God. Does the image make sense only within that framework? If the right hand of God is a strictly metaphorical description, then where is Jesus' risen body and why is he there?

Questions such as this one may seem to miss the point of the ascension. The angels sternly correct the witnesses of the ascension, "Men of Galilee, why do you stand looking into heaven? This Jesus, who was taken up from you into heaven, will come in the same way as you saw him go into heaven" (Acts 1:11). Since Jesus will come again in eschatological glory, the community of believers cannot simply stand around wondering where he is. The community receives the Holy Spirit on the day of Pentecost, so as to be found holy and blameless on the eschatological Day of the Lord. It might seem that theological questions about Jesus' ascension to the right hand of God have not been helpful for sustaining the eschatological focus of the Christian community. Has Christian eschatology thereby been cut off at its roots?

Two further theological developments can appear to make this concern more plausible: the doctrine of merit and the doctrine of the spiritual soul. The Council of Trent is well known for its insistence that Christian believers, thanks to the indwelling Holy Spirit, do indeed merit the reward of eternal life. The *Catechism of the Catholic Church* explains, "Filial adoption, in making us partakers by grace in the divine nature, can bestow *true merit* on us as a result of God's gratuitous justice" (§2009). Even though we cannot merit justifying grace, we do merit "the graces needed for our sanctification, for the increase of grace and charity, and for the attainment of eternal life" (§2010). In its discussion of merit, the Catechism alludes once to Romans 8, without citing it, but otherwise the Catechism's sources are the Roman Missal, Augustine, the Council of Trent, and Thérèse of Lisieux. Are there biblical grounds for understanding our meritorious actions as our participation through the Holy Spirit in Christ's saving work, so that his passage from death to life remains always the source of ours?

The difficulty is equally acute for the doctrine of the spiritual soul. Here the Catechism does pause explicitly to reflect on the relationship of this doctrine to biblical revelation. In two highly compressed sentences, citing (in footnotes) three texts from Matthew, two from John, and one from Acts, the Catechism argues, "In Sacred Scripture the term 'soul' often refers to human *life* or the entire human *person*. But 'soul' also refers to the innermost aspect of man, that which is of greatest value in him, that by which he is most especially in God's image: 'soul' signifies the *spiritual principle* in man" (§363). After a brief discussion of body-soul unity, drawing on the Aristotelian doctrine of the soul as the form of the body, the Catechism repeats the teachings of the fourteenth-century Council of Vienna and the sixteenth-century Fifth Lateran Council to the effect that God creates each soul immediately (the parents do not produce the soul) and that the soul is immortal. Neither of these teachings, however, is easily found in the New Testament. Nor is it clear how these teachings ensure the connection between our passage from death to life and Jesus' resurrection and ascension. If we have an immortal soul, isn't our passage automatic, arising from our own spiritual potencies?

Lastly, the doctrine of the spiritual soul undergirds the Catechism's understanding of an eternal life as marked above all by beatific vision. But Jesus himself does not refer to the beatific vision, preferring instead to describe the world to come in terms of images of banqueting, the many rooms of his Father's house, sitting on thrones judging and reigning, and the hundredfold replacement of goods that believers have sacrificed for Jesus' sake in this life. Arguing that the "mystery of blessed communion with God and all who are in Christ is beyond all understanding and description" (§1027), the Catechism interprets these biblical images as metaphorical expressions of a transcendent reality. Without referring to Scripture, the Catechism states, "Because of his transcendence, God cannot be seen as he is, unless he himself opens up his mystery to man's immediate contemplation and gives him the capacity for it. The Church calls this contemplation of God in his heavenly glory 'the beatific vision'" (§1028). But if Scripture is "the soul of theological studies," as both the Second Vatican Council and Pope Benedict XVI say must be the case, then where does the Church get this understanding of the "beatific vision"?

One likely candidate, of course, is the philosophy of Plato. In Plato's *Symposium*, Socrates is led by his teacher Diotima to ascend from contemplation of physical beauty to contemplation of the eternal spiritual form of beauty. Diotima asks Socrates whether if "it were given to man to see the heavenly beauty face to face, would you call his . . . an unenviable life, whose eyes had been opened to the vision, and who had gazed upon it in true contemplation until it had become his own forever?"[21] If one finds Plato here at the pinnacle of the Church's eschatology, it can easily come to seem that Plato is the driving force behind the whole of the Church's eschatology. Thus the account of Christ's descent into hell relies upon Christ's separated soul and a community of conscious souls waiting for the resurrection of the body: where did all these active separated souls come from, if not from Platonic imaginations? Theological reflection on Jesus' resurrection, too, draws upon philosophy and has in the past crowded out the study of Jesus' resurrection by historians and biblical scholars. Similarly, in accounting for where Jesus is now, theological reflection on Jesus' ascension to the right hand of the Father makes distinctions between spirit and matter that derive from Platonic philosophy. The Church too can seem less an eschatological community and more a community shaped by Platonic care of the soul through interactions with the souls of the saints. The notion of merit has roots in the virtue of justice that Socrates, Plato, and Aristotle sought for themselves and their hierarchically ordered cities. Most troubling of all, the doctrine of the beatific vision can seem to relativize the biblical promises of bodily resurrection, last judgment, and new creation.

GREEK PHILOSOPHY AND THE FUTURE
OF CHRISTIAN ESCHATOLOGY

Should the first task of implementing Pope Benedict's vision therefore be to revise the Church's eschatology along more biblical lines? One gets this impression from N. T. Wright's *Surprised by Hope: Rethinking Heaven, the Resurrection, and the Mission of the Church*. He argues that for centuries Christians have mistakenly depended on "Plato's factory" for their "mental furniture."[22] Beginning in the early patristic period, believers developed a "Platonized Christianity (or was it Christianized

Platonism?)" that, in Wright's view, distorted Christian eschatology in an otherworldly direction.[23] This position mirrors that of the mid-twentieth-century biblical scholar Oscar Cullmann, who contrasted the biblical doctrine of resurrection with the Greek doctrine of immortality and argued that the latter too often prevails among Christians.[24] The philosopher Martin Heidegger, among others, concurred: "Soon after the end of the first centuries the eschatological problem was concealed. Afterward, the original meaning of Christian concepts was not recognized. In contemporary philosophy too, the Christian formations of concepts are concealed behind the Greek attitude."[25] We might also think of Tertullian's trenchant remark against the Gnostic and Marcionite heretics: "What indeed has Athens to do with Jerusalem? . . . Away with all attempts to produce a mottled Christianity of Stoic, Platonic, and dialectic composition!"[26]

Agreeing with Cullmann and Wright, contemporary theologians often criticize the use of Greek philosophy in Christian eschatology. Singling out Thomas Aquinas, but with the broad sweep of traditional Christian eschatology in view, Jürgen Moltmann articulates this standard criticism: "Thomas did not translate the biblical language into any other language or mode of thought, but basically liquidated it. His 'theology of hope' is in truth not the theology of a biblical 'hope' but the anthropology of the natural desire (*appetitus naturalis*) of the inner self-transcendence of human beings which finds its answer in the metaphysical theology of the supreme good (*summum bonum*)."[27] Despite his own criticisms of Moltmann's eschatology as overly horizontal, Hans Urs von Balthasar expresses from quite a different perspective a broadly similar concern: "Platonism clearly dominated Western, even Christian, thinking down to the threshold of modern times; we have only to think of the stress laid on the 'immortality of the soul', and how the resurrection was held to be an almost unnecessary 'accidental blessedness' superadded to the substantial blessedness already possessed."[28] The philosophical sources of Balthasar's eschatology, like Moltmann's, are generally not Greek but German, especially G. W. F. Hegel and Martin Heidegger. Other major twentieth-century theologians, such as Sergius Bulgakov, Karl Barth, and Karl Rahner, also rely upon German idealism and its existentialist offshoots for philosophical underpinnings in eschatology.[29] R. R. Reno's recent commentary on Genesis sums up the concern that the Platonic search for "the sweet nectar of the eternal that will palliate our vulnerability to decay and death" will lead us away from the divine Son who became incarnate, suffered, and died for us in order to give "us a new future in the flesh, not a new metaphysical location."[30]

As a young professor, Joseph Ratzinger sought in his own way to develop a "'de-Platonized' eschatology."[31] Although his mature eschatology retains many points in common with his German contemporaries, he concludes that Scripture itself does not permit de-Platonization: "the more I dealt with the questions and immersed myself in the sources, the more the antitheses I had set up fell to pieces in my hands and in their place I saw the inner logic of the Church's tradition stand forth."[32] In his *Eschatology*, he argues against portraits of Plato "as an individualistic, dualistic thinker who negates what is earthly and advocates a flight into the beyond."[33] In his 2006 Regensburg Lecture as Pope Benedict XVI, he emphasizes that Greek philosophical thought is inscribed within Scripture itself, from "the later wisdom literature" through the New Testament: "biblical faith, in the Hellenistic period, encountered the best of Greek thought at a deep level, resulting in a mutual enrichment."[34]

Does this view of Scripture as related fruitfully to Greek philosophical thought find support from other scholars?[35] Treating what he terms "the perennial issue of the Christian encounter with Hellenism" in his Gifford Lectures on the Cappadocian Fathers' natural theology, Jaroslav Pelikan observes that words such as "logos" (John 1:1) and "hypostasis" (Heb 1:3) came "to the Septuagint and then to the Christian vocabulary from the language of Classical and Hellenistic philosophy and science."[36] Similarly, in his *Judaism and Hellenism*, Martin Hengel describes how the Wisdom of Solomon, which significantly influenced the New Testament texts, has affinities with Stoic philosophy.[37] Richard Bauckham notes the Stoic influence on a key text for traditional Christian eschatology, 2 Peter 1:4, "he has granted to us his precious and very great promises, that through these you may escape from the corruption that is in the world because of passion, and become partakers of the divine nature."[38] Elsewhere Bauckham examines the use of "Hellenistic true-god-language" in the Letter to the Hebrews.[39] We might also point to Ben Witherington III, whose *Jesus the Sage* makes clear the Hellenistic influences in late Second-Temple Jewish and Christian texts.[40]

Consider Paul's claim that "this slight momentary affliction is preparing for us an eternal weight of glory beyond all comparison, because we look not to the things that are seen but to the things that are unseen; for the things that are seen are transient, but the things that are unseen are eternal" (2 Cor 4:17-18). Paul's emphasis on an "eternal weight of glory beyond all comparison" (or "beyond all measure") calls to mind the transcending of this-worldly limitations that Plato is known for evoking. When Paul tells the Corinthians that by "beholding the glory of the Lord" they are "being changed into his likeness from one degree of glory to another" (2 Cor 3:18), his expressions likewise resonate with Platonic and Stoic notions, without thereby ceasing to be uniquely Christian. Yet when N. T. Wright, whose opposition to Platonism we noted above, interprets 2 Corinthians 3–4, he finds that our "glory" means simply that we are not overcome by suffering, because we will be vindicated by God. In his view, the "glory of God" refers to the work of the Spirit in the hearts of believers. Christians are changed into Christ's likeness "from one degree of glory to another" when Christians "reflect God's glory to one another and so enable an honest and open-faced ministry to take place."[41] It will be clear that Wright makes very little of the "eternal weight of glory beyond all comparison" that Paul promises us. But if Paul is right that our glory is to be "beyond all comparison," it may be that Wright overemphasizes the horizontal dimension of glory and underestimates its transcendent dimension.

An emphasis on the horizontal dimension also appears in Wright's portrait of resurrection life. He states, "There will be work to do and we shall relish doing it. All the skills and talents we have put to God's service in this present life . . . will be enhanced and ennobled and given back to us to be exercised to his glory."[42] This description of the enhancement of our skills and talents does not evoke a life utterly "beyond all comparison." Wright imagines the new "work to do" not in terms of the "things that are unseen," but emphatically in terms of the things that are seen. The transcendent dimension found in Paul seems strongly muted in Wright. If we emphasize the renewed material creation and a new set of cosmic adventures, we risk turning eternal life into something quite banal.[43] Who wants to repeat forever, no matter in how elevated a fashion, our earthly experiences of banqueting and evangelization?

• • •

How then to describe the hope of Christians without falling into an unhelpful dichotomy between the horizontal and the transcendent or between biblical narrative and Greek philosophical culture? It seems to me that Thomas Aquinas can help us here. Rooted in Scripture, the Apostles' Creed, and the Fathers' insights, and benefiting from a critical appreciation of Greek philosophy, Aquinas' contemplation of the mysteries of faith generates rich insight into Jesus' passage and ours. We will explore Jesus' descent into hell, his resurrection, and his ascension to the right hand of the Father. Jesus enables the Church, as his eschatological people, to share in his passage by sending the Holy Spirit to sanctify us and to enable us to perform works of love. By tracing this path, I hope to gain insight into how Christians can appropriately speak about "the hope set before us" (Heb 6:18).

As we begin this study, then, let us pray with the psalmist: "You have said, 'Seek my face.' My heart says to you, 'Your face, Lord, do I seek'" (Ps 27:8). In the joys and trials of this life, "The Lord is the strength of his people, he is the saving refuge of his anointed. O save your people, and bless your heritage; be their shepherd, and carry them for ever" (Ps 28:8-9).

Part I

THE PASSAGE OF JESUS CHRIST

1

Christ's Descent into Hell

∽

Jesus suffered and died on the cross for our sins, but what happened to him when he died?[1] Was he "gathered to his people" (Gen 49:33) like Jacob, or was he "brought down to Sheol, to the depths of the pit" (Isa 14:15)? As many biblical scholars point out, the eschatology of both Second-Temple Judaism and early Christianity affirmed the existence of a conscious intermediate state in which the dead await resurrection.[2] When Jesus died, then, he entered this intermediate state. Jesus' resurrection cannot be separated from his solidarity as a dead man with those whom Hebrews calls the "great cloud of witnesses" (Heb 12:1).

In making this case, I begin by examining N. T. Wright's view, representative of numerous other biblical scholars and theologians, that the New Testament requires us to believe in an intermediate state that contains all the Christian dead, who are conscious, happy, equal, and inactive. Interestingly, although Wright warns against understanding life after death in terms of "a salvation that is essentially *away from* this world," Wright's portrait of the intermediate state is profoundly otherworldly, to the point that he does not mention that Jesus himself entered into this state.[3]

The polar opposite of Wright's otherworldliness is the dramatic theology of Holy Saturday offered by Hans Urs von Balthasar, whose position has become influential in theological circles today. Many Fathers of the Church, too, emphasize the importance of Jesus' preaching among the dead, and the best contemporary Orthodox theology retains this emphasis. After examining these views, I turn to Thomas Aquinas' position that Jesus' entrance into the intermediate state inaugurates the liberation of the holy Israelites who were there waiting for him. I argue that the vindication of holy Israel in the intermediate state provides a crucial context for Jesus' resurrection, which is the first fruits of the resurrection—the "great Passage"[4]—of God's whole people.

N. T. WRIGHT ON THE INTERMEDIATE STATE

Why does Wright believe that an intermediate state exists, and how does he conceive of it? Wright observes that "any Jew who believed in resurrection, from Daniel to the Pharisees and beyond, naturally believed also in an intermediate state in which some kind of personal identity was guaranteed between physical death and the physical re-embodiment of resurrection."[5] Quoting Philippians 1:23—"My desire is to depart and be with Christ, for that is far better"—he affirms that Paul is "thinking of a blissful life with his Lord immediately after death," prior to bodily resurrection.[6] He likewise cites Jesus' words on the cross to the repentant thief, "Truly, I say to you, today you will be with me in Paradise" (Luke 23:43), as well as Jesus' words to his disciples about there being "many rooms" (the Greek *monē* indicating a temporary dwelling) in his Father's house (John 14:2). On the basis of these passages and others like them, Wright finds the biblical evidence for the existence of an intermediate place to be conclusive. As he says, Scripture speaks of "the dead waiting patiently, and sometimes not so patiently, for the time when they will finally be raised to new life."[7]

Wright argues that "the Christian dead" go to this disembodied paradise, whereas those who reject God's love enter into an animal-like condition.[8] All who die in Christ "are in substantially the same state, that of restful happiness."[9] While they wait for bodily resurrection, they experience "the conscious love of God and the conscious presence of Jesus Christ."[10] Paul sometimes uses the metaphor of sleep to describe the condition of those who have died in Christ (see 1 Cor 15:18, 20, 51). Yet as Wright points out, such sleep is not "unconsciousness," or else Paul could not affirm that to die and be with Christ "is far better" than continuing in life in the flesh (Phil 1:23). Wright considers that the metaphor of sleep describes the death of the body, "while the real person—however we want to describe him or her—continues."[11] In this regard, Wright's position is the largely same as that of John Calvin, who disagreed with Martin Luther's view that those who die in Christ are "asleep" until the day of resurrection. For Calvin, "the souls of the righteous, after their warfare is ended, obtain blessed rest where in joy they wait for the fruition of promised glory."[12]

Wright thinks that "soul" in the New Testament means the "whole person or personality" rather than a spiritual entity.[13] According to 2 Timothy 1:10, he points out, Christ Jesus "abolished death and brought life and immortality to light through the gospel," and so it does not seem appropriate to conceive of a distinct immortality of the soul.[14] Humans possess immortality only as a gift from God in Christ, not as "an innate possession."[15] Wright is willing to speak of an intermediate state with "souls, spirits or angel-like beings," but only insofar as these souls or spirits are "held in that state of being not because they were naturally immortal but by the creative power of YHWH."[16]

According to Wright, all the Christian dead know and love in the intermediate state in the same way and to the same degree. In defense of this position, he appeals to Jesus' frequent observation that "many that are first will be last, and the last first" (Mark 10:31). In Wright's view this means that there will be no "first" or "last," because the Christian dead will all be the same as regards knowing and loving God and Christ. He argues that "we shouldn't be surprised at this lack of distinction between the postmortem state of different Christians."[17] Christian believers do not earn, through good works, higher positions in a heavenly hierarchy: "there is no reason whatever to say, for instance, that Peter or Paul, Aidan and Cuthbert, or even, dare I say, the mother of Jesus herself is more advanced, closer to God, has achieved more spiritual growth, or whatever, than those Christians who have been martyred in our own day or indeed those who have died quietly in their beds."[18] All are as they are simply by being in Christ. Anyone who is in Christ has attained the fullness of what there is to be attained. Thus all living or dead persons who are in Christ are "saints," and no saint is closer to Christ than any other saint. If any person happens to be closer to Jesus in this life, death is the great equalizer for those who are in Christ: "Death itself gets rid of all that is still sinful. . . . There is nothing then left to purge."[19] Here too Wright's view is similar to that of Calvin, who holds that the experience of death suffices to purify and perfect believers who were unable to attain Christian perfection in this life.[20]

Yet if a person in Christ devotes his or her life to radical self-giving love by the grace of the Holy Spirit, why would this not involve (after death) a certain continuity according to which the dead person in Christ resonates more deeply with "the conscious love of God and the conscious presence of Jesus Christ"? The issue is not simply whether death purges all one's sins away. Rather, the issue is whether, by the grace of the Holy Spirit, a life lived in particular closeness to Christ enables one to enjoy Christ's presence in the intermediate state more deeply than can one who on earth lived in Christ but did not do so particularly closely. Why would not the person who actively and at great sacrifice loves more here also love more in the life to come?[21]

On the related topic of "purgatory," Wright's central reason for rejecting a purgatorial intermediate state is his commitment to grounding "one's beliefs in scripture itself."[22] In his view, Paul rules out the medieval notion of purgatory when he states, "There is therefore now no condemnation for those who are in Christ Jesus" (Rom 8:1). For Paul this means that "the law of the Spirit of life in Christ Jesus has set me free from the law of sin and death" (Rom 8:2), so that Paul, like all believers, can "live according to the Spirit" and set his mind "on the things of the Spirit" (Rom 8:5). It seems to me, however, that Paul is not here teaching a doctrine of the absolute spiritual sameness of all who are in Christ, either in this life or after death.

Wright grants the possibility that the Christian dead in the intermediate state have an interest in what happens on earth. In Revelation 6:9, the Seer is shown "under the altar the souls of those who had been slain for the word of God and for the witness they had borne; they cried out with a loud voice, 'O Sovereign Lord, holy and true, how long before you will judge and avenge our blood on those who dwell upon the earth?'" (6:9-10). This passage leads Wright to speculate that in the intermediate state the Christian dead, already in some way reigning with Christ, not only call for justice but also intercede with the Father on our behalf. But he emphasizes that this is mere speculation. Scripture does not make clear what exactly it is that the Christian dead in the intermediate state are doing on our behalf, if anything. As a result, he holds that humans alive today are not warranted in calling upon the intercession of the Christian dead.[23]

When Wright interprets the Old Testament notion of Sheol, he describes it as a place where the dead experience utter isolation and sorrow, but he does not explicitly connect it to the intermediate state.[24] In *Surprised by Hope*, he does not say anything about the intermediate state prior to the salvation wrought by the cross. He describes Jesus' experience of being dead as "the silent rest of the seventh-day sabbatical in the tomb," but he does not say more.[25]

CHRIST'S DESCENT INTO HELL: SALVATION-HISTORICAL PERSPECTIVES

Given that there is a conscious intermediate state, as Wright supposes, must we assume that Jesus' entrance into it was completely uneventful? It seems that the intermediate state should be more connected to human history, and especially to the history of salvation, than Wright supposes in his portrait of a placid and otherworldly intermediate state. This was the view of the Fathers of the Church, and it has recently been revived in an unusually dramatic form by Hans Urs von Balthasar.

According to Balthasar, all of the dead prior to Jesus' cross experienced the punishment of the damned. Jesus, then, adopted a position of radical solidarity with those experiencing damnation in Sheol. When Jesus entered the intermediate state bearing the burden of our sin, he did so as the most completely damned soul of all in order to enclose all others in his love.[26] For Balthasar, the incarnate Son can go to the bitterest lengths of alienation because of his unique relationship with the Father, which includes infinite distance as well as infinite unity. Citing Ephesians 4:9, "he had also descended into the lower parts of the earth," Balthasar argues that Jesus "went through an experience of forsakenness that took him far beyond Sheol and Gehenna," bad as those were.[27] He agrees with Adrienne von Speyr's conclusion that Jesus' descent into hell introduces him interiorly to all the sin that he has conquered. On this view, the dead Jesus is no mere passive observer of sin, but rather encounters it from within: "He undertakes this journey in pure 'wordlessness' (for, after all, the Incarnate Word of God is dead) and also in 'pure obedience', for 'the Father is not merely, as was the case on the Cross, veiled and lost to view, but now the Son is forced to enter into that which is the opposite of the Father', into the pure essence of sin that has been separated from the world, into what has been condemned by God, in which God cannot be found."[28] In the dead Son's engagement with "the pure essence of sin" through his descent into hell, the bearer of divine mercy experiences the full punishment of sin (damnation). In this experience of intra-Trinitarian dereliction, sin is "burned up" as by fire.[29]

Balthasar argues that this portrait does more justice to the condition of death than does the view of "a joyful encounter between Jesus and the prisoners," which he considers to go "beyond what theology can affirm."[30] Yet even if he succeeds in connecting Jesus' entrance into the intermediate state with the drama of salvation, his account of Jesus undergoing damnation seems itself to go well "beyond what theology can affirm."[31]

Do the Fathers offer a better account of Jesus' descent into hell? Many Fathers focus their attention on 1 Peter 3:18-19, "For Christ also died for sins once for all, the righteous for the unrighteous, that he might bring us to God, being put to death in the flesh but made alive in the spirit; in which he went and preached to the spirits in prison," and 1 Peter 4:6, "For this is why the gospel was preached even to the dead, that though judged in the flesh like men, they might live in the spirit like God." Contemporary biblical scholars root these passages in the worldview of apocryphal texts such as *1 Enoch* and the *Gospel of Peter.* In his commentary on 1 Peter 3:18-19, Ben Witherington III concludes, "We certainly do not find here any sort of second-chance, beyond-death theology, not least because the text is about angels and not humans; and Peter does not tell us that the resurrected Jesus went and preached any good news to anyone."[32] Witherington considers that 1 Peter has in view the glorified Christ who judges the powers of evil, rather than a supposed spiritual existence of Christ between his death and resurrection. Other biblical scholars are more willing to consider patristic interpretations. Thus Joel Green finds that, although the meaning of 1 Peter 3:18-19 and 4:6 remains obscure, "we need not jettison early Christian interpretation of Peter's work and the tradition it represents."[33]

In the view of Clement of Alexandria, "the Lord descended to Hades for no other end but to preach the Gospel," so that even in Hades, "all the souls, on hearing the proclamation, might either exhibit repentance, or confess that their punishment was just, because they believed not."[34] Clement has in view the fate of those who lived and died before Christ, without ever hearing anything about the salvation he offers. Similarly, in his *Epistle to Epictetus*, Athanasius affirms that after Jesus' death, the Word did not part from either his body or his soul, but instead went "to preach, as Peter says, also to the spirits in prison."[35] The same point is made by John of Damascus, among many others: "The deified soul went down into hell so that, just as the Sun of Justice rose upon those on earth, so also might the light shine upon them under the earth who were sitting in darkness and the shadow of death." Damascene explains that "to them that believed He became a cause of eternal salvation, while to them that had not He became a refutation of unbelief, and so also to them in hell, 'That to him every knee should bow, of those that are in heaven, on earth, and under the earth' [Phil 2:10]."[36]

This view of Jesus' entrance into the intermediate state is articulated in a contemporary vein by Metropolitan Hilarion Alfeyev, in his *Christ the Conqueror of Hell: The Descent into Hades from an Orthodox Perspective*.[37] After briefly indicating the New Testament roots of the doctrine, especially 1 Peter and Ephesians 4:9, as well as its presence in the Apocrypha, Metropolitan Hilarion turns to the theology of the Fathers and to Orthodox liturgical texts. He concludes that Christ's descent into hell and his preaching to the dead are "an inseparable part of the dogmatic tradition of the Church."[38] According to Metropolitan Hilarion, Jesus among the dead offered salvation to all and "opened for *all* the doors to paradise."[39] Through his descent into hell, Jesus destroyed hell, the power of Satan, and the power of death. Metropolitan Hilarion states, "After Christ, hell is no longer the place where the devil reigns and people suffer but is a prison for the devil himself as well as for those who have voluntarily decided to stay with him and share his fate."[40] On this view, those who die without learning about or accepting Christ receive another chance in hell, where all hear Christ's preaching.[41] The key point is that Christ's descent into hell inaugurated the movement of deification: "As the last stage in Christ's divine descent (*katabasis*) and self-emptying (*kenosis*), his descent into Hades became the starting point of humanity's ascent toward deification (*theosis*). Since this descent, the path to paradise is opened for both the living and the dead."[42]

Although I agree with Metropolitan Hilarion's emphasis that Jesus' descent into hell is "the starting point of humanity's ascent toward deification," I differ from his view that the intermediate state offers humans a second chance to accept Jesus. In part, this is because I think that implicit faith in Jesus is possible in this life, and so the question of how those can be saved who have not heard of Jesus is not as urgent as it appeared, for example, to Clement of Alexandria.[43] My central concern, however, is that the intermediate state, in which body-soul unity has been ruptured and souls await the resurrection of the body, cannot be a new historical life with a new opportunity for hearing the Gospel. There cannot be one life for the human person as a soul-body unity, followed by another life—with the same fundamental choice at stake—as a separated soul.

THOMAS AQUINAS ON CHRIST'S DESCENT INTO HELL

Aquinas' theology of Christ's descent into hell charts a helpful course between Wright's ahistorical portrait of the intermediate state and the fully historicized accounts of Christ's damnation or Christ's preaching in the intermediate state.[44] Like Augustine, Aquinas thinks that 1 Peter 3 does not describe the dead Jesus' preaching in the intermediate state. For Augustine, drawing upon Psalm 16:10, "It is established beyond question that the Lord, after he had been put to death in the flesh, 'descended into hell.'"[45] But Augustine considers that the meaning of 1 Peter 3:18-21 consists in its emphasis, in light of the story of Noah, on the urgent importance of baptism. This interpretation allows Augustine and Aquinas to move away from a fully historicized account of Christ's activity in the intermediate state.

Like all the dead, Jesus in his separated soul went to the intermediate state to await the resurrection of his flesh.[46] In the intermediate state he encountered the saints of Israel and those non-Israelites united to holy Israel by faith in God. In his understanding of holy Israel, Aquinas follows Hebrews' teaching that God's holy people "conquered kingdoms, enforced justice, received promises, stopped the mouths of lions, quenched raging fire, escaped the edge of the sword, won strength out of weakness, became mighty in war, put foreign armies to flight" (Heb 11:33-34).[47] Regarding these people, Hebrews testifies that "God is not ashamed to be called their God, for he has prepared for them a city" (11:13).

None of their holy deeds, however, was enough to redeem and renew Israel, because they still labored under original sin. Aquinas reasons that the individuals described in Hebrews' catalogue of faith were "cleansed from sin, so far as the cleansing of the individual is concerned. Nevertheless the faith and righteousness of no one of them sufficed for removing the barrier arising from the guilt of the whole human race."[48] Before Jesus died for us, people who died in faith still lacked full holiness. They could not yet "see" God; the Temple curtain had not yet been torn in two. As Aquinas says, the penalty of original sin was still owed, because "the price of man's redemption was not yet paid."[49]

According to Aquinas, then, when Jesus died and his soul (united hypostatically to the divine nature in the Person of the Son) entered the intermediate state, he freed the saints of Israel to enjoy fully the divine presence that they sought. He thereby inaugurated the restoration of Israel, the holy people. Aquinas states that "upon the holy fathers detained in hell solely on account of original sin, He shed the light of glory everlasting."[50] Recall that this light of glory is the interior illumination by which the blessed enter into the most intimate relationship possible with Jesus Christ and with each other. In describing this fulfillment of Israel through the Messiah's descent into hell, Aquinas quotes a variety of Old Testament passages: "Surely he has borne our griefs and carried our sorrows" (Isa 53:4); "As for you also, because of the blood of my covenant with you, I will set your captives free from the waterless pit" (Zech 9:11); "Lift up your gates, O ye princes" (Ps 24:7; RSV: "Lift up your heads, O gates!").[51] Aquinas reads these texts through Colossians 2:15, "He [God] disarmed the principalities and powers and made a public example of them, triumphing over them in him [Christ]."[52]

In broad accord with Aquinas' position, although from a strictly historical perspective, Larry Hurtado argues that the salvation of the Old Testament saints would have been the meaning of Jesus' descent into hell for the first Christians:

> Jesus' descent to hades to announce to the Old Testament saints the benefits of his victorious redemptive work dramatically asserts his lordship over all spheres of creation, vividly illustrating the confession in Philippians 2:9-11 that he is to be acknowledged "in heaven, and on earth and under the earth." The motif also portrays the conviction that "to this end Christ died and lived again, so that he might be Lord of both the dead and the living" (Rom 14:9). In addition, Jesus' descent asserts that the Old Testament figures to whom he offers deliverance are part of the company of those redeemed through Jesus, being incorporated into the salvation he secured. That is, Jesus' hades descent affirms the fundamental unity of divine purpose in the Old Testament and in the churches, with Jesus portrayed as the one savior of all.[53]

This portrait of the Messiah's presence among his holy people in the intermediate state requires appreciating the waiting of Israel in history. Consider Luke's depiction of Simeon, who "was righteous and devout, looking for the consolation of Israel, and the Holy Spirit was upon him" (2:25). The Holy Spirit revealed to Simeon that the consolation or restoration of Israel through the Messiah would come about during Simeon's lifetime, and he rejoiced greatly upon seeing the baby Jesus in the Temple: "Lord, now let your servant depart in peace, according to your word; for my eyes have seen your salvation which you have prepared in the presence of all peoples, a light for revelation to the Gentiles, and for glory to your people Israel" (2:29-32). Similarly the prophetess Anna had been waiting for years in the Temple "with fasting and prayer night and day" (Luke 2:37), and her waiting too was rewarded. Seeing the baby Jesus, "she gave thanks to God, and spoke of him to all who were looking for the redemption of Jerusalem" (2:38).

Is it legitimate to imagine the joy of Abraham, Isaac, and Jacob—that is, the inauguration of the "consolation of Israel" and the "redemption of Jerusalem"—when Christ Jesus came to them in the intermediate state? If one holds with Wright and Metropolitan Hilarion that there is an intermediate state, as I do, then it should indeed be a place of joy for those who love God. Even so, the waiting of holy Israel in the intermediate state, like that of Simeon and Anna in the Temple, must have entailed some suffering "through their glory being delayed."[54] Aquinas adds, however, that their suffering would have been mitigated by having "great joy" from the faithful hope with which they awaited the Messiah's victory.[55] In this regard he quotes Jesus' description of Abraham's joy: "Your father Abraham rejoiced that he was to see my day; he saw it and was glad" (John 8:56).[56]

Aquinas does not think that all the inhabitants of the intermediate state are in the same condition. Due to the grace of the Holy Spirit, the "great cloud of witnesses" (Heb 12:1) is ready for Christ at his coming into the intermediate state. But others are not. Readiness for Christ's coming depends upon one's relation to his Passion, his act of love for sinners. Because of his faith, the good thief joins Christ in the intermediate spiritual paradise; in Aquinas' view, this is what Jesus means by telling the good thief, "Truly, I say to you, today you will be with me in Paradise" (Luke 23:43).[57] It is the grace of the Holy Spirit that enables the good thief to respond to Christ in faith. Speaking about the intermediate state, Aquinas comments that after his death Christ visited the holy dead "in place, according to his soul," because he visited them "interiorly by grace, according to his Godhead."[58]

Christ acts as King of his holy people Israel not by this-worldly power but by the power of his cruciform love, enacted on the cross. As Aquinas states, "Christ's descent into hell was one of deliverance in virtue of his Passion."[59] This royal power can be rejected. When Christ entered the intermediate state, therefore, his presence did not compel the dead to love him. Those whose love is still divided (even after the scourging of death) undergo in the intermediate state a further purification of their loves. Aquinas comments that "they who were such as those who are now in Purgatory, were not set free from Purgatory by Christ's descent into hell."[60] This does not mean that Christ's presence had no impact among those who as yet could not fully welcome him. It simply means that they were unable to fully welcome him, and his love worked, as it always does, to heal them gradually of this deficiency. Since Christ visited the whole intermediate state by enabling all the dead to recognize his paschal victory of love, the dead who rejected him were put "to shame by their unbelief and wickedness," whereas those being purified were inspired by further "hope of attaining to glory."[61]

Aquinas finds, then, that by entering the intermediate state at the moment of his redemptive death, Christ led those who welcomed him into the spiritual paradise "by enlightening them with the light of glory in hell itself."[62] Nonetheless, Aquinas also makes clear that "the consolation of Israel" and "the redemption of Jerusalem" are incomplete without bodily resurrection—Christ's and ours. The spiritual paradise cannot take the place of the "earthly corporeal paradise" that is to come. God has made us so that we might praise him forever in the body. In the words of Metropolitan Kallistos Ware, "man is not saved *from* his body but *in* it; not saved *from* the material world but *with* it."[63] The martyrs of Israel will receive "life and breath" anew from the Creator (2 Macc 7:22). As Paul puts it, "our commonwealth is in heaven, and from it we await a Savior, the Lord Jesus Christ, who will change our lowly body to be like his glorious body, by the power which enables him even to subject all things to himself" (Phil 3:20-21).[64]

CONCLUSION

Wright emphasizes the eschatological renewal of space, time, and matter; he fears eschatologies that overspiritualize our future with God. At the same time, he holds that the New Testament attests to an intermediate state in which the dead are conscious prior to the general resurrection. He portrays this intermediate state as a place of uneventful happiness, and he denies that the intermediate state involves purification. By contrast, Balthasar envisions Christ experiencing all sin in solidarity with the damned in Sheol. Numerous Fathers, followed by Metropolitan Hilarion, understand the intermediate state as marked by Christ's preaching, opening up the possibility that those who reject Christ in this life may accept him in the intermediate state.

Aquinas likewise affirms the existence of an intermediate state. At the moment of his redemptive death, Jesus entered into the intermediate state and liberated the holy people of God who were waiting for him. His resurrection thus reveals the vindication not only of Jesus, but also of the people of God who welcome Jesus as the messianic King. The happiness of those who welcome him accounts for Jesus' promise to the good thief that "today you will be with me in Paradise" (Luke 23:43) and for Paul's remark that he "would rather be away from the body and at home with the Lord" (2 Cor 5:8). Although people can be happy in the intermediate state, nonetheless death retains its bitterness: Jesus experienced the separation of body and soul as a profound privation.[65] In this regard at least, Aquinas' position is not contrary to Calvin's view that Jesus' "descent into hell" describes his suffering the terrible penalty of death on behalf of all sinners.[66]

Aquinas' connection of Jesus' entrance into the intermediate state with the vindication of holy Israel avoids Wright's otherworldly portrait of inactive sameness. At the same time, Aquinas' position does not overly historicize Jesus' presence in the intermediate state. Jesus works in the intermediate state by the power of his Passion without having to undertake a new ministry or undergo further desolation. When Christ the king arrived in the intermediate state to await his resurrection as the first-fruits of ours, the joyful passage of faithful Israel—of all who "died in faith, not having received what was promised, but having seen it and greeted it from afar, and having acknowledged that they were strangers and exiles on the earth" (Heb 11:13)—had indeed begun.

2

The Resurrection of Jesus Christ

∽

Discussing Paul's (and the Nicene Creed's) use of "in accordance with the scriptures" (1 Cor 15:4) to describe Jesus' resurrection, Christopher Seitz argues that this "accordance" cannot be discovered by proof-texting but rather involves carefully sifting the Old Testament witness to God's covenantal relationship with Israel, in light of the New Testament witness to Jesus.[1] The accordance of Jesus' resurrection with the Scriptures of Israel does not require us to enumerate the Old Testament texts that teach the doctrine of resurrection. What the accordance requires, instead, is the recognition that Israel's covenantal relationship with God is fulfilled in and through God's raising of Jesus from the dead. Does Jesus' resurrection, however, accord with the promised deliverance and restoration of the *whole* people of God?

This chapter seeks to show why the answer is yes. As an event that breaks into time and overthrows death, Jesus' resurrection truly accomplished the end of exile through the upbuilding of the people of God by the risen Christ. The first step is to show how this event accorded with the hopes and expectations of those who awaited the victory of the God of life. With regard to the hopes of Israel, the doctrine of the resurrection of the dead has been recently defended by the Jewish exegete and theologian Jon Levenson. When contemporary Christian biblical scholars investigate the New Testament witness to Jesus' resurrection, they similarly focus upon the expectations of the people of God. This chapter therefore begins with a survey of Levenson's understanding of resurrection and the restoration of Israel, and then briefly examines three historical-critical reconstructions—by N. T. Wright, Dale Allison, and James D. G. Dunn—of the first Christians' proclamation of Jesus' resurrection. From this perspective, I turn to Aquinas' way of expositing the New Testament witness to the resurrection of Jesus. I find that a similar attention to the people of God—Israel and the Church—guides his exposition of why the resurrection on the third day was "necessary" in God's plan, why the risen Jesus manifested himself only to a chosen few, and why Jesus rose with a glorified body. By showing how Jesus' resurrection belongs to God's plan for the glorification of his whole people, Aquinas leads us into the heart of Jesus' passage from death to eternal life.

RESURRECTION AND THE RESTORATION OF ISRAEL

Israel's Scriptures and Resurrection

In defending the view of the rabbis that the Torah teaches the doctrine of resurrection, Jon Levenson begins by arguing that "Sheol" expresses in the Hebrew Bible a negative, untimely death, rather than death itself. While granting that a few passages describe Sheol as the place of all the dead, he points out that almost always those who are said to go down to Sheol are those who have lost the favor of God. Furthermore, God can rescue people from Sheol, if only by rescuing them from approaching death and by restoring their worldly fortunes. While Levenson criticizes the rabbis for failing to recognize that the Hebrew Bible generally considers death to be the end of the individual's existence, he makes clear that Sheol is a mark of disfavor and more fluid and open than many scholars have supposed.[2]

This openness is enhanced by the status of Israel's Temple as a new Eden. Levenson observes that "death is as alien to the Temple, indeed, as repugnant to the Temple, as it is to Eden."[3] This is so because of the opposition between holiness and death. God's activity in and through the Temple is life-giving, not death-dealing. Psalm 133 teaches that everlasting life flows from the Temple, and the Hebrew Bible consistently portrays the Temple as an Edenic place of life, innocence, rejuvenation, and divine protection. Worshippers in the Temple experience a "temporary immortality" rooted in the Temple's justice, inviolability, and eternity.[4] According to Levenson, to yearn to dwell in the Temple is to yearn for this embodied immortality.

Not only are Sheol and the Temple open to God's victory over death, but also this possibility is confirmed by the story of Elisha's raising of the only son of the Shunammite woman (2 Kgs 4). Here resurrection from the dead through God's miraculous activity is connected with biblical commonplace of survival through descendents, so that resurrection and the restoration of Israel go together. Israel's God loves Israel as a son, and so when Israel is lost YHWH is both "the bereft father and the omnipotent Deity who aids bereft fathers."[5] Levenson also points out that in Isaiah 43:6-7, God promises to "bring my sons from afar and my daughters from the end of the earth, every one who is called by my name, whom I created for my glory, whom I formed and made."[6]

The description of exile as Israel's death appears strikingly in Ezekiel 37, where Ezekiel receives a vision of a valley of dry bones and the promise that they will be resurrected. Levenson holds that this vision expresses not a literal event but the promise that Israel will return from Babylonian exile and will be re-created by God as a people (now with an obedient "heart of flesh," as Ezek 36:26 says). The terms of the vision, however, indicate a cultural acceptance of resurrection as a possibility.[7] Resurrection here does not mean immortality, but it does mean that God unconditionally promises to restore the people Israel to "life," and not only to the normal course of life but to a transformed and re-created life.

For those who obey God, God promises life (see Deut 30:19-20; Lev 18:5; Prov 3–4). Although "life" here may simply mean long life in God's favor, nonetheless if God is Israel's healer, why would he allow death, which Israel never conceives of as a good, to have the last word for Israel? In this regard, Levenson suggests that 1 Samuel 2:6, where Hannah praises God as the one who "kills and brings to life; he brings down to Sheol and raises up," is an interpretation of Deuteronomy 32:39, "I kill and I make alive." Levenson argues that 1 Samuel 2:6 means that even though God brings death upon all, he will miraculously raise up some. If God governs death, one cannot rule out that God will rescue Israel, especially repentant Israel (see Ezek 18), from death. Although this is not yet "a full-fledged doctrine of the resurrection of the dead," it is a powerful statement about "the God who promises life."[8]

Levenson considers Daniel 12:1-3 to be the first clear statement of
the resurrection of the dead in the Hebrew Bible. He notes that Daniel
12:1-3 "leaves it beyond doubt that the postmortem fate of the righteous
is one of resurrection—the reanimation of corpses rather than vindication in the heavenly realm with a conferral of life."[9] This "reanimation of corpses" transforms bodiliness. Levenson cites the third-century
Talmudic sage Rav, who teaches that the world to come involves "'neither eating nor drinking nor sexual relations nor business transactions
nor jealousy nor hatred nor rivalry. Rather, the righteous sit with their
crowns on their heads and enjoy the radiance of the Divine Presence.'"[10]
Reading Daniel 12:1-3 in light of Isaiah 52:13 and Isaiah 66:22-24,
Levenson shows that at issue is the vindication of God. Although the
enemies of God and his people may prosper in this life, God has in view
an eschatological reversal of fortunes.[11]

In his interpretation of Daniel 12, Levenson argues at length that
rather than being attributable to "the martyrdom of faithful tradition-
alists under Antiochus IV around 167 B.C.E."[12] or to the influence of
Persian Zoroastrianism—to name two widespread theories—the Jewish
doctrine of the resurrection of the dead emerged in the Second-Temple
period for reasons internal to the faith of Israel. Belief in the resurrection of the dead accords with the faith and practice of a people who worship the God who governs life and death and who rescues his beloved
people Israel from death-like situations, the God whose prophets could
perform miracles of raising the dead and whose Temple prompted long-
ing for everlasting life with God.[13] In the deepest possible sense, obeying the Torah is life-giving, and disobeying the Torah is death-dealing.
Because of this connection with the God of life, Levenson concludes
that the near-sacrifice of Isaac (suggestive of the "resurrection" of the
beloved son) and the covenant at Sinai anticipate, as the rabbis taught,
the resurrection of the dead and the restoration of Israel.[14]

Jesus' Resurrection and His Mission

N. T. Wright has shown that during the Second-Temple period many
Jews believed that the conditions of exile still prevailed.[15] God had given
Israel his Torah so that Israel could be his people and dwell peacefully in
the land, but the Gentiles now ruled the land and the people were not
holy. The question was how God was going to rescue and restore Israel.
Most Jews expected that God's restoration of Israel would forgive Israel's

sins, renew the Temple, cleanse the holy land, and reunite the people of Israel in perfect observance of Torah. God would thereby accomplish a new exodus and firmly establish his holy people in the holy land. This restoration of Israel would bring about the renewal of the entire creation through Israel, and God would establish Israel as the true Adam, the priest-king of all creation.[16]

Having identified this basic story or worldview, Wright asks how Jesus relates to it.[17] Jesus announced the imminent action of God to inaugurate the kingdom of God (the restoration of Israel).[18] Indeed, Jesus made clear that he would be the one to do what only YHWH could do. Through Jesus' action, YHWH would truly become Israel's king. The restored Israel, brought back from exile and reordered around Jesus, would truly be the kingdom of YHWH. Yet Jesus' kingdom-inaugurating action, as his parables and teachings suggest, pivoted para-doxically on the event of his being rejected and killed.

In calling upon Israel to repent, Jesus was urging Israel to avoid the eschatological judgment that would accompany the inauguration of the kingdom. Jesus took upon himself the authority to forgive the people's sins (and end the exile), rather than centering this eschatological for-giveness around allegiance to Torah and Temple. Similarly, Jesus called for belief or faith not only in the reality that God's action was imminent but also in his own enactment of God's action. Jesus redefined the Torah through his teachings about the actions and interior dispositions appro-priate to members of the eschatological kingdom. Henceforth the Torah would be fulfilled by following Jesus. In short, the imminent eschato-logical judgment and vindication of Israel through Jesus' action would redefine Israel around Jesus, as Jesus suggested through his prophecy of the fall of Jerusalem and the destruction of the Temple.[19]

Wright also examines Jesus' teachings about Israel's most fundamen-tal identity markers, namely Sabbath observance, the food laws, loyalty to nation and to family, the holy land, and the Temple and its sacrificial cult. In every case Jesus challenged his Jewish followers to renounce their allegiance to these identity markers in favor of allegiance to him in a kingdom whose borders now included, in principle, even the Gentiles. In cleansing the Temple and prophesying its destruction, Jesus symboli-cally enacted God's eschatological judgment upon it for having become a center of violent nationalism.[20] The Passover meal in the upper room constituted Jesus and his twelve disciples as the eschatologically restored

Israel, with Jesus himself at the center. Jesus understood himself as the one in and through whom YHWH was returning to Zion. In inaugurating the kingdom through the eschatological tribulation, Jesus expected to suffer a sacrificial death for the sins of Israel—a death that would replace the cultic function of the Temple—and then to be vindicated. He would even be exalted to the very throne of God. In the kingdom that Jesus would bring about, to be loyal to Israel's God would mean to be loyal to Jesus. In Wright's portrait, Jesus' resurrection fits quite well: had Jesus not actually been resurrected, then a crucified Messiah whose death seemingly changed nothing could hardly have been acclaimed by Jews as victorious over evil and as inaugurating the kingdom.

Historical Evaluation of the Testimony to Jesus' Resurrection

In his *The Resurrection of the Son of God*, Wright fills out this view that the only way to account historically for the emergence of the Christian movement in the particular form it took is to affirm Jesus' resurrection. After showing that the ancient world had no direct parallels to the apostles' claim that Jesus had been raised from the dead, Wright demonstrates that the apostles' claim was something new and unexpected even within the messianic Jewish context. As a matter of historical explanation, Wright argues that the proclamation of Jesus risen (and the worship of Jesus by believers in Israel's God) could not have come about absent either the empty tomb or the appearances of the risen Jesus.[21] Mere hallucinatory visions would have produced an otherworldly religion rather than a religion of new creation.[22] Since bereaved people quite often sense the presence of the dead loved one, Wright concludes, "The more 'normal' these 'visions' were, the less chance there is that anyone . . . would have said what nobody had ever said about such a dead person before, that they had been *raised from* the dead. Indeed, such visions meant precisely, as people in the ancient and modern worlds have discovered, that the person was dead."[23] Paul experienced a vision of the exalted Jesus, but he did so within the context of the early Christians' proclamation of the empty tomb and the bodily resurrection of Jesus.

Furthermore, the resurrection narratives in the gospels do not present the risen Jesus as shining like a star (as might have been expected from Daniel 12), but instead present him as both confirming the reality of his bodiliness and doing things such as appearing and disappearing at will and passing through locked doors. If the evangelists had simply made up this "transphysicality," it should surprise us that they all described it in the same way.[24] Similarly, the resurrection narratives do not connect Jesus' resurrection with the future resurrection of believers, but instead focus on the evangelizing mission in this world that the risen Jesus gives his followers. By contrast, Paul emphasized the connection of Jesus' resurrection with ours. Had the resurrection narratives simply been invented, one would expect to see a connection to the future resurrection of believers.[25]

Not persuaded by Wright, Dale Allison argues in favor of the view that hallucinatory visions sparked the claim that Jesus had risen from the dead. For Allison, the resurrection narratives are what we would expect to find in wish-fulfilling descriptions molded by the "eschatological pattern" that Jesus aimed to embody.[26] The eschatological pattern requires not only suffering, rejection, abandonment, and death, but also miracles, crowds, wonder, and resurrection. On this view, the apostles and writers of the gospels followed the eschatological pattern in their proclamation of Jesus because they believed in Jesus' assertion of God's goodness and they affirmed "[h]is fundamental intuition . . . that the creator must be the redeemer, that the divine Father is good enough to ensure that those who mourn will be comforted, loving enough to guarantee that those who weep now will someday laugh."[27] Allison believes that God will indeed raise the dead at the end of time, but he thinks that the testimony to Jesus' resurrection came from bereaved and guilt-ridden disciples who experienced a sense of his presence after his death.[28]

James Dunn responds to positions such as Allison's by observing that "resurrection" would not have been the word applied to such visions. Noting that the ancient world contained precedents of visions of exalted dead heroes, Dunn points out, "A self-projected vision would presumably be clothed in imagery most closely to hand. That would include preeminently the imagery of Daniel 7:13-14, especially if it had been evoked by Jesus himself. We would then anticipate visions of Jesus in apocalyptic garb, clothed in dazzling white, and/or riding on the clouds of heaven."[29] The Gospels do not portray Jesus in this way; rather, Jesus' presence is strikingly corporeal. Furthermore, the apostles speak of resurrection rather than exaltation and thus use a language that visions of an exalted Lord would not have been likely to produce. The impact of the event led the first Christians to describe Jesus as bodily resurrected, and as Dunn says, "presumably there was something in what the first witnesses saw which they could bring to expression only with this term 'resurrection.'"[30] The appearances cannot be separated from the description "resurrection." Dunn concludes that the traditions set down in the New Testament make clear that "it was something perceived as having happened to *Jesus* (resurrection evidenced in the empty tomb and resurrection appearances) and not just something which happened to the *disciples* (Easter faith) which provides the more plausible explanation for the origin and core content of the tradition itself."[31]

As the apostles' interpretation of what they witnessed, Jesus' resurrection can only be affirmed by an act of faith. Dunn, however, considers this dependence on faith to be a strength rather than a weakness. In personal relationships, we depend on faith and trust. No matter how historically plausible, affirming the reality of the glorious resurrection of Jesus (not simply a resuscitation) requires faith, even for those who witnessed the risen Jesus.

AQUINAS ON JESUS' RESURRECTION

Wright and Dunn focus on the fact that some Jews, knowing that all Israel was to be resurrected on the last day and that the restoration of Israel would establish Israel's preeminence among the nations, nonetheless proclaimed that the crucified Jesus was risen from the dead. Why would God restore his people in this way? The theological tradition approached Jesus' resurrection in faith and asked questions about the nature of his risen body, his manifestation to his disciples, and the salvific causality of his resurrection. Arguing that such questions are too abstract, Otto Hermann Pesch concludes that Thomas Aquinas' theology of Jesus' resurrection contributes nothing today.[32] For his part, N. T. Wright warns theologians: "We must not back away from history, or seek to keep the theological handbrake on to prevent history running away with us."[33] The "theological handbrake" is the fear that when Jesus is seen within his Second-Temple context, his ambitions may appear bound too closely to the apocalyptic fervor and goals of those who zealously expected the final tribulation and the restoration of Israel.[34]

It is true that Aquinas' reflections on the resurrection do not apprehend the particular forms that eschatological fervor took in the Second-Temple period. Yet Aquinas does help us understand the "accordance" of Jesus' resurrection with God's promises to his people. This "accordance" complements the historical-critical scholarship of Levenson, Wright, and Dunn. Aquinas shows how Jesus' resurrection serves the people of God, precisely as a historical community (Israel and the church), on their passage from death to eternal life.

"Thus It Is Written": The "Necessity" of Christ's Resurrection

Aquinas' particular emphasis is evident in the *sed contra* of his first article on Jesus' resurrection. He quotes Luke 24:46, where the risen Jesus tells his apostles, "Thus it is written, that the Christ should suffer and on the third day rise again."[35] Taken as a whole, Luke 24:44-47 underscores that Jesus' resurrection points backward to God's covenantal relationship with Israel and forward to the salvation of all nations in the risen Lord. In Luke 24:44, after having shown his disciples that his risen body was physical rather than ghostly, Jesus says, "These are my words which I spoke to you, while I was still with you, that everything written about me in the law of Moses and the prophets and the psalms must be fulfilled." The risen Jesus must open his disciples' "minds to understand the scriptures" (24:45) before they can understand why his dying and rising fulfilled all that had been written in the Old Testament. Jesus goes on to command that "repentance and forgiveness of sins should be preached in his name to all nations, beginning from Jerusalem" (24:47). Jesus thereby fulfills and restores Israel (without negating it) and establishes the path of his church.

In this vein, Aquinas offers five reasons for why it was "necessary" for Jesus to rise from the dead. The first reason is the vindication of God's justice, which as Levenson observes characterizes Daniel 12:1-3 among many other texts. By raising Jesus, God showed that his justice triumphs over evildoing and thereby answered a central plaint of Israel. God also showed that Jesus is the just one who has borne Israel's sins and in whom Israel is restored. The next three reasons have to do with how Jesus' resurrection builds up the people of God through faith, hope, and love: the second reason is to confirm our faith that Jesus is the Son of God, the third reason is to inspire our hope that we too will be raised from the dead, and the fourth reason is that the power of the risen Jesus enables us to become holy. Lastly, the fifth reason parallels the first. Just as Jesus' resurrection vindicated God's justice toward the humble Jesus, so the fifth reason states that God will exalt those who follow Jesus in humility: God "deliver[s] us from evil" by the cross and "advance[s] us toward good things" by the resurrection.[36]

The exaltation of Jesus exhibits the path of the exaltation of the whole people of God.

The biblical texts that inform these five reasons also display the fulfillment or restoration of Israel and the upbuilding of the Church. Regarding the first reason, the vindication of God's justice as regards those who suffer for his name, Aquinas quotes Mary's Magnificat: "he has put down the mighty from their thrones, and exalted those of low degree" (Luke 1:52).[37] Mary praises God for helping "his servant Israel, in remembrance of his mercy, as he spoke to our fathers, to Abraham and to his posterity for ever" (1:54-55). In justly raising Jesus, God fulfilled his merciful promises to Israel. Aquinas links Luke 1:52 with Philippians 2:8-9, although he echoes the latter passage rather than directly quoting it. He observes that a "glorious resurrection" befits the "love and obedience to God" that Christ demonstrates in his self-humbling for the sake of sinners.

To these New Testament passages about the exaltation of the humble, Aquinas adds Psalm 139:2, "You know when I sit down and when I rise up."[38] Psalm 139 praises the all-encompassing character of God's knowledge and care for his people and concludes by asking God to punish the wicked and establish perfect justice. In accord with patristic exegesis, Aquinas understands this psalm to have Christ as its speaker. He suggests that the meaning of this verse is God's foreknowledge of Christ's "humiliation and Passion" and Christ's "glorification in the resurrection."[39] If Psalm 139:2 is about Christ's cross and resurrection, the remainder of the psalm shows how these mysteries of Christ's life consummate God's providential plan for the establishment of justice.

The second reason for the necessity of Jesus' resurrection is to instruct the Church in faith. Jesus' resurrection confirmed that the God who governs life has dwelt among us and has conquered sin and death. Aware of the centrality of Jesus' resurrection in Paul's letters, Aquinas cites 2 Corinthians 13:4, "For he was crucified in weakness, but lives by the power of God," and 1 Corinthians 15:14, "If Christ has not been raised, then our preaching is in vain and your faith is in vain."[40] As Israel's Messiah, Jesus is the "first fruits" (1 Cor 15:23) of the restoration of God's people that will occur fully when Jesus returns in judgment. The resurrection shows that Christ lives "by the power of God" (2 Cor 13:4), and this power ensures the future of the people of God.[41]

Levenson would not be surprised that in the same context Aquinas also quotes Psalm 30:9, "What profit is there in my death, if I go down to the pit? [Vulgate: What profit is there in my blood, while I go down into corruption?]" Sheol cannot hold the righteous; God rescues from Sheol.[42] Jesus' resurrection is necessary for faith in God because Israel's God does not abandon the righteous to Sheol, and Jesus is supremely righteous. Aquinas comments that the "necessity" here involves our faith in Christ: how could the crucified Christ reveal to his people God's victory, if his body simply rotted in the grave?

The third reason for the necessity of Jesus' resurrection is to stimulate the Church in hope. Aquinas cites 1 Corinthians 15:12, where Paul argues that the position of the Sadducees is no longer tenable, now that Jesus has risen from the dead. Aquinas also quotes Job 19:25, which in the Vulgate reads, "I know that my redeemer lives, and in the last day I shall rise out of the earth."[43] Although Levenson believes that the Book of Job does not teach resurrection, he points out that Job's frequent complaint that God does not rescue him is reversed at the end of the book where God does rescue Job. Hope arises from the knowledge that God has in fact rescued Jesus from death.

Aquinas supports his fourth and fifth reasons for the necessity of Jesus' resurrection by quotations from Romans 6 and 4, respectively. He accepts Paul's teaching that the life-giving righteousness required of God's people comes through Christ's fulfillment of the Law. Participating in Christ's cross, we are "dead to sin" with him (Rom 6:11); participating in Christ's resurrection, we are "alive to God" and "walk in newness of life" (Rom 6:4, 11).[44] Even now we share proleptically in the life of glory through the Holy Spirit. Similarly Romans 4:25, which states that Christ was "raised for our justification," reveals our path of life.[45] At issue is how the resurrection of Jesus shapes his members in holiness and advances the Church in her own "passage" configured to his love.[46]

In sum, Aquinas' five reasons for the necessity of Jesus' resurrection provide a biblical theology rooted in the vindication of Israel's God, which inspires faith, hope, and love. Faith, hope, and love incorporate us into the justice of God revealed in the risen Messiah. Aquinas' five reasons for the necessity of Jesus' resurrection illumine the path by which Israel's God, in Levenson's words about the promise of resurrection, "replaces sterility with fertility, childlessness with new descendants (and the return of lost descendants), hopelessness with a radiant future—death with life."[47] By revealing this path of life, Jesus' resurrection accords profoundly with the scriptures of Israel.

Learning from the Little Things: The Third Day, Christ's Scars

In proposing that it was "fitting" that Jesus rose on the "third day," Aquinas appeals to Acts 2:24, "God raised him up, having loosed the pangs of death, because it was not possible for him to be held by it," and Matthew 20:19, "[they will] deliver him to the Gentiles to be mocked and scourged and crucified, and he will be raised on the third day."[48] Acts 2:24 comes from Peter's speech on Pentecost, where he announces the fulfillment of Joel's prophecy about the outpouring of the Spirit prior to the coming of the day of the Lord. Peter proclaims that through Jesus' death and resurrection, accomplished "according to the definite plan and foreknowledge of God" (Acts 2:23), Jesus has been exalted to God's right hand, from whence he pours forth the Spirit. The promised restoration has arrived, and all those who repent and receive baptism will be saved. Matthew 20:19 stands at the beginning of Jesus' final journey to Jerusalem. Jesus explains to his uncomprehending disciples what is going to happen, including his crucifixion and resurrection. The third day, the day of resurrection, will bring about the eschatological "kingdom" (20:21) that Israel's prophets have foretold. By raising Christ on the third day, God acted to restore his people.

The third day therefore evokes for Aquinas the eschatological fulfillment of Israel. Through mystical interpretation, Aquinas expands this to a full-scale theology of history. He points to the three stages of history (before the Law, under the Law, and under grace) as well as the three states under which God's people live: the figures of the Law, the truth of faith, and the eternity of glory. Jesus' resurrection on the third day means that humans now stand under the "light of glory": the eschaton has been inaugurated.[49] Joseph Ratzinger finds similar resonances in the motif of the third day: "the third day is the time for theophany, as, for example, in the central account of the meeting between God and Israel on Sinai," the marriage at Cana "on the third day" (John 2:1), and the resurrection of Jesus.[50] The theophany of Jesus' resurrection reveals the full meaning of the earlier theophanies.

Although these interpretations of the "third day" are mystical rather than historical, the theology of history that emerges is similar to Wright's: Jesus' resurrection brings about the eschatological kingdom for which Israel had been waiting. As Wright emphasizes, this kingdom is attained by self-sacrificial love rather than by violent power. The same point is made by Aquinas' reflection on why Jesus' risen body retains the scars of his Passion (see John 20:27). The scars are "trophies [insignia] of his power."[51] The scars reveal that Jesus' power is that of the good shepherd who freely sacrifices himself for us.[52] As trophies of his self-sacrificial power, the scars tell of his eschatological judgment and restoration of the people of God through his supreme love.[53]

The Manifestation of Christ's Resurrection

The manner in which Jesus manifested his risen body constituted the restored people of God as an interdependent community of faith, hope, and love rather than a collection of enlightened individuals. Because Christ rose to glory rather than being resuscitated to earthly life, he showed his risen body only to chosen witnesses, and even these witnesses did not see him rise from the dead. His followers learned of his glorious resurrection from angels.[54] Like Dunn, Aquinas insists that faith is even required for the apostles: doubting Thomas, for example, saw the risen Jesus' visible wounds, and believed in Jesus' invisible divinity: "My Lord and my God!" (John 20:28).[55] The content of doubting Thomas' confession required faith rather than being established by physical sight alone. The risen Jesus showed his glorified body to his disciples and made clear that his body was a true body.[56] Yet he did not live with them "constantly as he had done before, lest it might seem that he rose unto the same life as before."[57] By rising to glory rather than merely to ongoing earthly life, he showed that the restored people of God have the life of glory as their end.

The risen Jesus also appeared at least once in such a way that his disciples "were kept from recognizing him" (Luke 24:16; cf. Mark 16:12). Agreeing with Gregory the Great, Aquinas thinks that Jesus appeared in this way to the disciples on the Emmaus road because of their weak faith. Before showing himself to them and strengthening their faith, he rebuked them, "O foolish men, and slow of heart to believe all that the prophets have spoken!" (Luke 24:25).[58] To the manifestation of the resurrection, Aquinas applies Paul's dictum, "The unspiritual man does not receive the gifts of the Spirit of God, for they are folly to him, and he is not able to understand them because they are spiritually discerned" (1 Cor 2:14).[59] To come to know Christ's passage we must begin to share in it.

Although it might seem that the strongest demonstrations of Jesus' resurrection are his appearances, Aquinas suggests that the authority of God's word is actually the strongest demonstration.[60] When Jesus explained his resurrection by appealing to Israel's Scriptures, he made his *strongest* case. Jesus not only interpreted Israel's Scriptures directly to his disciples (as he did in Luke 24:27), but he also speaks to us through Israel's Scriptures, as in Micah 7:8, "Rejoice not over me, O my enemy; when I fall, I shall rise."[61] In a similar way, the angels' testimony to Jesus' resurrection (Matt 28:2-7; Mark 16:5-7; Luke 24:4-7; John 20:12) is related to the Old Testament testimony. Indebted to such passages as Galatians 3:19, Acts 7:53, and Hebrews 1–2, Aquinas observes that the Torah "was given by God through the angels."[62] The testimony of the angels to Christ's resurrection can be seen as fulfilling the message of the Torah about God's plan for Israel and the world.

In addition to angelic and scriptural testimony, Jesus showed his followers "signs" that made clear both the real bodiliness and the glory of his risen body. Jesus gave these signs because the disciples were hesitant to believe; in this regard Aquinas quotes Mark 16:14, "Afterward he appeared to the eleven themselves as they sat at table; and he upbraided them for their unbelief and hardness of heart, because they had not believed those who saw him after he had risen."[63] The "signs" made the disciples eyewitnesses of Jesus' resurrection, as indicated by 1 John 1:1's claim to speak about that "which we have heard, which we have seen with our eyes, which we have looked upon and touched with our hands."[64] The signs were of two kinds: signs that showed that his body was a true human body, with nutritive and sensitive capacities; and signs that showed that his body was glorified.[65]

As an example of the latter, the risen Jesus entered into the upper room despite the doors being shut (John 20:19). Similarly, he "vanished out of their sight" (Luke 24:31) after breaking bread with the disciples who were journeying to Emmaus. For Aquinas, these events served to direct the disciples' attention to the glory of the resurrection. This glory had already been manifested, in anticipation, in Jesus' transfiguration, when "his face shone like the sun, and his garments became white as light" (Matt 17:2). Had he appeared in this way after his resurrection, however, he might have seemed to have an unreal body. Instead of showing his disciples the glorious clarity of his risen body, therefore, he exhibited other signs of bodily glory.[66]

Aquinas remarks that Jesus' risen body glorifies God by its sheer goodness. As Jesus says in the Gospel of John in preparation for his Pasch, "Father, the hour has come; glorify your Son that the Son may glorify you" (John 17:1).[67] The glory that Jesus asks from the Father is "the glory which I had with you before the world was made" (John 17:5). Jesus' risen body partakes in this glory. Aquinas comments that "[t]he more fully anything corporeal shares in the divine goodness, the higher its place in the corporeal order, which is order of place."[68] In the order of glory, whose organizing principle is love, Jesus' risen body is above the angels (cf. Eph 1:20-21; Heb 1:4).

Furthermore, Jesus glorifies the Father by bringing his people, united to his holy humanity, into the communion of glory. The Father gives Jesus "power over all flesh, to give eternal life to all whom you have given him" (John 17:2). Aquinas states that "the Word of God first bestows immortal life upon that body which is naturally united with himself, and through it works the resurrection in all other bodies."[69] As the head of his body, Jesus enables his people to share in his glory and to glorify the Father with him through the Holy Spirit. Christ's resurrection is the cause of ours.[70]

CONCLUSION

Levenson shows that the Hebrew Bible/Old Testament portrays Israel's faith in the God of life in such a manner that the vindication of this God will involve the resurrection of his people—the accomplishment of the fullness of life suggested already by the Temple. According to Levenson, the Torah's internal logic is in accord with later Old Testament passages that teach the resurrection of the body more clearly. Wright portrays the late Second-Temple period as one in which many Jews were expecting the return of YHWH to Zion, the forgiveness of the people's sins, the renewal of the Temple, the ingathering of the people, the restoration of the land, and (in short) the end of exile. This was the context in which Jesus redefined Israel around himself and sought to do for Israel and for the world what only YHWH could do. On the cross, Jesus accomplished the victory of God, and God vindicated Jesus' claims by raising him from the dead. Both Wright and Dunn find the resurrection of Jesus to be the most credible way of explaining the particular character of the early church's witness.

Aquinas' theology of Jesus' resurrection supports this emphasis on the accomplishment of God's eschatological purposes through Jesus' resurrection. According to Aquinas, Jesus' resurrection vindicates God's justice and inspires the faith, hope, and love that unite the Church in history to Jesus' passage. The testimony of the angels and apostles to Jesus' resurrection underscores that we receive resurrection faith not as independent individuals but as the people of God. The ways in which the risen Jesus manifested his body show that our glorified bodies will be true bodies but also radically different from bodies as we experience them now. The beauty and goodness of Jesus' risen body, including the scars that testify to his love, glorify God. As the deliverance and restoration of the people of God, whereby God calls his whole people to the perfection of embodied interpersonal love, God's raising Jesus from the dead did indeed take place "in accordance with the scriptures" of Israel. In sum, Aquinas' reflections on the resurrection offer a theology of glory, rooted in the history of God's people and manifested in the body of the Messiah.

3

Sitting at the Right Hand of the Father

ᔑ

Thus far we have discussed two stages of Jesus' passage from death to eternal life. As we argued, he transformed the intermediate state by leading to the vision of God the holy people who had preceded him, and he then rose from the dead to manifest God's justice and to establish his kingdom. After appearing to his disciples "during forty days" (Acts 1:3), he completed his passage by ascending in his glorified flesh to the right hand of the Father. As N. T. Wright states, "Jesus has gone ahead of us into God's space, God's new world, and is both already ruling the present world as its rightful Lord and also interceding for us at the Father's right hand."[1]

Yet, how could Jesus in the flesh sit by the incorporeal Father? Regarding glorified bodiliness, Wright criticizes Plato for causing us "to take for granted a basic ontological contrast between 'spirit' in the sense of something immaterial and 'matter' in the sense of something material, solid, physical."[2] Surely, however, the claim that Jesus sits at the right hand of God requires this "basic ontological contrast" between immaterial and material. Without denying that matter can be (as Pierre Benoit puts it) "transformed, penetrated, and dominated by the Spirit,"[3] we need to account for the reality that the Father does not have a "right hand" and that the human "sitting" of Jesus requires some kind of place.[4] The mystery of the ascension is that the Father is utterly immaterial, and yet Jesus, in his flesh, is now at the Father's "right hand."[5] In addition, the New Testament's descriptions of the ascended Jesus draw especially upon Psalm 110:1, "The Lord says to my lord: 'Sit at my right hand, till I make your enemies your footstool.'" A problem here is that biblical scholarship generally holds that Psalm 110:1 has in view a bodily God.

Addressing these issues, this chapter first surveys the New Testament's references to Psalm 110:1 along with relevant biblical scholarship. I then examine how Aquinas and the Fathers of the church treat the problems that arise in conceiving of Jesus' ascension in terms of the biblical descriptions of God's right hand. As we will see, the "descent" or incarnation of the Son of God culminates in his ascension to what Douglas Farrow describes as "Israel's throne *and* the throne of the Presence from which the Spirit goes forth."[6] Having ascended in the flesh to the divine "throne," Jesus enables his people to join him.

JESUS AT THE RIGHT HAND OF GOD: NEW TESTAMENT TEXTS
AND OLD TESTAMENT CONTEXT

Let us first survey the role of Psalm 110:1 in the New Testament. Making implicit reference to Psalm 110:1 and to Daniel 7:13-14 (the vision of the coming to the divine throne of "one like a son of man"), Jesus answers the high priest's question regarding whether he is the Messiah: "I am; and you will see the Son of man sitting at the right hand of Power, and coming with the clouds of heaven" (Mark 14:62; cf. Matt 26:64; Luke 22:69).[7] Similarly, in making the argument that the messianic Son of David is David's Lord, Jesus cites Psalm 110:1 (Matt 22:44; Luke 20:42-43). The parable of the talents portrays the Son on his glorious throne, and the redeemed "at his right hand" (Matt 25:33).

Moving from the Gospels to Acts, Peter's speech on Pentecost proclaims that the risen and ascended Jesus now lives "exalted at the right hand of God" (Acts 2:33) and from thence pours out the Holy Spirit.[8] Stephen's speech on the day of his martyrdom ends when Stephen, "full of the Holy Spirit, gazed into heaven and saw the glory of God, and Jesus standing at the right hand of God; and he said, 'Behold, I see the heavens opened, and the Son of man standing at the right hand of God'" (Acts 7:55-56). This statement leads Stephen's hearers—with

Saul (later Paul) among the leaders—to seize him, carry him out of Jerusalem, and stone him to death.

In Paul's letters, he affirms that the risen Jesus "is at the right hand of God" and "intercedes for us" (Rom 8:34). Describing the blessings bestowed upon the saints in God's eternal plan of predestination or election, Paul rejoices in the fact that God raised Jesus "from the dead and made him sit at his right hand in the heavenly places, far above all rule and authority and power and dominion" (Eph 1:20-21). In Colossians Paul likewise teaches that Jesus is "seated at the right hand of God" (Col 3:1).

We find the same affirmation in Hebrews: after Jesus "had made purification for sins, he sat down at the right hand of the Majesty on high" (Heb 1:3; cf. Heb 8:1, 10:12-13, 12:2). Hebrews also quotes Psalm 110:1 directly with reference to Jesus (Heb 1:13).[9] First Peter observes that the risen Jesus "has gone into heaven and is at the right hand of God, with angels, authorities, and powers subject to him" (1 Pet 3:22). In short, as James Dunn says of Psalm 110:1, "This verse runs like a gold thread through much of the New Testament, and is so interwoven into the language of the New Testament writers that it evidently was a primary starting point or stimulus for the strong strand of New Testament christology summed up in the confession, 'Jesus is Lord.'"[10]

A Bodily God?

Many biblical scholars, however, consider that the psalmist believed that God actually has a right hand. The biblical archeologist Mark Smith, for example, connects Psalm 110 with the pre-exilic period of the Davidic monarchy, in which "Yahweh ensured national well-being, justice, and fertility (Psalms 2, 72, 89, 110), while the king in turn guaranteed national cult to Yahweh (1 Kgs 8; 2 Kgs 12)."[11] On this view, YHWH is a "national deity," preeminent among the gods (monolatry), who ensures the military and economic success of Israel against the nations.[12] In the period of the late monarchy, Smith says, "depiction of Yahweh became decreasingly anthropomorphic to some extent."[13] Even so, Psalm 110 could envision YHWH's "right hand" not only as his divine power but also as a physical reality. Smith argues that in Exodus 33:22, for example, "The divine hand suggests a super-human appendage that can cover a human being," an understanding of

YHWH rooted in "the older Levantine tradition of describing divinities of superhuman scale."[14]

In his *The Bodies of God and the World of Ancient Israel*, Benjamin Sommer observes, "The God of the Hebrew Bible has a body. This must be stated at the outset, because so many people, including many scholars, assume otherwise. The evidence for this simple thesis is overwhelming, so much so that asserting the carnal nature of the biblical God should not occasion surprise."[15] Sommer cites a wide variety of anthropomorphic texts, beginning with Genesis 1:26 and including Genesis 2:7, 3:8, 11:5, Exodus 33:20, Isaiah 6:1, Amos 9:1, and many more. In his view, according to the Hebrew Bible YHWH actually has various bodies, located at various places in the world. Why then have many theologians and exegetes interpreted the Hebrew Bible/Old Testament as revealing an incorporeal God? According to Sommer, the answer is partly the acceptance of "hackneyed misrepresentations of Jewish scripture that grew out of medieval Christian supersessionism."[16] But the answer also involves medieval Jewish embarrassment with the notion of a corporeal God. In this regard he cites Saadia Gaon and Maimonides, for whom "the denial of God's corporeality was a crucial aspect of monotheism."[17] Sommer grants that the Hebrew Bible does not make explicit that its anthropomorphic language about YHWH is *not* metaphorical. But given its consistent silence about its use of anthropomorphic language, he holds that this language must consistently be taken literally rather than metaphorically.

Smith finds that monotheistic claims emerged from monolatry at the time of Second Isaiah, shortly before the Babylonian Exile.[18] For Sommer, by contrast, Israelite monotheism accepts the existence of many gods but affirms that one god (Israel's) is and always has been absolutely sovereign over other gods and over matter, and was not created or born from something prior.[19] The gods are those who possess free causality and immortality, and thus they can include angels and even humans. Polytheism on this view consists in worshipping many gods rather than only one of them.[20]

The research of Smith and Sommer is relevant to the affirmation of Jesus' sitting at the right hand of the Father, because these issues were already of concern to the first Christians, as indeed to most Second-Temple Jews.[21] Richard Bauckham has shown that Greek philosophical culture sharpened Jewish articulation of God's unique identity in the

Second-Temple period.[22] Bauckham observes that "the overwhelming tendency in Second Temple Judaism was to depict God as absolutely unique, to differentiate God as completely as possible from all other reality, and to understand the exclusive worship of God as marking, in religious practice, the absolute distinction between God and all creatures."[23] In his magisterial study of Psalm 110:1 in Scripture and the early Church, Martin Hengel notes that early Christian apologists such as Justin Martyr feared that the verse might offend the philosophically minded among both pagans and Jews.[24] Not only does the image that suggests that God has a "right hand," but also Jesus has been exalted *in the flesh* to God's right hand, leading to the possibility of a conflation of divinity and humanity. Indeed, although Douglas Farrow faults patristic interpretation for remaining "trapped by the underlying competition between the divine and the creaturely,"[25] worshipping Jesus who sits in the flesh at the Father's "right hand" inevitably raises questions about the relationship between God and his bodily creatures. Put another way, Jesus' sitting at the right hand of the Father so as to pour forth the Holy Spirit upon his people requires reflection upon the nature of God and upon the Incarnation.

AQUINAS ON JESUS' SITTING AT THE RIGHT HAND OF GOD

Interpreting Scripture's Language about God

The third question that Aquinas treats in the *Summa theologiae*, after treating *sacra doctrina* and God's existence, is whether God is bodily. Not surprisingly, in the objections that he gives to his own position, he cites a number of the biblical texts to which scholars such as Smith and Sommer appeal: Genesis 1:26, "Let us make man in our image, after our likeness"; Psalm 34:15, "The eyes of the Lord are toward the righteous, and his ears toward their cry"; Psalm 118:15, "The right hand of the Lord does valiantly"; Job 40:9, "Have you an arm like God, and can you thunder with a voice like his?"; Isaiah 3:13, "The Lord has taken his place to contend, he stands to judge his people"; and Isaiah 6:1, "I saw the Lord sitting upon a throne, high and lifted up; and his train filled the temple."[26] In response to passages such as these, Aquinas adduces other biblical texts, above all Exodus 3:14 and John 4:24, that he considers to be normative. In Exodus 3:14, God names himself, "I am who am." God is not a particular kind of being, a limited mode of being, as he would be if he were in any sense bodily. Aquinas reasons metaphysically that it is "impossible that in God there should be any potentiality," which would be the case for a finite body.[27] This truth is also confirmed, Aquinas thinks, by Jesus' words to the Samaritan woman, "God is spirit, and those who worship him must worship in spirit and truth" (John 4:24).

Aquinas does not thereby ignore the signs in the Old Testament that Israel might have worshipped a corporeal YHWH. He argues that in order to teach certain truths to a philosophically uneducated audience, Scripture at times speaks of God as though God were corporeal: "Corporeal parts are attributed to God in Scripture on account of His actions, and this is owing to a certain parallel. For instance the act of the eye is to see; hence the eye attributed to God signifies His power of seeing intellectually, not sensibly; and so on with other parts."[28] God's authorship of Scripture means that its literal sense may have more than one meaning.[29] Aquinas also points out that the human authors of the biblical writings did not know all the truths that the Holy Spirit intended and that later expositors rightly discern.[30]

Even so, why did God allow biblical authors to use language that suggests that God is bodily? Since we require sense images in order to know intellectual truths, God teaches us according to our capacities.[31] The consequences of sin, too, make it more difficult for us to apprehend intelligible realities. The Holy Spirit wills "that spiritual truths be expounded by means of figures taken from corporeal things, in order that thereby even the simple who are unable by themselves to grasp intellectual things may be able to understand it."[32] The "figures" that express "spiritual truths," however, are only rightly understood when taken metaphorically. This discernment of metaphorical predication is an important task of philosophical reasoning in biblical exegesis. Citing 2 Corinthians 10:5, "We destroy arguments and every proud obstacle to the knowledge of God, and take every thought captive to obey Christ," Aquinas holds that our created rationality "should minister to faith as the natural bent of the will ministers to charity."[33]

Sitting at the Right Hand of the Father

When Aquinas treats Jesus' sitting at the right hand of the Father, he begins by testing his view against three objections, all of which revolve around the issue of corporeality. The first objection argues that since God is not corporeal, it is impossible for Christ, even in his human nature, to be on the "right" or "left" of God the Father. God the Father has no "right" or "left" side. Here Aquinas refers back to his discussion in the *prima pars* of God's incorporeality, and he cites John 4:24, "God is spirit." He concludes, "Therefore it seems that Christ does not sit at the right hand of the Father."[34]

The second objection raises a quite different problem: if Jesus in his exalted flesh is at the Father's right hand, "it follows that the Father is seated on the left of the Son."[35] Given that it is an honor for the incarnate Son to sit at the Father's right hand, does this honor diminish the Father's priority in the Trinity by placing the Father at the Son's left hand? It would seem that Jesus' sitting at the right hand of the Father has the unfortunate consequence of placing the Father and the Son in competition for glory, with the Son winning the competition. For this reason the objector feels compelled to reject the biblical language entirely.

The third objector fully embraces the divine corporeality implied in the biblical language. The objector quotes Stephen's words in Acts 7:56 and takes them literally: "Behold, I see the heavens opened, and the Son of man standing at the right hand of God."[36] But if these words are to be taken literally, then Scripture contradicts itself. After all, Mark 16:19 observes that "the Lord Jesus, after he had spoken to them, was taken up into heaven, and sat down at the right hand of God." If Jesus is sitting, how can he be standing? As Aquinas puts it, "sitting and standing savor of opposition."[37]

How does Aquinas address these exegetical and theological issues? He first affirms the truth of Mark 16:19: the risen Jesus does indeed sit at the right hand of the Father. Aquinas affirms this truth guided by John Damascene, who writes in *The Orthodox Faith*:

> Now, we say that Christ sat in His body at the right hand of the Father, yet we do not mean a physical right hand of the Father. For how would He who is uncircumscribed have a physical right hand? Right and left hands belong to those who are circumscribed. What we call the right hand of the Father is the glory and honor of the Godhead in which the Son of God existed as God and consubstantial with the Father before the ages and in which, having in the last days become incarnate, He sits corporeally with His flesh glorified together with Him, for He and His flesh are adored together with one adoration by all creation.[38]

In these reflections Damascene is drawing upon Gregory of Nazianzus; in turn, Gregory is drawing upon Aristotle. Damascene earlier employs Aristotle's demonstration of a "first mover" to show that God cannot be bodily because a body could not be "limitless, boundless, formless, impalpable, invisible, simple, and uncompounded."[39] It follows that the Father does not have a right hand except in the sense of his eternal "glory and honor." The Father's "right hand" is not a place but a way of speaking about the divine glory.[40] As Aquinas concludes, the meaning of Jesus' sitting at the right hand of the Father is that Jesus now shares unchangeably "in the Father's bliss."[41] As regards Jesus himself, the goal of his descent into hell and resurrection has been attained.

In his analysis, Aquinas draws also upon Augustine, Acts 2, and Psalm 16. In proclaiming that Jesus is "exalted at the right hand of God" (Acts 2:33; cf. 2:27), the Apostle Peter quotes Psalm 16:10-11, "For you do not give me up to Sheol, or let your godly one see the Pit. You show me the path of life; in your presence there is fulness of joy, in your right hand are pleasures for evermore." Augustine comments on this psalm: "Your favor and your bounty are our delights on this life's journey; they will lead us to the height of glory in your own presence."[42] Guided by Augustine, Aquinas interprets the psalmist's "fulness of joy," the "pleasures for evermore" in the Father's "right hand," as "the Father's bliss."[43] As Damascene suggests, were the Father's bliss changeable, then God would in some sense be a body, whereas in fact "God is spirit" (John 4:24). In the flesh, Jesus has entered into the Father's bliss.

Aquinas also holds that "Christ is said to sit at the right hand of the Father inasmuch as He reigns together with the Father, and has judiciary power from Him; just as he who sits at the king's right hand helps him in ruling and judging."[44] This interpretation of sitting at the king's right hand has affinities with the original meaning of Psalm 110:1 as applied to David.[45] The remainder of Psalm 110 shows how the Davidic king, at the Lord's right hand, shares in the Lord's rule: "The Lord sends forth from Zion your mighty scepter. Rule in the midst of your foes! . . . The Lord is at your right hand; he will shatter kings on the day of his wrath" (Ps 110:2, 5). Beyond these images of military conquest, the Lord also promises the Davidic king, "The Lord has sworn and will not change his mind, 'You are a priest for ever, after the order of Melchizedek'" (Ps 110:4). To sit at God's "right hand" involves both royal and priestly power. The "right hand" of God is the just and merciful "ruling and judging" of the God who is love. In this sense, as Aquinas says (quoting Augustine), God is nothing but "right hand."[46] This befits a love that, in Damascene's words, is "limitless, boundless, formless, impalpable, invisible, simple, and uncompounded." When Jesus attains the goal of his descent into hell and his resurrection, he enjoys the Father's bliss as the priest-king who leads creation to share in this bliss.

Sitting and Standing

Reflecting on the difference between Jesus' "sitting" and "standing" at the right hand of God, Aquinas calls to mind a homily by Gregory the Great on the ascension.[47] In this homily, Gregory proposes that these two descriptions indicate the relationship of humans to God, who is both judge and advocate. Gregory considers that Mark's description of Jesus sitting has to do with the expectation of Jesus' return in judgment to bring all things to a glorious consummation. Since a judge normally sits, Gregory reasons, so does Jesus in Mark's portrait. Likewise, Stephen's vision of Jesus standing corresponds to the fact that humans normally stand to help others, and Jesus is helping Stephen during his ordeal, just as he helps the whole Church attain to the Father's bliss through the royal road of suffering. In his *Commentary on the Epistle to the Hebrews*, Aquinas argues that sitting is the posture of "authority" and "stability" (or "immobility") as regards judicial power and "regal dignity."[48] The posture of standing signifies the power to help: "He stands to oppose with strength. Hence, He was standing, as it were prepared to help Stephen in his agony."[49] For Aquinas, then, the metaphors of "sitting" and "standing" at the right hand of the Father teach us about how Jesus leads the people of God into the Father's bliss. Descriptions of his posture depict not his bodily position but rather the authority and power that he, with the Father, now exercises for us.[50]

Does Jesus sit "at the right hand of God" only after his resurrection and ascension? According to Hebrews, the one "through whom" God the Father "created the world" (1:2), the one who "reflects the glory of God and bears the very stamp of his nature" (1:3), is also the one who "sat down at the right hand of the Majesty on high" (1:3) after making purification for sins. It follows both that Jesus' sitting at the right hand of the Father signifies his human sharing in the divine power to rule and judge, and that Jesus does not *merely* attain to a share in God's glory. Rather, as the Son, Jesus is the one through whom the Father creates all things. As Richard Bauckham remarks, "for Hebrews, Jesus' high priesthood entailed both true divinity and true humanity."[51] The Son must be eternally at the "right hand of the Father" insofar as this image signifies "the glory and honor of the Godhead in which the Son of God existed as God and consubstantial with the Father before the ages."[52] Through his paschal mystery, the incarnate Son ascends to the right hand of the Father in order to exercise, in the flesh, the royal and priestly work of ruling and judging all creation, that is, of bringing the Church, as "the body of Christ" (1 Cor 12:27), to share in the Father's bliss through the Holy Spirit.

The Father's Right Hand

In the writings of the Fathers, the divine Son sometimes receives the name of the Father's "right hand." Aquinas argues that this name is given to the Son "by appropriation," that is, in order to shed light on the names that designate personal properties of the Son (Word, Image).[53] For example, Irenaeus depicts the Son and Spirit as the Father's "hands," in order to affirm against the Gnostics that God needed no help from lesser beings to make all things.[54] Similarly, *Discourse IV against the Arians*, a pro-Nicene tract written around 340 that has been mistakenly attributed to Athanasius, interprets Psalm 74:11's reference to "God's hand" as a description of the Son of God.[55] In light of God's delay in vindicating his people, Psalm 74:11 asks God, "Why do you hold back your hand, why do you keep your right hand in your bosom?" *Discourse IV* connects this psalm with John 1:18, "No one has ever seen God; the only Son, who is in the bosom of the Father, he has made him known." The one who is "in the bosom of the Father" is the Father's "right hand."

This connection seems less far-fetched in light of the context of Psalm 74, which begins, "O God, why do you cast us off for ever?" Psalm 74 is a lament for the loss of the temple, which has been burned to the ground. In addition, Psalm 74 laments the loss of God's presence through the prophets: "We do not see our signs; there is no longer any prophet, and there is none among us who knows how long" (74:9). The psalmist begs God to redeem and restore his people Israel: "Have regard for your covenant; for the dark places of the land are full of the habitations of violence. Let not the downtrodden be put to shame; let the poor and needy praise your name" (74:20-21). According to *Discourse IV*, therefore, in Jesus Christ God's "right hand" came forth from his "bosom" to fulfill the petitions of the people of God. When God's "right hand" came forth, God vindicated his covenantal promises, lifted up the downtrodden, and led the poor and needy to praise God's name. In the flesh, Jesus now sits at the right hand of God so as to raise his people to God's right hand.

Discourse IV has its eye upon the Arian teaching that the Son is not coequal with the Father, and so its treatment of God's "right hand" focuses upon Christ's divinity, the fact that this "hand" is "in the bosom of the Father" (John 1:18; cf. Ps 74:11). Thus it argues that when Psalm 77:10 complains that "the right hand of the Most High has changed"— as if God could have "forgotten to be gracious" or "in anger shut up his compassion" (77:9)—the meaning is that the Father's "right hand" has become incarnate. The Incarnation is the change, as it were, by which the Father's "right hand" comes forth to save. The Father's "right hand" is the incarnate Son, and this Son is co-equal to the Father in divinity. As *Discourse IV* puts it, "if the hand is in the bosom, and the Son in the bosom, the Son will be the hand, and the hand will be the Son."[56]

When Mark 16:19 speaks of Jesus as sitting at God's "right hand," Aquinas too has in view Jesus' divinity and the danger of subordinating the Son to the Father. He states that "three things can be understood under the expression *right hand*. First of all, as Damascene takes it, *the glory of the Godhead*; secondly, according to Augustine, *the beatitude of the Father*; thirdly, according to the same authority, *judiciary power*."[57] Aquinas also notes that the Gloss on Romans 8:34 ("Christ Jesus . . . who is at the right hand of God") explains that being at God's "right hand" means "equal to the Father in that honor whereby God is the Father."[58] The Gloss on Hebrews 1:3 ("sat down at the right hand of the Majesty on high") makes the same point, explaining that the phrase means that the Son "is in equality with the Father over all things, both in place and dignity."[59] The fact that it is this same Son, the divine creator and sustainer of the universe, who in the flesh "made purification for sins" and then "sat down at the right hand of the Majesty on high" (Heb 1:3), indicates the consummation of the Incarnation in the divine Son Jesus' exercise of priestly and royal power at the Father's right hand.[60]

Aquinas emphasizes that for the Son to be "at the right hand" of the Father implies no subordination of the Son to the Father. Only if the Son is fully divine can the Son possess, "unchangeably and royally," the Father's glory, beatitude, and judiciary power.[61] The incarnate

Son's sitting at the right hand of the Father cannot be separated from the Son's identity as the one "who is in the bosom of the Father" (John 1:18). The preposition "at" indicates not a spatial reality—since the Father has no "right hand"—but rather "personal distinction and order of origin."[62] Thus the preposition "at" does not indicate "degree of nature or dignity, for there is no such thing in the divine Persons."[63] Divinity does not admit of degree: the Son is either God, or a mere creature. Since the power of generation in the Father is perfect, the Father as the "principle" of the Son generates a perfect image who perfectly possesses the divine nature.[64] Were this not the case, then as Aquinas points out there would have been no kenosis in the Incarnation, contrary to Philippians 2:6.[65]

In his *Commentary on the Epistle to the Hebrews*, Aquinas notes that the phrase "sat down at the right hand" can refer either to Jesus' divinity or his humanity. As regards Jesus' divinity it signifies his "equality with the Father"; as regards Jesus' humanity it signifies his created goodness.[66] Indeed, compared with any other creature, Jesus' human nature is "superior simply speaking,"[67] as Hebrews goes on to say: "having become as much superior to angels as the name he has obtained is more excellent than theirs" (1:4). Admittedly, there is a Nestorian or adoptionist temptation here: it could seem that in the ascension, the man Jesus joins up with the Son who dwells eternally at the "right hand" of the Father. Aquinas avoids this error by arguing that the "grace of union" implies not only distinction of nature but also unity of Person.[68] Jesus is one Person, one acting subject, the Son of God. Jesus in his humanity is not adopted into the divine life as a reward for his making "purification for sins" (Heb 1:3). This is so because Jesus truly is the "Son, whom he appointed the heir of all things, through whom also he created the world" (Heb 1:2).

Does this mean, however, that Jesus' sitting down at the right hand of God, after making purification for sins, adds nothing to Jesus in his humanity? Aquinas affirms that Jesus' sitting (as man) at the right hand of God means that "Christ as man is exalted to divine honor."[69] But Aquinas immediately adds that "nevertheless such honor belongs to him as God, not through any assumption, but through his origin from eternity."[70] Aquinas is here hard at work to preserve the unity of Jesus' two natures in his one Person, so as to avoid undermining the truth that "the Word became flesh and dwelt among us" (John 1:14). This Chalcedonian insistence on the Incarnation does not, however, evacuate the drama of Jesus' exaltation "to divine honor." Morna Hooker suggests that Mark 16:19 refers to Jesus as sitting at the right hand of God because this description, drawn from Psalm 110:1, had become a standard way for the early Church to express Jesus' Lordship.[71] Once Jesus' Lordship is properly understood, then Aquinas' insistence that "Christ as man is the Son of God, and consequently sits at the Father's right hand"[72] can be seen to ground the transhistorical drama in which Jesus ascends to the right hand of the Father and exercises priestly and royal power so as to bring the creation to its consummation.

Jesus and the Holy Spirit

The grace of the Holy Spirit renders Jesus, in his humanity, fit to be the "head" of his body the Church, the people of God.[73] As the "one mediator between God and men" (1 Tim 2:5), Jesus is the sole Savior of humankind, in every time and place.[74] From eternity, the mission of the Holy Spirit in perfecting the holy humanity of the Son has as its goal the eschatological consummation of the whole Church. Aquinas holds that all humans "have received grace on account of his grace, according to Romans 8:29, 'For those whom he foreknew he also predestined to be conformed to the image of his Son, in order that he might be the first-born among many brethren.'"[75] Reflecting upon the outpouring of grace through Jesus, Aquinas comments that "it behooved him to have grace which would overflow upon others, according to John 1:16, 'And of his fulness we have all received, and grace for grace.'"[76]

In this historical drama, Jesus' charity and humility in his Passion merit the glorious exaltation of his humanity. Aquinas sees this connection between Jesus' Passion and resurrection in Philippians 2:8-11, among other places: "And being found in human form he humbled himself and became obedient unto death, even death on a cross. Therefore God has highly exalted him and bestowed on him the name which is above every name, that at the name of Jesus every knee should bow . . . and every tongue confess that Jesus Christ is Lord, to the glory of God the Father."[77] Discussing the reward of Jesus' charity, Aquinas reasons that "when any man through his just will has stripped himself of what he ought to have, he deserves that something further be granted to him as the reward of his just will."[78] While the language here is philosophical, the thought is biblical. Aquinas quotes Jesus' promise in Luke 14:11, "For every one who exalts himself will be humbled, and he who humbles himself will be exalted."[79] Out of supreme love, Jesus accepts suffering and death, endures mockery, suffers persecution, and descends into hell. This fourfold kenosis merits a fourfold exaltation, consisting in his resurrection from the dead, his ascension into heaven, his sitting at the right hand of the Father and being acknowledged as God, and his attainment of judiciary power.[80]

On this view, Jesus' sitting as our priest-king at the right hand of the Father flows from what Jesus merits by his kenotic Passion. Isaiah 52–53 offers crucial insight here. The Servant's "appearance was so marred, beyond human semblance, and his form beyond that of the sons of men. . . . He was despised and rejected by men; a man of sorrows, and acquainted with grief; and as one from whom men hide their faces he was despised, and we esteemed him not" (52:14, 53:3). Describing Jesus' sitting at the right hand of the Father, Aquinas quotes Isaiah 52:13, "Behold, my servant shall prosper, he shall be exalted and lifted up, and shall be very high."[81] This prophecy applies, Aquinas thinks, to Jesus at the right hand of the Father: the Servant is revealed to be "very high," indeed to possess the very Godhead of the Father.[82]

Because he is the incarnate Son, the grace of the Holy Spirit "is more fully in Christ than in all other creatures, so much so that human nature in Christ is more blessed than all other creatures, and possesses over all other creatures royal and judiciary power."[83] Through his "royal and judiciary power," he builds up the people of God. Aquinas states that "the very showing of himself in the human nature which he took with him to heaven is a pleading for us; so that for the very reason that God so exalted human nature in Christ, he may take pity on them for whom the Son of God took human nature."[84] He took "his heavenly seat as God and Lord" not in order to lord it over rational creatures who have not received the "mightier gifts" that he received in his humanity.[85] Rather, as befits the supreme charity of his Passion, he took his heavenly seat so as to "send down gifts upon men, according to Ephesians 4:10: 'He ascended above all the heavens, that he might fill all things,' that is, 'with his gifts,' according to the gloss."[86] As Farrow puts it, "it is plainly towards this sacred ascension as high priest and king that he [Jesus] moves on his way to the destiny of man. . . . Through his resurrection and ascension he will realize in the presence of God the fruit of the work he accomplished here with us."[87]

Do the Blessed Sit at the Right Hand of the Father?

Aquinas connects Micah 2:13, "He who opens the breach will go up before them"—a verse that in context has Christological and ecclesiological resonances—with Jesus' statement in John 14:2-3, "In my Father's house are many rooms; if it were not so, would I have told you that I go to prepare a place for you? And when I go and prepare a place for you, I will come again and take you to myself, that where I am you may be also."[88] Since Jesus sits at the right hand of the Father, it seems that we will do so too; otherwise we could not be where Jesus is. Aquinas also quotes Ephesians' statement that God, in his merciful love, "made us alive together with Christ (by grace you have been saved), and raised us up with him, and made us sit with him in the heavenly places in Christ Jesus" (2:5-6).[89] Ephesians promises that we will sit with the Father in Christ Jesus. Aquinas adds that the seer of the Book of Revelation reports a similar promise made by the risen Jesus to the church in Laodicea: "He who conquers, I will grant him to sit with me on my throne, as I myself conquered and sat down with my Father on his throne" (3:21).[90]

This extraordinary promise receives surprisingly little attention in contemporary commentaries on the Book of Revelation. Judith Kovacs and Christopher Rowland, for example, do not mention Revelation 3:21 in their commentary, despite their attention to the Church's exegetical tradition.[91] Robert Mulholland remarks only that "citizenship in New Jerusalem is participation in the victory of Jesus over the fallen order, it is ruling with him. But the churches are reminded of the nature of Jesus' throne; it is one that is gained through death."[92] Similarly, Ben Witherington comments without elaboration, "The victor gets to have ongoing fellowship with Christ and to sit with him on his throne."[93] Sitting with Jesus on his throne, however, sounds like sitting at the right hand of the Father. It sounds as though we will gain a share in his divinity with the Father and the Holy Spirit. Is this the goal that Jesus, as the priest-king of all creation, aims to accomplish for us?

Aquinas addresses this question by adducing a further biblical text, Hebrews 1:13, which follows shortly after Hebrews 1:3's affirmation that the risen Jesus sits at the right hand of God.[94] Hebrews 1:13 asks rhetorically, "But to what angel has he ever said, 'Sit at my right hand, till I make your enemies a stool for your feet?'" Clearly the implied answer is that God has said this to no angel, and to no human other than Jesus. Only the Son, through whom the Father created the world and who "reflects the glory of God and bears the very stamp of his nature" (Heb 1:3), sits at the right hand of God. Aquinas argues for the absolute uniqueness of Jesus' sitting at the right hand of God, not only as regards Jesus' divinity but also as regards his humanity. No other human is the Son of God, and no other human receives the perfection of beatitude and judicial power that Christ receives in his humanity. As Aquinas puts it, Jesus as God "is on equality with the Father," while as human "he excels all creatures in the possession of divine gifts."[95] In this sense, it belongs to Jesus alone to sit at the right hand of God.

What then does Ephesians 2:6 mean, or Revelation 3:21? If we do not sit with Jesus at the right hand of God in the same way that Jesus does, how are we "fellow heirs with Christ" (Rom 8:17)? Aquinas answers that even if the beatitude of Jesus in his humanity is greater than that of any angel or of any other human, nonetheless in another sense "it can be said that every saint in bliss is placed on God's right hand; hence it is written (Matt 25:33): 'He shall set the sheep on his right hand.'"[96] Given the truth of such passages as Ephesians 2:6 and Revelation 3:21, we can say that the beatitude of the blessed differs only by degree from the beatitude of Jesus in his humanity. The "light" of divine glory makes "deiform" the intellect of the blessed.[97] Glorified humans truly know God in himself, rather than knowing merely a created intermediary. Nothing less than this could fulfill the intimacy promised also by 1 John 3:2, "Beloved, we are God's children now; it does not yet appear what we shall be, but we know that when he appears we shall be like him, for we shall see him as he is," and Revelation 21:23, "And the city has no need of sun or moon to shine upon it, for the glory of God is its light, and its lamp is the Lamb."[98] The fact that Jesus' sitting at the right hand of the Father is unique does not mean that no others participate in the beatitude that he enjoys in his humanity.

Aquinas considers that in Revelation 3:21, Christ's sitting on the Father's throne refers to Christ's judiciary power. In support of this view, he quotes Ephesians' testimony that the Father "has put all things under his [Jesus'] feet and has made him the head over all things for the church" (1:22) as well as Acts 10:42, where Peter proclaims that the risen Jesus "commanded us to preach to the people, and to testify that he is the one ordained by God to be judge of the living and the dead."[99] Jesus uniquely judges all rational creatures as the compassionate high priest (Heb 4:15) and supreme "king of peace" (Heb 7:2) who suffered and died to fulfill all justice.[100] Insofar as Jesus, at the Father's right hand, sends the Holy Spirit upon us so as to configure us to his cruciform love, we will share eschatologically in his judging as well. Jesus promises Peter and the disciples, "Truly, I say to you, in the new world, when the Son of man shall sit on his glorious throne, you who have followed me will also sit on twelve thrones, judging the twelve tribes of Israel" (Matt 19:28).[101] Paul similarly tells the Corinthians, "Do you not know that the saints will judge the world?" (1 Cor 6:2).[102] Yet Paul also affirms the uniqueness of God's judging: "For we shall all stand before the judgment seat of God" (Rom 14:10).[103]

In ascending to the right hand of the Father, Jesus works to accomplish the consummation of all things in God. For the evangelist Matthew, according to W. D. Davies and Dale Allison, "the future was above all two things: Christ and Israel. The παλιγγενεσία for him meant the world in which Christ reigns, a world with a redeemed Israel."[104] Without possessing a Second-Temple understanding of the restoration of Israel, Aquinas too thinks of the new creation as "the world in which Christ reigns, a world with a redeemed Israel." The Messiah's judgment, in which the blessed will share, will establish the new creation, the fullness of the kingdom of God.[105] Whereas bodies as we know them now primarily manifest material order, glorified bodies will primarily manifest spiritual order, the supreme wisdom and charity of Trinitarian communion. Aquinas adds that because the actions of every human have an influence down through the ages, "the body remains subject to change down to the close of time: and therefore it must receive its reward or punishment then, in the last judgment."[106]

CONCLUSION

After his descent into hell and his resurrection, Jesus ascended to the right hand of the Father. To express the reality of Jesus' ascension, the New Testament authors drew upon Psalm 110:1 and its corporeal image for God. As we have seen, the problems raised by modern historical-critical scholarship regarding such images for God were not unknown in Second-Temple Judaism and the early Church. For Aquinas, as for the first Christians, Scripture's bodily portraits of God are metaphorical: God the Father does not have a "right hand." In another sense, God is nothing but "right hand," just and merciful judgment.[107] In yet another sense, the Son always sits at the Father's "right hand" because of his equality of nature and distinction of Person. The posture of the incarnate Son expresses his judiciary power and his intercession for us, which he accomplishes as king and priest of the people of God. Sitting at the right hand of the Father signals Jesus' authority and power to establish his people in righteousness and to bring us to share in the divine life. Indeed, because of the communion between head and body, the Church already participates in Jesus' reign, both in the sense that the royal exaltation of the head will entail the exaltation of his body and in the sense that humans approach God's "right hand" by sanctifying grace and the indwelling of the Holy Spirit, which Jesus supremely possesses and which we receive through his priestly intercession.[108]

Does Jesus' humanity fade into the background, as Douglas Farrow fears may be the case in certain patristic doctrines of the ascension?[109] When Jesus ascends in the flesh to the right hand of the Father, this ascension belongs to none other than the Son of God, who is eternally at the right hand of the Father. Yet it is as the divine Son made man that, in the economy of salvation, he rules and judges all other creatures so as to bring about the kingdom of God. The grace of the Holy Spirit comes to us through his human reign and intercession. By his passage in the flesh to his Father, the Son prepares a place for all those who receive "from his fulness . . . grace upon grace" (John 1:16; cf. John 14:3). As the Father's "right hand" at work in Israel and the Church, he brings his members to the "right hand" that is the eternal divine glory.

Jean Daniélou reminds us that the mystery of Jesus' sitting at the right hand of the Father "is contemporary with ourselves."[110] At the Father's right hand, Jesus pours forth his Holy Spirit upon the Church. Through faith, the sacraments, and works of love, the Church is already united to Jesus. At the same time, the Church yearns in eschatological tension for the consummation of this supreme friendship. By his descent into hell, resurrection, and ascension to the right hand of the Father, Jesus works to accomplish our passage from death to eternal life. Our passage, therefore, is the theme to which we now turn.

Part II

THE PASSAGE OF CHRIST'S PEOPLE

4

A People in Passage
Faith, Eucharist, Almsgiving

∾

We have seen that Jesus' passage always has in view our participation in it. The Son of God undertook his paschal journey for our sake. If so, however, what should the life of believers be like as we await the glorious return of Jesus (Acts 1:11) and the consummation of all things? What characterizes the Church as a people in passage?

The Second Vatican Council's Dogmatic Constitution on the Church, *Lumen Gentium*, seeks to answer this question. *Lumen Gentium* states, "Rising from the dead (cf. Rom. 6:9) he sent his life-giving Spirit upon his disciples and through him set up his Body which is the Church as the universal sacrament of salvation. Sitting at the right hand of the Father he is continually active in the world in order to lead men to the Church and, through it, join them more closely to himself."[1] Jesus unites us to himself through the gift of faith, through which we affirm "not the mere word of men, but truly the word of God (cf. 1 Th. 2:13), the faith once for all delivered to the saints (cf. Jude 3)."[2] In faith the Church celebrates the Eucharist, in which "the unity of believers, who form one body in Christ (cf. 1 Cor. 10:17), is both expressed and brought about" so as to make us "partakers of his glorious life."[3] The Holy Spirit provides the Church with "hierarchic and charismatic gifts" that enable members of the Church to "serve each other unto salvation so that, carrying out the truth in love, we may through all things grow unto him who is our head (cf. Eph. 4:11-16)."[4] *Lumen Gentium* emphasizes that "the Church encompasses with her love all those who are afflicted by human misery and she recognizes in those who are poor and who suffer, the image of her poor and suffering founder. She does all in her power to relieve their need and in them she strives to serve Christ."[5]

Does *Lumen Gentium*'s view of the Church retain the first Christians' eschatological stance, or have the centuries tamed the eschatological witness of the believing community? In favor of the latter view, Larry Hurtado argues that in the fourth century "imperial Christianity lost the earlier understanding of itself as the provisional witness to the Kingdom of God, and quickly imagined itself to be that Kingdom in its own structures and earthly prominence (which had in fact been established under Constantine by very familiar use of imperial force)."[6] Similarly, N. T. Wright proposes that Christians quickly abandoned first-century eschatology, which was all too often replaced by the hope for an "escape from the present universe into some Platonic realm of eternal bliss enjoyed by disembodied souls after the end of the space-time universe."[7] Wright grants that some first-century Jews had a Hellenized expectation of an intermediate state (see chap. 1 above), but he warns that "it would be a great mistake to regard a Hellenized expectation as basic, and to place the socio-political hope in a secondary position."[8] From a more radical perspective, but with the same connection between eschatology and radical politics, John Howard Yoder states, "Christendom does not merely need improvement around the edges; it has become disobedient at the heart. The unfaithfulness is at the same time ritual, dogmatic, moral, ecclesiastical, etc."[9] Other scholars such as Richard Horsley suggest that the New Testament itself is the problem, because it too often fails to protest the structures of the Roman Empire.[10]

By contrast, I think that the Church has remained faithful to the New Testament marks of the eschatological community, namely the apostolic teaching and fellowship, eucharistic worship, and sharing of possessions (Acts 2). Without denying the value of other elements such as baptism or of more systematic approaches to the mystery of the Church, I wish to examine how these three elements effect the Church's eschatological orientation "toward the coming dawn of Christ's redemptive victory and the summing up of all things in Christ."[11] This chapter first explores the three elements according to the Book of Acts, the Gospel of John, and the letters of Paul. In light of this biblical survey, I then address faith, the Eucharist, and almsgiving in Thomas Aquinas' theology. Aquinas illumines for us the eschatological community that, awaiting the return of the risen and ascended Christ, was "filled with the Holy Spirit and spoke the word of God with boldness" (Acts 4:31).[12]

NEW TESTAMENT MARKS OF THE ESCHATOLOGICAL COMMUNITY

The Book of Acts

The Book of Acts states that the risen Jesus, prior to his ascension, appeared to his disciples and spoke to them "of the kingdom of God" (1:3). His disciples ask him when the kingdom will arrive: "Lord, will you at this time restore the kingdom to Israel?" (1:6). He replies that although the Father does not will that the disciples should know the "times or seasons" (1:7), they will "receive power when the Holy Spirit has come upon you; and you shall be my witnesses in Jerusalem and in all Judea and Samaria and to the end of the earth" (1:8).[13] Having said this, he ascends into heaven. Two men in white robes instruct the disciples that they should cease gazing after him and that they should expect his return. Shortly thereafter, on the Jewish feast of Pentecost, the sound of wind and the appearance of tongues of fire signal the outpouring the Holy Spirit upon them, so that they begin to speak in foreign languages and are able to communicate to the Jews of the Diaspora who had assembled in Jerusalem for the feast. Speaking on behalf of all the disciples, Peter proclaims the resurrection and exaltation of Jesus to the assembled multitude (Acts 2:36).[14]

Wondering whether the kingdom has arrived, the multitude asks Peter what they should do. Peter urges them to repent and be baptized. Now that the Spirit has been poured out, as Joel prophesied would happen prior to the coming of "the day of the Lord" (Acts 2:20, quoting Joel 2:30), repentance and baptism in the name of Jesus brings the gift of the Holy Spirit that will save the people from the coming eschatological judgment.[15]

But what to do after repentance and baptism, once the Holy Spirit has been received? Acts states that the newly baptized "devoted themselves to the apostles' teaching and fellowship, to the breaking of bread and the prayers" (2:42). Here we see the fundaments of the eschato-logical community: apostolic teaching and fellowship, and the litur-gical celebration of the Eucharist.[16] The eschatological community is also known by its sharing of possessions so that all have a sufficiency: "And all who believed were together and had all things in common; and they sold their possessions and goods and distributed them to all, as any had need" (2:44-45; cf. 4:32-35).[17] Everyday life as a believer in Jesus involves receiving the apostolic teaching, the liturgical breaking of bread together, and sharing possessions. Acts observes that "day by day, attending the temple together and breaking bread in their homes, they partook of food with glad and generous hearts, praising God and having favor with all the people" (2:46-47).

Peter gives another speech proclaiming the resurrection of Jesus and the need for repentance in preparation for Jesus' eschatological return in judgment. Repentance, Peter says, will free the people from their sins and give them "times of refreshing" (Acts 3:19).[18] On the day of the Lord, God will "send the Christ appointed for you, Jesus, whom heaven must receive until the time for establishing all that God spoke by the mouth of his holy prophets from of old" (3:21). Peter's words lead many of his auditors to believe in Jesus. The leaders of the Jewish commu-nity in Jerusalem, however, consider that Peter has led the people astray by teaching Jesus' resurrection, with the result that the apostles spend a night in prison.

This beginning of persecution is paralleled by the discovery of self-ishness and falsehood within the community of believers. Ananias and Sapphira die as soon as their lies are discovered, in sharp contrast with those who experience healing through their faith in Jesus. Shortly there-after, the apostles are arrested again and dissension spreads within the community of believers, when "the Hellenists murmured against the Hebrews because their widows were neglected in the daily distribution" (Acts 6:1).[19]

The first martyr is the deacon Stephen, who preaches about the longstanding infidelity of God's people Israel and affirms that the risen Jesus is the eschatological "Son of man standing of the right hand of God" (Acts 7:56) in preparation for the day of judgment.[20] His auditors, thinking that they have heard blasphemy, formally punish Stephen by stoning him to death. As a result, "a great persecution arose against the church in Jerusalem; and they were all scattered throughout the region of Judea and Samaria, except the apostles" (8:1). This persecution again is paralleled by dissension within the Church itself. After Paul's conversion, he joins the apostolic community in Jerusalem, but when "he spoke and disputed against the Hellenists" (9:29), they try to kill him. Paul is sent back to Tarsus.

Herod kills James the brother of John and imprisons Peter, who miraculously escapes. Paul begins his mission to the Jewish Diaspora; in Lystra he is stoned nearly to death (Acts 14:19). Dissension arises about whether salvation requires circumcision, and some believers in Jesus, belonging to "the party of the Pharisees" (15:5),[21] argue that the answer is yes. The apostles and elders formally meet in Jerusalem to decide the question. Peter and Paul argue that salvation comes through "the grace of the Lord Jesus" rather than Torah observance. James proposes the compromise that wins the day: gentile believers are to "abstain from what has been sacrificed to idols and from blood and from what is strangled and from unchastity" (15:29).[22]

Paul, along with his companions and converts, receives further beatings and imprisonments but continues to spread the gospel. Taking leave of the elders of the church of Ephesus, Paul urges them to be strong in the face of coming dissensions: "Take heed to yourselves and to all the flock, in which the Holy Spirit has made you guardians, to feed the church of the Lord which he obtained with his own blood. I know that after my departure fierce wolves will come in among you, not sparing the flock; and from among your own selves will arise men speaking perverse things" (Acts 20:28-29).[23] From the community of believers will come false believers who will seek to lead others astray, out of the desire for power and self-aggrandizement.[24]

Given the inevitable presence of "fierce wolves" both within and without, how do believers avoid becoming what Peter describes as "this crooked generation" (Acts 2:40), unprepared for the eschatological consummation? The answer, Acts suggests, has to do with the marks of the eschatological community. Specifically, the apostolic community is united by apostolic teaching, eucharistic worship, and a recognition that all possessions are God's gift to be shared with others according to need. Despite the persecutions and dissensions, these marks continue to unite believers in preparation for the eschatological judgment.

The Gospel of John

The Gospel of John gives us further insight into these three marks. First, the importance of the apostolic teaching appears in the risen Jesus' thrice-repeated injunction to Peter to shepherd Jesus' sheep (John 21).[25] Jesus prays for the disciples' faithfulness to his word. He asks the Father, "Sanctify them in the truth; your word is truth" (17:17). The truth of the apostolic teaching unites believers to God. Jesus teaches that "this is eternal life, that they know you the only true God, and Jesus Christ whom you have sent" (17:3). Rooted in this knowledge, the apostolic community mediates the forgiveness of sins that Jesus offers all humans. The risen Jesus breathes forth his Spirit upon the apostles and tells them, "Receive the Holy Spirit. If you forgive the sins of any, they are forgiven; if you retain the sins of any, they are retained" (20:22-23). The Holy Spirit given by the Father and the Son ensures the apostolic community's mediation of saving truth to the world. At his last supper, Jesus tells his disciples that "I will pray the Father, and he will give you another Counselor, to be with you for ever, even the Spirit of truth" (14:16-17).[26]

Second, the importance of the "breaking of the bread" appears in the Gospel of John in Jesus' teaching that he is the true manna, the true bread from heaven. By eating this "bread," believers possess eternal life. In this manner believers already enjoy an eschatological participation in the divine life, the communion of Father, Son, and Holy Spirit.[27] Jesus teaches the multitude by the Sea of Galilee, "He who eats my flesh and drinks my blood has eternal life, and I will raise him up at the last day. . . . He who eats my flesh and drinks my blood abides in me, and I in him. As the living Father sent me, and I live because of the Father, so he who eats me will live because of me" (6:54, 56-57). This life will be full only "at the last day." Even so, as Jesus says, "he who believes has eternal life. I am the bread of life" (6:47-48). For those who believe, the "breaking of the bread and the prayers" provide a foretaste of the eschatological consummation.[28]

The third mark is almsgiving, sharing one's possessions. Jesus sends his disciples into the world just as he has been sent into the world by the Father, and the disciples must manifest the love of the Son just as Jesus manifests the love of the Father (see John 17:18, 23, 26). Jesus requires his disciples to imitate his own love for them: "This is my commandment, that you love one another as I have loved you. Greater love has no man than this, that a man lay down his life for his friends" (15:12-13).[29] Each believer in Jesus must be prepared to share not only possessions, but indeed his or her own life for the sake of others. This commandment, as Jesus recognizes, is repellent to those who live for themselves. Those who live for themselves do not want their deeds to "be exposed" (3:20) by the light of Jesus' love. The eschatological judgment is thus already present in Jesus: "And this is the judgment, that the light has come into the world, and men loved darkness rather than light, because their deeds were evil" (3:19).

In the Gospel of John, Jesus promises that the apostles' teaching will be sustained by the Holy Spirit, whom the Father will send through the Son. The truth communicated by Jesus and the Spirit already constitutes a participation in the eschatological consummation, as does the community's reception of the bread of life and its radical sharing of possessions in love (see John 14:23). The repentant community of believers manifests to the world the inbreaking of God's salvation.

The Letters of Paul

Paul explains the position of the believer in Jesus: "since we are justified by faith, we have peace with God through our Lord Jesus Christ. Through him we have obtained access to this grace in which we stand, and we rejoice in our hope of sharing the glory of God" (Rom 5:1-2). Is Paul's hope-filled waiting for the eschatological consummation ("sharing the glory of God") marked by the elements of apostolic teaching and fellowship, liturgical breaking of bread, and radical sharing of possessions that we find in Acts and John (both written after Paul's letters)?[30]

As himself an apostle (1 Cor 1:1), Paul warns against dissensions that come from following particular apostles rather than Christ himself. He emphasizes that the apostles teach not themselves but "Christ crucified" (1 Cor 1:23). The apostles are under divine compulsion (see 1 Cor 8:16) to spread the gospel of God's mercy, by which God frees us from our sins in Christ Jesus and makes us in the Spirit "children of God, and if children, then heirs, heirs of God and fellow heirs with Christ, provided we suffer with him in order that we may also be glorified with him" (Rom 8:16-17).[31] God has chosen to spread the gospel through the apostles' teaching. As Paul says in a series of rhetorical questions: "But how are men to call upon him in whom they have not believed? And how are they to believe in him of whom they have never heard? And how are they to hear without a preacher? And how can men preach unless they are sent?" (Rom 10:14-15). As "ministers of a new covenant" (2 Cor 3:6), commissioned by God and sealed by the Holy Spirit, the apostles have received the eschatological mission of proclaiming Jesus Christ in whom "all the promises of God find their Yes" (2 Cor 1:20).

Paul has in view "[a]ll the churches of Christ" (Rom 16:16), and he reminds the Corinthians of "the daily pressure upon me of my anxiety for all the churches" (2 Cor 11:28). The role of the apostle differs from that of a mere teacher, because the apostles' teaching is not separable from their fellowship. Thus Paul does not simply ask his communities to listen to him; he also claims authority over his communities. He admonishes the Corinthian community by letter so that, as he says, "when I come I may not have to be severe in my use of the authority which the Lord has given me for building up and not for tearing down" (2 Cor 13:10).[32] When controversy arises over his teaching, Paul goes up to Jerusalem and, along with his co-worker Barnabas, receives "the right hand of fellowship" (Gal 2:9) from James, Peter, and John. This fellowship, rooted in "the ministry of reconciliation" (2 Cor 5:18), is an eschatological one: "he who sows to the Spirit will from the Spirit reap eternal life" (Gal 6:8). Paul emphasizes that all true "manifestations of the Spirit" result in "building up the church" (1 Cor 14:12).

What about the second mark, the liturgical breaking of bread? The communal "breaking of bread" is not supposed to be for satisfying hunger. The community must not mistake the Eucharist for an ordinary meal. Instead, Paul explains that in the Eucharist, the community is obeying Jesus' command at the Last Supper. He recounts that "the Lord Jesus on the night when he was betrayed took bread, and when he had given thanks, he broke it, and said, 'This is my body which is for you. Do this in remembrance of me.' In the same way also the cup, after supper, saying, 'This cup is the new covenant in my blood. Do this, as often as you drink it, in remembrance of me'" (1 Cor 11:23-25). This remembrance, Paul makes clear, has eschatological significance: "For as often as you eat this bread and drink the cup, you proclaim the Lord's death until he comes" (1 Cor 11:26).

When the community of believers shares in the bread and cup in remembrance of Jesus, this sharing must include all members of the community equally. Paul observes that the divisions that have overtaken the Corinthian community mean that some are receiving the bread and cup in abundance, whereas others are too impoverished to receive. Paul therefore admonishes the community: "When you meet together, it is not the Lord's supper that you eat. For in eating, each one goes ahead with his own meal, and one is hungry and another drunk. What! Do you not have houses to eat and drink in? Or do you despise the church of God and humiliate those who have nothing?" (1 Cor 11:20-22). Failure to ensure that the entire community is able to partake in the Eucharist is a failure of love, and thus is a failure truly to "remember" Christ's body and blood in anticipation of his return in glory. As Paul says, "Whoever, therefore, eats the bread or drinks the cup of the Lord in an unworthy manner will be guilty of profaning the body and blood of the Lord" (1 Cor 11:27). If at the eucharistic table a person lacks love, that person "eats and drinks judgment upon himself" (1 Cor 11:29). In relation to the eschatological judgment, such a person is spiritually "weak and ill" or even dead (1 Cor 11:30).[33]

The community's union in love, Paul emphasizes, is expressed and built up in the "breaking of bread and the prayers." When the community of believers comes together for the Eucharist, the community with its many members shares in "one bread" and therefore shows itself to be "one body" (1 Cor 10:17). The sharing of bread is a sign of inclusion in Christ's Pasch. This inclusion actually comes about in the sharing of bread, so the sharing is not merely a sign, but a sign that brings about the eschatological reality. In this vein Paul asks rhetorically, "The cup of blessing which we bless, is it not a participation in the blood of Christ? The bread which we break, is it not a participation in the body of Christ?" (1 Cor 10:16).[34] To break the bread and bless the cup together provides the community with a participation in the Pasch of Christ, a participation that is similar to a marital union: "For, as it is written, 'The two shall become one.' But he who is united to the Lord becomes one spirit with him" (1 Cor 6:16-17).[35]

This participation, Paul points out, differentiates Christian worship from that of the altar of the Jerusalem Temple. Just as Jews who partake in the Temple sacrifices are "partners in the altar" (1 Cor 10:18), so also Christians become "partners in the altar" of Christ, the sacrificial altar of the cross. Paul adds that participation in Christ differentiates Christian worship from the idolatrous sacrifices of the pagans: "You cannot drink the cup of the Lord and the cup of demons" (1 Cor 10:21).[36] He then explains the difference between sharing liturgically in a sacrificial meal and merely eating dinner at the house of an unbeliever, where some of the meat bought at market may have been offered in pagan sacrifice. To eat dinner with an unbeliever is acceptable, whereas to share liturgically in pagan sacrifice is to unite oneself to demons. He sums up this distinction by urging that "whatever you do, do all to the glory of God" (1 Cor 10:31).

With respect to the third mark, the sharing of possessions, Paul expects the members of his communities to pay taxes (Rom 13:6), and his communities do not hold property in common.[37] He supported himself in Corinth by working with his fellow tentmakers Aquila and Priscilla, in addition to receiving money from Macedonian friends (see Acts 18:3; 1 Cor 9:14; 2 Cor 11:8; 1 Thess 2:19). Even so, Paul does insist that believers must share their possessions. He tells the Corinthians that this sharing should be a regular weekly practice rather than merely an occasional gift: "On the first day of every week, each of you is to put something aside and store it up, as he may prosper, so that contributions need not be made when I come" (1 Cor 16:2). The size of each person's gift (in this case to the collection for the Jerusalem church) should depend upon how that person has prospered during the week. Possessions are not an end in themselves, but rather should be shared freely and "bountifully" (2 Cor 9:6) in order to ensure a bountiful reward from God, the giver of all.

Paul makes clear that sharing possessions is a central way that believers imitate Jesus Christ. As Paul explains, "genuine" love will imitate "the grace of our Lord Jesus Christ, that though he was rich, yet for your sake he became poor, so that by his poverty you might become rich" (2 Cor 8:8-9).[38] Paul envisions the giving away of material possessions as a way to gain spiritual possessions in Christ. Those who receive the gift of material possessions will amply reward the givers by their prayers, and in this exchange the grace of God will be manifested and glorified. Those who give away material possessions should trust that God will reward them both materially and spiritually (see 2 Cor 9:8-11).[39] Thus the sharing of possessions, too, has eschatological overtones.

Receiving through Christ "access in one Spirit to the Father" (Eph 2:18), the church both participates already in the Trinitarian life and awaits the eschatological fullness, the "day on which he [God the Father through the risen Christ] will judge the world in righteousness" (Acts

17:31). As Paul puts it, "we must all appear before the judgment seat of Christ, so that each one may receive good or evil, according to what he has done in the body" (2 Cor 5:10). Awaiting the return of Christ, the believer is already caught up through Christ in the Spirit to the Father. Such life can no longer be merely human life; it must be a supernatural life marked by the inauguration of the eschaton, while taking the form of participation in the suffering of Christ so as to share in his glorious resurrection and ascension.

THOMAS AQUINAS AND THE ESCHATOLOGICAL COMMUNITY

How does Aquinas interpret these New Testament portraits of the eschatological character of Christian life? With respect to the apostles' teaching and fellowship, I will explore Aquinas' theology of faith; with respect to the breaking of bread and prayers, I will explore Aquinas' theology of the Eucharist; and with respect to the community's sharing of possessions, I will explore Aquinas' theology of almsgiving. Indebted to the theological tradition, Aquinas helps to clarify the eschatological form that our passage takes between the resurrection of "Christ the first fruits" and "the end, when he delivers the kingdom to God the Father after destroying every rule and every authority and power" (1 Cor 15:23, 24).

Faith and Eschatology

Aquinas supposes that at all times and places, some humans have had at least implicit faith in Christ Jesus and belonged to the Church.[40] What difference then does the apostles' teaching make? The apostles' teaching spreads the knowledge of the true God and of the forgiveness of sins (see Jer 31:34).[41] The transformative power of this teaching consists in the grace of the Holy Spirit that is poured out abundantly at Pentecost.[42] Aquinas takes seriously Jesus' promise that "[w]hen the Spirit of truth comes, he will guide you into all the truth" (John 16:13).[43] What the apostles teach in the inspired Scriptures about the mysteries of Christ's life, the sacraments, life in Christ, resurrection and eternal life, and so forth belongs to the "law of the Spirit of life" (Rom 8:2) in the sense that these realities "dispose us to receive the grace of the Holy Spirit, and [pertain] to the use of that grace."[44]

For the apostles as for us, faith involves an evangelizing mission: public witness to Jesus glorifies God and serves our neighbor.[45] Having received the Holy Spirit "sooner and more abundantly than others," the apostles bear witness to Jesus by preaching and by writing the books of the New Testament.[46] The apostles thereby proclaim the saving truth about God. The apostles teach both about who this God is (the Father, Son, and Holy Spirit), and also about the path by which this God draws us to himself ("all those things which God dispenses in time, for man's salvation").[47] At the Last Supper, Jesus promises Peter his divine assistance in leading the apostolic community: "I have prayed for you that your faith may not fail; and when you have turned again, strengthen your brethren" (Luke 22:32).[48] Believers can count upon the truthful preservation of the apostles' teaching within the apostolic fellowship of the church because of the power of Jesus' prayer, confirmed by his Holy Spirit.

Aquinas emphasizes that the apostles received their teaching from the Lord: "It is not human knowledge, but the divine truth that is the rule of faith."[49] In devoting ourselves to the apostles' teaching and fellowship, we receive an eschatological communion in God's truth. Although our faith employs propositions, "the act of the believer does not terminate in a proposition, but in a reality," Truth in person.[50] We already enjoy in faith the union with God that will be made complete in eternal life, when we will see "the unveiled truth to which our faith cleaves."[51] Commenting on the relationship between faith and hope as set forth in Hebrews 11:1, Aquinas remarks that "in us the first beginning of things to be hoped for is brought about by the assent of faith."[52] Faith aims at its perfection, vision. Since faith is an interpersonal communion with the triune God who is love, faith lives through charity.[53]

Eucharist and Eschatology

When Aquinas discusses the second mark, the "breaking of bread and the prayers," he observes that Jesus causes the life of grace not only by coming into the world in the Incarnation, but also by "coming sacramentally into man."[54] Just as Jesus' entrance into the world in the Incarnation poured out "grace and truth" upon the world, so that "from his fulness have we all received, grace upon grace" (John 1:16-17), so also Jesus' entrance into the believer in the sacrament of the Eucharist pours forth the grace of the Holy Spirit. By partaking in the sacrament of the Eucharist, believers receive the fruit of Christ's Pasch, namely the "forgiveness of sins" (Matt 26:28) and "eternal life" (John 6:54). In this regard Aquinas also cites Hebrews 9:15, which describes Jesus as "the mediator of a new covenant, so that those who are called may receive the promised eternal inheritance."[55] The Eucharist unites us to "the promised eternal inheritance."

The Eucharist gives eternal life in two other related ways. First, the Eucharist sacramentally represents nourishment, since "it is given by way of food and drink."[56] No more than baptismal water aims to cleanse the body does the Eucharist aim to nourish the body. Rather, Jesus in the Eucharist nourishes the recipient's spiritual life "by sustaining, giving increase, restoring, and giving delight."[57] Jesus describes this spiritual sustenance in John 6:55, "For my flesh is food indeed, and my blood is drink indeed."[58] Spiritual sustenance differs from material sustenance in that our bodies quickly grow hungry and thirsty again, and also in that our bodies ultimately decay and corrupt. By contrast, spiritual food and drink lift us up toward the fullness of spiritual life, which is not corruptible. The Eucharist's spiritual nourishment fuels our attainment of eternal life in union with Christ.

Second, the Eucharist's symbols of bread and wine represent the uniting of many members into one. Aquinas delights in Augustine's observation that the many grains of wheat that constitute the bread, and the many grapes from which comes the wine, symbolize the unity of the Church that the Eucharist brings about. Quoting Augustine, he praises the Eucharist as the "sign of unity" and the "bond of charity."[59] The fact that the sacramental representation takes place under the symbols of bread and wine bespeaks the Eucharist's effect, namely charity. Charity unites believers to God and to each other. In this life, we cannot possess the full perfection of charity, because we cannot always contemplate God and love him. We can only habitually love God "by neither thinking nor desiring anything contrary to the love of God."[60] In eternal life, by contrast, we will enjoy the perfection of charity. To share in God's eternal communion requires that "man's whole heart is always actually borne towards God."[61] Aquinas suggests that this is why Paul embraces the prospect of death (see Phil 1:23; 2 Cor 5:8).[62] The Eucharist configures us to Christ's sacrificial death so that, in charity, we can share fully in his resurrection with all the members of his mystical body.

As Aquinas notes, the Eucharist of course does not bring us immediately into eternal life. The Eucharist is called "viaticum," food for the journey, because it "does not at once admit us to glory, but bestows on us the power of coming unto glory."[63] Reading typologically, Aquinas interprets 1 Kings 19:8 as a figure of the Eucharist as viaticum.[64] In 1 Kings 19, Elijah is fleeing from Queen Jezebel, who has promised to kill him. Resting on his journey under a broom tree, he begs the Lord to take away his life; he feels that he has failed, just as his predecessors and nation have. Instead, he is awakened from sleep by an angel who provides him with "a cake baked on hot stones and a jar of water" (19:6) and who nourishes him twice with this food and drink. Elijah then "went in the strength of that food forty days and forty nights to Horeb the mount of God" (19:8). Peter Leithart points out that the only other place the Bible uses the word for "hot stones" is Isaiah 6:6, where Isaiah sees the Lord "sitting upon a throne" and an angel purifies Isaiah by touching his lips with a "burning coal" from the altar of the Temple.[65] By uniting us with the altar of Christ's Pasch, the spiritual food that is the Eucharist strengthens humans for the journey toward resurrection and the new creation.[66]

When Aquinas introduces the sacraments in the *Summa theologiae*, he observes that "God gives grace to man in a way which is suitable to him."[67] In order to gain knowledge, we depend upon our senses. Furthermore, original sin focuses us on what we experience empirically rather than on God. It is fitting then that "the healing remedy should be given to a man so as to reach the part affected by disease."[68] Corporeal sacraments lead us toward spiritual realities that we would otherwise neglect. Indeed, Aquinas observes that "if man were offered spiritual things without a veil, his mind being taken up with the material world would be unable to apply itself to them."[69] The effect of the Eucharist in drawing us into eternal life flows in part from the corporeal character of the sacrament. By practicing certain "bodily actions,"[70] above all the eucharistic liturgy, we are enabled to raise our minds and hearts to eternal life.

All the sacraments of the New Law, including the Eucharist, prefigure the state of glory. No sacrament, not even the Eucharist, will be needed in eternal life. Instead the Eucharist unites believers to the power of Jesus' Pasch, so as in this life to provide us with spiritual "nourishment, whereby life and strength are preserved."[71] Aquinas draws an analogy between the sacramental life and the individual and communal dimensions of bodily life. Generation, growth, nourishment, healing, and restoration pertain to the individual body, while government and the raising of children pertain to the community. The point is that

the entire sacramental organism is ordered to the eschatological fulfillment of human individual and communal life in communion with God.
As Jean-Pierre Torrell describes Aquinas' sacramental theology, "The
historical Christ, today glorified, touches us by each of the acts of his
earthly life, which is thus the bearer of a divinizing life and energy."[72]
The Eucharist is the greatest sacrament, according to Aquinas, because
it is a figure of "the union of Christ with the Church" that will be perfected in eternal life.[73]

As "the consummation of the spiritual life,"[74] the Eucharist unites
us to God and to each other and "foreshadows the divine fruition, which
shall come to pass in heaven."[75] Aquinas recognizes numerous figures of
the Eucharist in the Old Testament, but he considers the most significant figure to be the paschal lamb.[76] The Israelites escape the plague of
the death of the firstborn by painting the sacrificial blood of the paschal
lamb upon their doorposts, so that God's punishment passes over them
(Exod 12:13). The first Christians recognized the crucified and risen
Jesus, the Savior, as the fulfillment of the figure of the paschal lamb. He
is the "Lamb of God" (John 1:29) and the "Lamb standing, as though
it had been slain" (Rev 5:6). By paying the penalty of sin for us by his
blood, Jesus in his supreme charity opened the way by which God will
pass over us in the eschatological judgment.[77] In the Eucharist, prefig-
ured by the paschal lamb and prefiguring the heavenly banquet celebrat-
ing the marriage of the Lamb (see Rev 21), we are therefore "inebriated
with the sweetness of the divine goodness, according to Cant. 5:1: 'Eat,
O friends, and drink, and be inebriated, my dearly beloved.'"[78]

Almsgiving and Eschatology

Regarding the third mark, sharing possessions, Aquinas inquires especially into two issues: First, should Christians distribute their wealth to
all equally, or primarily take care of family members and members of
the church who are in need? Second, are Christians required to have a
common purse rather than private property?[79]

In seeking to answer these questions, Aquinas highlights Galatians
6:10, "So then, as we have opportunity, let us do good to all men, and
especially to those who are of the household of faith."[80] To do good
to others is to act benevolently toward them, and such benevolence, in
whatever concrete form it takes, is "an effect of love in so far as love
moves the superior to watch over the inferior."[81] Can only those who

are superior, then, exercise beneficence? Aquinas responds that among humans (as opposed to angels), persons who are superior in one respect will be inferior in another. All humans therefore are in need of beneficence in some respect. Given the limitations of human nature, we can only act beneficently toward some others, since we can only do good in a particular time and place. Insofar as time and place allow, however, we must be prepared to do good to all others.[82] There is one way in which we can already do good to all others, namely by praying for all people.

Do Christians owe beneficence to all equally, or first to those in need within the Christian community? On behalf of the former view, Aquinas cites the injunction of Jesus: "When you give a dinner or a banquet, do not invite your friends or your brothers or your kinsmen or rich neighbors, lest they also invite you in return, and you be repaid. But when you give a feast, invite the poor, the maimed, the lame, the blind, and you will be blessed, because they cannot repay you" (Luke 14:12-14).[83] If we are supposed to help only those who cannot repay us, then familial and communal bonds will not be the basis of beneficence. Inevitably, however, we do more good to friends and relatives than we do to others. Regarding the good that parents do for their children, for example, Jesus asks, "what man of you, if his son asks him for bread, will give him a stone?" (Matt 7:9).

In doing good first to our children, we do not sin against charity. Indebted to Augustine, Aquinas argues that there is an order of charity, rooted in the order of nature. God should be loved above all, and we should love ourselves and our neighbors as partakers in the goodness of God. Relatives and friends possess a particular claim upon our beneficence because of their closeness to us.[84] People can be close to us in different ways, and "we ought in preference to bestow on each one such benefits as pertain to the matter in which, speaking simply, he is most closely connected with us."[85] Normally, for example, we ought to feed our father before feeding strangers, although this precept can vary according to circumstances, as when a stranger is in extreme need and our father not so. What about Jesus' injunction to give banquets not for friends or family members, but for the poor? Aquinas considers that Jesus is warning against making invitations for the purpose of being invited ourselves. Such a motive would turn our benevolence into cupidity. If those closest to us are not in need, "we ought to give alms to one who is much holier and in greater want, and to one who is more useful to the common weal, rather than to one who is more closely united to us."[86]

Like Paul, Aquinas does not think that Christians need to share a common purse or eschew private property. Nonetheless, he argues that some Christians are called to do so. Drawing upon Ephesians 4:11-12, he remarks that the Church should contain diverse "states of life" that express the way in which "the fulness of grace, which is centered in Christ as head, flows forth to his members in various ways, for the perfecting of the body of the Church."[87] Different actions and duties require different states of life. The counsels of poverty, chastity, and obedience aim at freeing the mind's affections so that they can tend wholly to God.[88] The "state of perfection" involves following these counsels in communal life, thereby living out Jesus' call to the rich young man: "If you would be perfect, go, sell what you possess and give to the poor, and you will have treasure in heaven; and come, follow me" (Matt 19:21).[89]

By contrast, a married person's state of life involves different duties. Aquinas teaches that persons who do not have a vocation to the religious life should seek to maintain sufficient private possessions to ensure their ability to fulfill their duties according to their station in life. In this regard Aquinas quotes 1 Timothy 5:8, "If any one does not provide for his relatives, and especially for his own family, he has disowned the faith and is worse than an unbeliever," as well as 2 Corinthians 8:13, "I do not mean that others should be eased and you burdened."[90] In his first work as a magister in Paris, *Contra impugnantes dei cultum et religionem*, Aquinas vigorously defends the counsel of poverty as practiced in the religious life of the mendicant orders that depend entirely on alms. Yet even for the mendicants, giving away their money and property does not mean depriving themselves entirely of material possessions, since food and clothing are necessary even for the mendicant state of life.[91] As regards those persons whose state of life does not allow for the observance of the counsels, Aquinas explains that "[i]t does not belong to a liberal man so to give away his riches that it is left for his own support, nor the wherewithal to perform those acts of virtue whereby happiness is acquired."[92]

Given that most members of the Church should have private possessions, how should they share these possessions? Almsgiving reveals the love of the eschatological community.[93] Aquinas notes that the place of almsgiving in the life of charity is emphasized by 1 John 3:17: "But if any one has the world's goods and sees his brother in need, yet closes his heart against him, how does God's love abide in him?"[94] This statement occurs in 1 John's discourse about the already/not yet character of the eschaton. As 1 John observes, the community of believers already experiences the eschaton even while awaiting the final fulfillment: "Beloved, we are God's children now; it does not yet appear what we shall be, but we know that when he appears we shall be like him, for we shall see him as he is" (3:2). A similar eschatological context characterizes Hebrews 13's injunction to give alms. Having exhorted believers to remember that "here we have no lasting city, but we seek the city which is to come" (13:14), Hebrews explains how believers should behave while awaiting this "lasting city": "Do not neglect to do good and to share what you have, for such sacrifices are pleasing to God" (13:16).[95]

Almsgiving belongs to charity because to give alms is an act of mercy, and mercy (along with joy and peace) is an effect of charity. By giving alms, believers imitate the mercy that God has shown us in Christ Jesus. Because mercy consists in helping others in their neediness, "mercy is accounted as being proper to God: and therein his omnipotence is declared to be chiefly manifested."[96] Almsgiving, in other words, makes our works to be like God's. Describing God's supreme mercy in Christ, Aquinas cites Ephesians 2:4-5, "God, who is rich in mercy, out of the great love with which he loved us, even when we were dead through our trespasses, made us alive together with Christ (by grace you have been saved)."[97] The eschatological resonances become clear when one recalls the remainder of Paul's sentence: "and raised us up with him, and made us sit with him in the heavenly places in Christ Jesus, that in the coming ages he might show the immeasurable riches of his grace in kindness toward us in Christ Jesus" (Eph 2:6-7). Formed by God's gift in Christ and the Spirit, believers must be a community of gift. Indeed, when Aquinas identifies the Person of the Holy Spirit by the name "Gift," he explains that "love has the nature of a first gift, through which all free gifts are given. So since the Holy Spirit proceeds as love . . . he proceeds as the first gift."[98] When we give material or spiritual alms to others in need, we manifest the eschatological indwelling of the Holy Spirit, by whom we are gifted.

Sharing material possessions requires the virtue of liberality with money, which allows a person to make use of money "whether for himself, or for the good of others, or for God's glory."[99] According to

Aquinas, Christians can virtuously possess the amount of money consistent with the needs of their "condition of life."[100] Possessing too much money, however, indicates a twofold problem: an undue possession of wealth vis-à-vis one's poorer neighbors, and an immoderate love of riches.[101] Regarding the immoderate love of riches, Aquinas quotes 1 Timothy 6:10, "the love of money is the root of all evils; it is through this craving that some have wandered away from the faith and pierced their hearts with many pangs."[102] Paul tells Timothy to enjoin wealthy people to be liberal with their money so as to "take hold of the life which is life indeed" (1 Tim 6:19), namely the life to come. Love of riches is the root of all evils in the somewhat attenuated, but still significant sense that all evils can and at times do arise from this love.[103]

Aquinas agrees with Ambrose's teaching that "God does not wish a man to lavish all his wealth at once, except when he changes his state of life."[104] Ambrose identifies Elisha as an example of a change in state of life. When Elijah called Elisha to follow him, Elisha killed his oxen and made a feast for the people (1 Kgs 19:21). Believers who are not called to change their state of life should simply give alms abundantly in proportion to their means. Here Aquinas cites Tobit's encouragement to his son Tobias to give alms so as to "[lay] up a good treasure for yourself against the day of necessity. For charity delivers from death and keeps you from entering the darkness" (Tob 4:9-10).[105] Almsgiving delivers from everlasting death for two reasons: it merits an everlasting reward in the order of grace, and the giver receives the prayers of the recipient.[106] It would be impossible to love one's neighbor without giving alms, since love requires not only well-wishing but also well-doing. Jesus therefore commands almsgiving and warns that those who neglect it will be condemned, as Aquinas notes with reference to Matthew 25:41-43.[107]

Does Christian perfection require giving away all one's possessions? Aquinas thinks not, but he does hold that the state of perfection requires being completely at the service of others. When Jesus warns that the rich can hardly enter the kingdom of God, Peter asks on behalf of the disciples, "Lo, we have left everything and followed you. What then shall we have?" (Matt 19:27).[108] Jesus answers by enumerating their reward both in this life and in eternal life. Through the grace of the Holy Spirit, the apostles dispossessed themselves completely in order to follow Jesus. Their successors the bishops, too, give their lives for

Jesus (or should do so), and so their office qualifies as a "state of perfection." They devote themselves entirely to "things pertaining to the love of their neighbor" and thereby lead their flock toward the eschatological consummation.[109] They do not, however, need to give away all of their personal possessions, let alone the possessions of their dioceses. Aquinas agrees with Ambrose in supposing that "[t]he goods of churches should not all be given to the poor, except in a case of necessity."[110] This is so because the Church has other necessary expenses, including maintaining its ministers and administering the divine worship. Bishops should ensure that a due portion of the Church's possessions, as of their own possessions, is given to the poor.

Aquinas cites Abraham as evidence that "the highest perfection is compatible with great wealth."[111] Voluntary poverty, then, serves spiritual perfection but is not required for it. The radicality of the Gospel is not diminished so long as all is ordered to the love of God and of neighbor in God. The sharing of possessions follows from faithful sharing in the apostolic teaching and in the Eucharist. Christian almsgiving flows from the communication of the Lord's presence in word and sacrament within the apostolic fellowship guided by the Holy Spirit. Indeed, the eschatological presence of Christ and the Spirit sustaining the truth of faith and the unity of the visible apostolic fellowship makes possible the sharing of possessions in a manner that bears spiritual fruit.

CONCLUSION

On the day of Pentecost, when the Holy Spirit filled the apostles, Peter proclaimed to the people of Israel, "This Jesus God raised up, and of that we are all witnesses. Being therefore exalted at the right hand of God, and having received from the Father the promise of the Holy Spirit, he has poured out this which you see and hear" (Acts 2:32-33). Peter called upon his fellow Jews to repent and be baptized so as to receive the forgiveness of sins and the gift of the Holy Spirit. Those who heeded Peter's call "devoted themselves to the apostles' teaching and fellowship, to the breaking of bread and the prayers" (Acts 2:42), and they "had all things in common" (Acts 2:44). From his place "at the right hand of God," Jesus nourishes by the Holy Spirit his eschatological community, marked by faith, eucharistic worship, and the sharing of possessions in love.

Given the utopian urgency with which secular eschatologies are often pursued today—despite the failure of what Richard Bauckham and Trevor Hart call "the myth of inevitable and unlimited human improvement"[112]—it might seem unlikely that Aquinas' vision of faith, the Eucharist, and almsgiving support an *eschatological* ecclesiology. For example, the Church's allowance for private property can seem to be lacking in eschatological zeal.[113] Aquinas shows, however, that the apostles' teaching and fellowship, received by faith, lifts us into an intimate relationship with the Father, Son, and Holy Spirit. The Eucharist, too, explodes the limits we impose upon interpersonal communion, and we embody this communion through the heroic almsgiving of some and the abundant almsgiving of all. The central eschatological reality is that we live already in union with Jesus and we allow our passage to be configured to his. As Joseph Ratzinger observes, "The bond with Jesus is, even now, resurrection. Where there is communion with him, the boundary of death is overshot here and now."[114] Living "at the end of the times" (1 Pet 1:20), our lives are already "hid with Christ in God" (Col 3:3).[115]

Aquinas' portrait of the Church as the eschatological community, however, raises two issues that we need to address before turning to the consummation of the Church when Christ returns in glory. First, the centrality of the sharing of possessions raises the issue of the eschatological value of our works of love, that is, the issue of merit. Second, the communion in faith that we have traced raises the issue of whether our rationality consists solely in physical processes, with the profound limitations thereby imposed upon intimacy with God, or whether we possess a spiritual soul whose capacities exceed those of physical processes. Our answers to these two questions will do much to determine how we envision the relationship of our passage to Christ's. In preparation for the book's final chapter on bodily resurrection and beatific vision, therefore, the next two chapters address the issues of merit and the spiritual soul.

5

Can We Merit Eternal Life?

⌒⌒

By participating in Jesus' passage through faith and works of love enabled by his Holy Spirit, do we merit eternal life? In his Sermon on the Mount, Jesus employs the image of a heavenly treasury: "Do not lay up for yourselves treasures on earth, where moth and rust consume and where thieves break in and steal, but lay up for yourselves treasures in heaven, where neither moth nor rust consumes and where thieves do not break in and steal. For where your treasure is, there will your heart be also" (Matt 6:19-21). Jesus attaches the promise of heavenly reward to certain actions. For example, he teaches, "Blessed are you when men revile you and persecute you and utter all kinds of evil against you falsely on my account. Rejoice and be glad, for your reward is great in heaven, for so men persecuted the prophets who were before you" (5:11-12). Likewise, those who love only their friends already have their reward, whereas those who love their enemies will receive a heavenly reward (5:46). Those who practice piety so as to be seen and praised by others "will have no reward from your Father who is in heaven" (6:1). Those who give alms, pray to God, and fast in secret without desiring a temporal reward, can be sure that "your Father who sees in secret will reward you" (6:4, 6, 18).[1]

This emphasis on reward, on storing up "treasures in heaven," is found also in the Gospel of Luke. Jesus warns against "all covetousness"

(Luke 12:15) and tells a parable designed to encourage his hearers to seek heavenly treasure. The parable presents a wealthy farmer who loves his temporal possessions more than he loves God, and who therefore is unprepared for eternal life: "'I will say to my soul, Soul, you have ample goods laid up for many years; take your ease, eat, drink, and be merry.' But God said to him: 'Fool! This night your soul is required of you; and the things you have prepared, where will they be?'" (12:19-20). Jesus concludes that people should strive to be "rich toward God" (12:21) by giving alms: "Sell your possessions, and give alms; provide yourselves with purses that do not grow old, with a treasure in the heavens that does not fail, where no thief approaches and no moth destroys" (12:33).

How should we understand Jesus' words? N. T. Wright comments that in reaction to the tendency of medieval theologians to see "everything in terms of merit," the Protestant Reformers placed the absence of merit at the heart of their theology.[2] In Wright's view, the concentration on merit's presence or absence distorts the message of Jesus. Wright explains that the "logic of merit" produces an understanding of "God as a distant bank manager, scrutinizing credit and debit sheets."[3] He emphasizes that Jesus, like Paul, thinks in terms of the "logic of love"—the outpouring of the Holy Spirit—rather than in terms of the "logic of merit."

Arguably, however, there is a place for both the logic of merit and the logic of love in theological reflection on how we participate in Christ's passage by building up "treasures in heaven" (Matt 6:20). This chapter first examines the biblical roots of the theology of merit, as set forth in Gary Anderson's *Sin: A History*. I then explore Thomas Aquinas' account of meriting eternal reward. By uniting merit and love, Anderson and Aquinas help us to see how the indwelling Holy Spirit configures our passage to Christ's.

GARY ANDERSON'S BIBLICAL THEOLOGY OF SIN AND MERIT

By means of historical reconstruction, Gary Anderson identifies a shift in the image of sin employed by biblical authors. His research suggests that prior to the sixth century B.C. and the rise of the use of Aramaic, biblical authors speak of sin as a weight or a burden. Later biblical authors, however, envision Israel's sin as a debt (in the context of debt slavery). Anderson observes, "Almost as soon as the idea of sin as a debt appears on the scene, so does its financial counterpart, credit."[4] To make this point, he discusses a variety of biblical passages, including Daniel 4:27, "Therefore, O King, may my advice be acceptable to you: Redeem your sins by almsgiving and your iniquities by generosity to the poor; then your serenity may be extended"; Proverbs 11:4, "Financial capital is of no avail on the day of wrath, but *sĕdāqâh* saves from death"; Proverbs 19:17, "He who is generous to the downtrodden makes a loan to the Lord; He will repay him his due"; Sirach 29:12, "Store up almsgiving in your treasury, and it will rescue you from all affliction"; and Tobit 4:7-11,

> Give alms from your possessions to all who live uprightly, and do not let your eye begrudge the gift when you make it. Do not turn your face away from any poor man, and the face of God will not be turned away from you. If you have many possessions, make your gift from them in proportion; if few, do not be afraid to give according to the little you have. So you will be laying up a good treasure for yourself against the day of necessity. For almsgiving delivers from death and keeps you from entering the darkness; and for all who practice it, almsgiving is an excellent offering in the presence of the Most High.

In these biblical passages, almsgiving functions as does credit in an accounting ledger. Thus, Daniel can assure King Nebuchadnezzar that credit balances debt; almsgiving pays the debts we owe for our sins. Regarding the notion of a "treasury" (Sir 29:12) or a "good treasure" (Tob 4:9) built up by acts of almsgiving, Anderson notes that this "treasury" is thought to stand as credit against the debts of our sins and to rescue us from God's wrath on the day of judgment. Turning to the New Testament, he finds very similar language in passages such as Luke 12 and Matthew 6, where Jesus urges his hearers to obtain heavenly treasure (credit) by means of good actions.

Drawing upon Ephrem the Syrian and Augustine, Anderson remarks that although God wills to reward our good works, nonetheless the reward far exceeds the works. In the heavenly treasury "[e]very dollar invested in yields growth by a hundredfold. The small amount deposited provides sufficient leverage to open the gates of immeasurable divine generosity (so Augustine: 'Give a little and receive on a grand scale. . . . Give the earth and gain heaven')."[5] Furthermore, it is God who establishes the "treasury" by his promises, so that our hope for a heavenly reward flows from our faith in God, whose grace "guarantees" the reward.[6]

Anderson treats at length the encounter of Jesus and the rich young man. When the rich young man asks Jesus how to gain eternal life, Jesus replies, "If you would be perfect, go, sell what you possess and give to the poor, and you will have treasure in heaven; and come, follow me" (Matt 19:21). The rich man goes away sad. In order to avoid being "last" (19:30) in the life to come, do we need to give away all our possessions, as Jesus requires of the rich young man?[7] Anderson answers that "Jesus's injunction to give alms was meant to turn the young man's earthly focus heavenward through the agency of the poor."[8] Comparing Jesus' words with similar injunctions in rabbinic Jewish literature, he distinguishes between "heroic almsgiving" and the proportionate almsgiving that is taught elsewhere in the New Testament.[9] Heroic almsgiving is the vocation of Jesus' inner group of disciples. Anderson points out that Jesus "had in his company a band of followers who had left their families to follow him. The radical demands of the kingdom for this inner circle precluded, at least for a time, any involvement with family."[10] As Anderson says, later Christians also recognized heroic almsgiving as a vocation for "men and women who were . . . leaving family behind in pursuit of the Kingdom of God."[11]

In the New Testament, not all followers of Jesus are called to heroic almsgiving. But all are called to proportionate almsgiving in imitation of Christ's sacrificial love. Jesus' parable of the last judgment (Matt 25:41-43) shows how this is so. Jesus portrays himself as sending away, at the final judgment, those who gave him no food when he was hungry, no drink when he was thirsty, no welcome when he was a stranger, no clothing when he was naked, and no care when he was in prison. By contrast, those who perform such acts of self-giving love will "inherit the kingdom prepared for you from the foundation of the world" (25:34). No one is excused on the grounds that they did not meet Jesus, for we meet Jesus in the poor: "Truly, I say to you, as you did it to one of the least of these my brethren, you did it to me" (25:40).

Even so, how can God give us such an extraordinary eschatological reward for comparatively small actions? Especially because "[w]e love, because he first loved us" (1 John 4:19), it hardly seems that our love—by which God "abides" in us (4:16) and gives us "confidence for the day of judgment" (4:17)—should have any relationship to the glorious reward. Anderson points out, however, that our almsgiving flows from and imitates God's own gifting. He states, "In light of the character of the heavenly treasury, it is hardly fair to say that a religious system of debits and credits stands outside the framework of a gracious and loving God. Indeed, in giving alms to the poor one is imitating those very same qualities that exist within God."[12] True, our debts are so enormous that it would seem that "no amount of almsgiving could ever make a dent in what was owed."[13] But once our debts have been paid by Jesus Christ, whose life has infinite value, we have an infinite source of "credit." When we are united to this source of "credit" by the grace of the Holy Spirit, our works of love merit a "treasure in heaven."

THOMAS AQUINAS ON MERIT AND ESCHATOLOGY

Anderson's exegesis challenges the view that the "logic of love" and the "logic of merit" need be in opposition. Even so, given the imperfection of our actions, our tendency to sin, and the lack of proportion between human actions and a glorious reward, it still seems difficult to suppose that our charitable actions really merit an eternal reward, "treasure in heaven" (Matt 19:21).[14] Anderson's portrait needs further theological development. In this regard, Aquinas' discussion of merit is particularly helpful.[15]

The Merited Reward of Jesus of Nazareth and Our Merit

At the center of Aquinas' theology of merit stands Jesus Christ, whose "predestination is the cause of ours" as regards both our adoptive sonship and the sanctifying grace that enables our meritorious actions.[16] God's eternal plan for our salvation has Jesus' Pasch at its center. Because Jesus "humbled himself and became obedient unto death, even death on a cross," Paul says, "God has highly exalted him and bestowed on him the name which is above every name, that at the name of Jesus every knee should bow, in heaven and on the earth and under the earth, and every tongue confess that Jesus Christ is Lord, to the glory of God the Father" (Phil 2:8-11).[17] Aquinas discusses this passage in light of Romans 4, where Paul explains that Abraham must have been justified by faith because "to one who works, his wages are not reckoned as a gift but as his due" (Rom 4:4). According to Philippians 2, Aquinas notes, the reward of Jesus' Passion—namely that "God has highly exalted him"—is Jesus' "due." In justice, the divine plan ensures that "he who humbles himself will be exalted" (Luke 14:11).[18]

The justice of Jesus' glorification corresponds to the injustice of Jesus' humiliation. Jesus certainly did not deserve to suffer and die the humiliating death of a criminal, nor did he deserve the mockery that he received on the cross. As Aquinas puts it, "when any man through his just will has stripped himself of what he ought to have, he deserves that something further be granted to him as the reward of his just will."[19] In his obedient endurance of suffering and death for love of us, Jesus showed himself to be the faithful "servant" of God (Phil 2:7).[20] As a faithful servant, he humbled himself in a way that merits reward from God. Since the grace of the Holy Spirit perfected Jesus not solely as an individual but as head of the Church, he merited eternal life for all his members.[21] But if Jesus has satisfied and merited for the entire human race, it might seem that we should not speak of further satisfaction and merit on the part of his followers. If all is God's gift, why confuse matters by claiming that "those who are made one with the crucified Christ" by "faith living through charity" merit eternal life?[22]

In his discussion of merit, Aquinas recalls Paul's suggestion that God's reward to him will correspond to what he deserves to receive from a just judge. In 2 Timothy 4:7-8, Paul is near death and tells Timothy, "I have fought the good fight, I have finished the race, I have kept the faith. Henceforth there is laid up for me the crown of righteousness, which the Lord, the righteous judge, will award to me on that Day, and not only to me but also to all who have loved his appearing."[23] Exercising just judgment, the Lord will award to Paul (and to all who have loved the Lord) a "crown of righteousness." Aquinas argues that Paul can make such a bold claim because of the realities of Trinitarian indwelling and adoptive filiation. Jesus promises that "if a man loves me, he will keep my word, and my Father will love him, and we will come to him and make our home with him" (John 14:23). To the Samaritan woman at the well, he speaks of the Holy Spirit as the "water" who fulfills our spiritual thirst and guides us to eternal life: "whoever drinks of the water that I shall give him will never thirst; the water that I shall give him will become in him a spring of water welling up to eternal life" (John 4:14). This "spring of water welling up to eternal life," Aquinas says, is the indwelling "Holy Spirit moving us to life everlasting" through our actions.[24] Regarding adoptive filiation, Paul observes that the Spirit of Christ bears "witness within our spirit that we are children of God, and if children, then heirs, heirs of God and fellow heirs with Christ, provided we suffer with him in order that we may also be glorified with him" (Rom 8:16-17). The indwelling Spirit makes us "children of God" and "fellow heirs with Christ." Aquinas explains that merit has its root in "grace and charity" and its reward in "the enjoyment of God."[25]

When God adopts us as his sons and daughters in the Son, our action comes to possess not one but two active principles, namely human free will and grace of the Holy Spirit. In light of these two principles, Aquinas distinguishes between "congruent" and "condign" merit. A reward earned in strict justice is earned condignly, while a reward given despite the conditions of strict justice not being met is earned congruously. Insofar as the charitable action proceeds from the human will, the action earns the reward of eternal life only "congruously," that is to say, only because God fittingly wills to give this reward to the charitable action. God gives the reward by a certain "equality of proportion," because the graced human person does what he or she can.[26] As regards the human will, no charitable action can merit the reward of eternal life by strict justice. Ontologically speaking, God and humans "are infinitely apart, and all man's good is from God. Hence there can be no justice of absolute equality between man and God."[27] With respect to human capacities, it would be ludicrous to suppose that our actions could deserve the reward of beatific communion in the Trinity.[28]

Yet given the indwelling of the Trinity and our adoptive sonship, a human action can also be viewed with respect to "the dignity of grace" and "the power of the Holy Spirit moving us to life everlasting."[29] From this perspective the action's value depends on the Holy Spirit as its principle. As the *Catechism of the Catholic Church* observes, "Grace, by uniting us to Christ in active love, ensures the supernatural quality of our acts and consequently their merit before God and before men."[30] Aquinas states that insofar as our work "proceeds from the grace of the Holy Spirit moving us to life everlasting, it is meritorious of life everlasting condignly."[31] Our work can be said to merit in justice the reward of eternal life, so long as we recognize that (in the *Catechism*'s words) our "good actions proceed in Christ, from the predispositions and assistance given by the Holy Spirit."[32] Thus Paul's labors to fight "the good fight" render him justly worthy of receiving the "crown of righteousness" at the judgment. As Paul says, "I know whom I have believed, and I am sure that he is able to guard until that Day what I have entrusted to him" (2 Tim 1:12).[33]

Since the indwelling Trinity enables us to merit, it will be clear that justifying grace itself, by which we receive the indwelling Trinity, cannot be merited.[34] Lest there be any doubt, Aquinas states that "a man can merit nothing from God except by his gift, which the Apostle expresses aptly saying (Rom 11:35): 'Who hath first given to Him, and recompense shall be made to him?'"[35] Aquinas grants that "God gives grace to none but to the worthy," but he adds "not that they were previously worthy, but that by his grace he makes them worthy."[36] We become worthy only when God makes us his adopted children in Christ. Far from competing with Christ's salvific action, our actions have meritorious value only when we are incorporated into Jesus' "superabundant satisfaction for the sins of the human race."[37] Paul depicts his own incorporation into Jesus' Passion: "I rejoice in my sufferings for your sake, and in my flesh I complete what is lacking in Christ's afflictions for the sake of his body, that is, the church" (Col 1:24). From eternity, God ordains this incorporation of believers into the crucified Christ. Describing God's plan of salvation, Paul says that "we are his workmanship, created in Christ Jesus for good works, which God prepared beforehand, that we should walk in them" (Eph 2:10). In his teaching about merit, Aquinas underscores this eternal ordination: "God ordained human nature to attain the end of eternal life, not by its own strength, but by the help of grace; and in this way its act can be meritorious of eternal life."[38]

When we have been made children of God by the grace of the Holy Spirit, our charitable actions merit progress in our relationship with God.[39] In this regard Aquinas cites Proverbs 4:18, "The path of the righteous is like the light of dawn, which shines brighter and brighter until full day."[40] Charitable actions dispose us to receive a more intimate relationship with God, an increased participation in the Holy Spirit and configuration to Christ.[41] Nonetheless, if we lose grace by mortal sin, no amount of previous charitable actions merits the renewal of justifying grace in us. This renewal can only be God's free gift. Furthermore, not even a lifetime of charitable actions can merit the grace of final perseverance. Our final attainment of glory, like our justification, is utterly God's free gift.[42]

Aquinas adds that only Jesus can merit justifying grace for others, since "Christ's soul is moved by God through grace, not only so as to reach the glory of life everlasting, but so as to lead others to it."[43]

Yet the works and prayers of holy persons on behalf of others can in a "congruous" fashion merit justifying grace for others. It is "in harmony with friendship" that God fulfill his friends' holy desires, in accord with God's ordination, "for the salvation of others."[44]

Almsgiving and Merit

In an example that could be taken directly from Anderson's book, Aquinas comments upon Jesus' words in Luke 16:9—"make friends for yourselves by means of unrighteous mammon, so that when it fails they may receive you into the eternal habitations"—by describing how those who receive alms can merit in "congruous" fashion for their benefactors. Aquinas states, "The poor who receive alms are said to receive others into everlasting dwellings, either by impetrating their forgiveness in prayer, or by meriting congruously by other good works, or materially speaking, inasmuch as by these good works of mercy, exercised towards the poor, we merit to be received into everlasting dwellings."[45] The prayers of beneficiaries rise up to God on behalf of benefactors, and God may have mercy on benefactors through such prayers.

When we give alms out of love for God and neighbor, it is the grace of the Holy Spirit in us that moves us to love the needy. In this regard Aquinas quotes 1 John 3:17, "If any one has the world's goods and sees his brother in need, yet closes his heart against him, how does God's love abide in him?"[46] Among the Old Testament texts that Anderson highlights, Aquinas attends particularly to Daniel 4:27 and Tobit 4:8. Daniel 4:27 describes almsgiving as a way of making satisfaction for sin, and thus as belonging to the virtue of justice.[47] In Tobit 4:8-9, Tobit instructs his son, "If you have many possessions, make your gift from them in proportion; if few, do not be afraid to give according to the little you have. So you will be laying up a good treasure for yourself against the day of necessity."[48] Aquinas concludes that under normal circumstances, almsgiving should be abundant but not heroic. This teaching accords with Paul's instruction to the Corinthians, "I do not mean that others should be eased and you burdened, but that as a matter of equality your abundance at the present time should supply their want, so that their abundance may supply your want" (2 Cor 8:13-14).[49]

CONCLUSION

It is commonplace to encounter criticisms of the medieval "emphasis on human merit" and the "clerical packaging of merits to meet the inevitable shortfall."[50] By contrast, Gary Anderson shows that merit is a profoundly biblical reality. As he makes clear through analysis of Old Testament passages, works of love function as credits against the debt of sins, although God mercifully helps to pay the debt for Israel's sins. In the New Testament, Anderson finds that earning credit (or merit) through works of love has a function even after Christ has paid the debt for all sins. God enables his adopted children, through the grace of the Holy Spirit, to be configured to Jesus by imitating his love and sharing in his reward. Praising "the surpassing grace of God" in the Corinthians, Paul tells them that "you will be enriched in every way for great generosity" (2 Cor 9:11, 14). Regarding the reward that those who give alms to the poor will receive, Jesus says that they will "inherit the kingdom prepared for you from the foundation of the world" (Matt 25:34), while those who fail to give alms will be condemned. Works of love have this role in the last judgment because they show that we share in the grace of the Holy Spirit, who makes us adopted children of God, "heirs of God and fellow heirs with Christ, provided that we suffer with him in order that we may also be glorified with him" (Rom 8:17).

Since human charitable actions come primarily from the Holy Spirit as their principle, Aquinas describes "life everlasting" as "the reward of the works of justice in relation to the divine motion."[51] As Aquinas shows, the action of the Holy Spirit in us enables us to merit this reward in justice, not because we have become self-sufficient, but because God rewards his work in us. Aquinas thereby accounts for the "treasure in heaven" (Matt 19:21) that Jesus urges his followers to seek.[52] In this light, Paul is not being arrogant when he supposes that because of the works that he has performed, "there is laid up for me the crown of righteousness, which the Lord, the righteous judge, will award to me on that Day, and not only to me but also to all who have loved his appearing" (2 Tim 4:8). Paul recognizes that God has stored up for him a heavenly treasure due to the actions that Paul accomplished by the grace of the Holy Spirit, "so that no human being might boast in the presence of God" (1 Cor 1:29). Through the indwelling Holy Spirit, those whom God adopts as sons and daughters in the Son are made worthy of "the free gift of God," namely, "eternal life in Christ Jesus our Lord" (Rom 6:23). Eternal life, then, is not something that we merely stumble into. At the right hand of the Father, Christ is making us even now to be worthy of his love by becoming people of love, "fit for the kingdom of God" (Luke 9:62).

6

Do We Have Spiritual Souls?

⌒

Lewis Ayres has pointed out that the spiritual soul constitutes the "anthropological context within which the structure of traditional discussions of grace and sanctification and the restoration of the *imago Dei* can be articulated."[1] In Ayres' view, this anthropological context is a fully biblical one.[2] The Church's affirmation of the reality of the spiritual soul,[3] however, is often thought to be the unbiblical byproduct of Platonic currents in patristic and medieval Christianity, made worse by the seventeenth-century philosopher René Descartes' splintering of body and soul.[4] For many Christians, contemporary neuroscience seems to have finally validated the anthropology of the skeptics depicted in the Wisdom of Solomon: "We were born by mere chance, and hereafter we shall be as though we had never been; because the breath in our nostrils is smoke, and reason is a spark kindled by the beating of our hearts. When it is extinguished, the body will turn to ashes, and the spirit will dissolve like empty air" (Wis 2:2-3).

In this regard, the work of Nancey Murphy has been particularly influential. Affirming the resurrection of the dead, Murphy strongly rejects the view that "[w]e were born by mere chance, and hereafter we shall be as though we had never been." She argues, nonetheless, that rationality is not a spiritual phenomenon but a physical one, albeit a far more complex phenomenon than "the beating of our hearts." As a Christian philosopher who hopes to contribute to contemporary theology, Murphy attends carefully to the history of biblical and theological arguments in favor of the spiritual soul. While recognizing the complexity of the biblical evidence, she agrees with Joel Green's view that the New Testament does not teach the doctrine of the spiritual soul.[5]

In this chapter, I first compare Murphy's critique of the spiritual soul with Thomas Aquinas' philosophical arguments in favor of the doctrine. Although Murphy disagrees with Aquinas, she praises Aquinas for providing "a high-water mark for both clarity and specificity" in comparison to other accounts of the spiritual soul.[6] In light of Aquinas' arguments, I suggest that the doctrine of the spiritual soul remains philosophically plausible. I then turn to Joel Green's exegetical analysis and propose, in conversation with the work of other biblical scholars, that his position on the spiritual soul does not do sufficient justice to New Testament eschatology. I conclude that Christians have affirmed the spiritual soul—and in this regard rightly sought the assistance of Greek philosophy—in faithful response to the promptings of biblical revelation.[7]

NANCY MURPHY AND THOMAS AQUINAS ON THE SOUL

In the preface to her *Bodies and Souls, or Spirited Bodies?*, Nancey Murphy asks, "Are human immortal souls temporarily housed in physical bodies, or *are* we our bodies?"[8] Although this way of phrasing the question does not leave room for the position of those who affirm the hylomorphic unity of body and soul, nonetheless it serves well to introduce her main point, which is that "there is no additional metaphysical element such as a mind or soul or spirit. . . . We are, at our best, complex physical organisms," although we are also, in some sense, "blown by the Breath of God's Spirit."[9]

Murphy sets forth her case for "nonreductive physicalism" in four chapters.[10] Her first chapter seeks largely to show that the denial that human beings possess a spiritual, immaterial component does not contradict the teaching of Scripture. The second chapter places Thomas Aquinas' hylomorphism in dialogue with three modern scientific developments: the seventeenth-century displacement of Aristotelian physics and formal causality by the atomism of modern physics (and the response of René Descartes); the nineteenth-century "Darwinian revolution" as regards the relation of humans to other animals; and present-day break-throughs in neuroscience. The third chapter argues that a nonreductive physicalist understanding of the human person does not do away with human free will and intelligent self-transcendence. Finally, the fourth chapter responds to some philosophical arguments in favor of "dualism" and suggests that nonreductive physicalism best corresponds to the available scientific evidence.

In Murphy's view, the notion of the spiritual soul arose as a "just so" story, a primitive accounting for unexplained phenomena whose gaps have now been better filled by contemporary neuroscience. Appealing to the extraordinary complexity of our brain processes, she distinguishes between atomistic, bottom-up accounts of causation—which are deterministic—and top-down or "downward" causation that avoids determinism by means of "selective activation of lower-level causal processes," as well as by appreciation for the influence of culture.[11] Since many have affirmed the existence of the spiritual soul partly so as to reject a deterministic account of human agency, her "nonreductive physicalism" requires her interlocutors to face more rigorously the question of why they posit a spiritual soul.

While she generally admires Aquinas' descriptions of the vegetative and sense powers of the soul, she disagrees with his contention that the human soul is spiritual. She grants that "[t]he functions Thomas attributed to the active intellect—abstraction, judgment, and reasoning—are less well understood in neuro-biological terms than are the faculties shared with animals."[12] Likewise, she recognizes that no "accumulation of data can ever amount to a proof that there is no immaterial mind or soul in addition to the body."[13] The data to which she is referring are twofold. First, there are data from brain imaging scans, and especially from patients who have suffered localized brain damage, that show that specific areas of the brain are engaged in the activities that Aquinas attributed to the rational soul's powers of intellect and will. When these areas of the brain are damaged, the seemingly spiritual activities (such as the identification of the human good) are impaired. Second, there are studies that have demonstrated the importance of particular areas in the brain for the development of human language abilities, and that reveal "the beginning of an understanding of the very complex brain processes that enable us to engage in language-based reasoning."[14] Among the cases she cites is that of a nineteenth-century railway worker, Phineas Gage, whose personality was permanently altered by damage of his prefrontal cortices. From these two kinds of data, Murphy concludes, "let us consider what characteristics your soul would have to retain for it to be recognizably *you* who gets to heaven. Your consciousness, your memories, your likes and dislikes, perhaps? But, as we have seen, these are all the province of brain studies."[15] In her view, therefore, humans "are purely physical organisms."[16]

For his part, Aquinas holds that the soul is the substantial form of the human being, by virtue of giving the matter its act of being. The one substantial form "makes man an actual being, a body, a living being, an animal, and a man."[17] This substantial unity does not require that humans have only a material nature. Aquinas maintains that every human act of understanding in this life requires sense images, that is, requires the body. At the same time, however, he states that the soul has "an operation and a power in which corporeal matter has no share whatever."[18] This is because the scope of human intellectual activity exceeds the power of even the most complex bodily processes. The rational or spiritual soul knows the individual material thing by abstracting its universal "form" from its individual matter.[19] If knowledge were itself material, then even granted our neurological complexity, such knowledge would not be able to attain to a universal form. Edward Feser explains this by comparing a mental image, which is a physical product of physical processes, to an intellectual concept (or universal form): "Any mental image is always going to be particular and individual in some respect, in a way that the concepts grasped by the intellect are not. For example, the mental image you form of a triangle is necessarily going to be of an equilateral, isosceles, or scalene triangle specifically; but the concept of a triangle that your intellect grasps is one that applies to all of these, precisely because it abstracts away from these properties."[20]

Any image produced by neural processes will itself be a material image, since the neural system is material. No matter how complex the interaction of neural processes, the neural image will be a physical image. We move beyond this physical image by abstracting the particular and individual properties from the image, that is to say by interpreting the image. The only way that we can move from neural processes to a universal concept, however, is by possessing a spiritual operation that transcends the material limits of the neural processes.[21] Here Norris

Clarke's warning is apropos: "The notion of a purely physical subject that exercises higher activities irreducible to the physical properties of the same subject cannot stand up under metaphysical analysis."[22] Derek Jeffreys makes the same point: "natures are limited in their causal powers, and by themselves cannot produce qualitatively superior natures."[23]

Rather than acting as yet another physical cause within the neural processes, the spiritual soul works as a formal cause, in Clarke's words, "by structuring, channeling, the pattern of energy flow."[24] The spiritual soul does not replace the neural processes, but rather organizes these processes in particular acts of knowing and willing.[25] It follows that the doctrine of the spiritual soul is not affected by whether neuroscience can show a physical correlate for every mental act. Indeed, Aquinas appreciates the significance of brain damage just as much as do philosophers informed by the example of Phineas Gage. Aquinas states, "When the act of the imagination is hindered by a lesion of the corporeal organ, for instance, in a case of frenzy; or when the act of memory is hindered, as in the case of lethargy, we see that a man is hindered from actually understanding things of which he had a previous knowledge."[26] It would not surprise Aquinas that brain imaging is able to register mental activity, since each act of understanding requires brain activity as regards the mental image.

Even so, as we saw in chapter 1, Aquinas holds that after the death of the body, human souls continue in conscious existence. How can this be possible if human knowing, as we have seen, depends upon sense images? In an objection to his view of the separated soul, Aquinas states that since "death destroys the senses and imagination," it would seem to follow that "after death the soul understands nothing."[27] Distinguishing his view from that of Platonic thinkers, he notes that if the embodiment of the soul (rather than the nature of the soul itself) caused the human soul to need the body, then after death the soul would be freed to know things without the body. As Aquinas points out, "In that case, however, the union of soul and body would not be for the soul's good, for evidently it would understand worse in the body than out of it."[28] He argues on the contrary that because the human soul is made to be the form of the body, it is for the soul's good that rational acts involve the body. To be separated from the body is against the soul's nature.[29]

Nonetheless, Aquinas posits that when the soul undergoes a change in its mode of existence, the soul likewise undergoes a change in its mode of activity. Separated from the body, the soul may turn directly to intelligible realities, although the knowledge gained in this way will be more "general and confused" than the knowledge that the embodied soul can obtain through turning to sense images.[30] Aquinas holds that God illumines the separated soul so that it remains able to know realities actively.[31] Our knowing and loving in the intermediate state is a special work of God, through which he sustains his communion with the spiritual souls that he has created.

SCRIPTURE, ESCHATOLOGY, AND THE SPIRITUAL SOUL

The above reflections on the intermediate state call to mind the inevitable connection between philosophical and theological argumentation as regards the spiritual soul. In this light, it is important to ask whether the New Testament gives support to the doctrine of the spiritual soul. Murphy lists four New Testament passages that especially seem to reflect a distinction between a material body and a spiritual soul: Matthew 10:28, "Do not fear those who kill the body but cannot kill the soul; rather fear him who can destroy both soul and body in hell"; Luke 16:22-23, "The poor man died and was carried by the angels to Abraham's bosom. The rich man also died and was buried; and in Hades, being in torment, he lifted up his eyes, and saw Abraham far off and Lazarus in his bosom"; Luke 23:43, "And he said to him, 'Truly, I say to you, today you will be with me in Paradise'"; and 2 Corinthians 5:6-8, "So we are always of good courage; we know that while we are at home in the body we are away from the Lord, for we walk by faith, not by sight. We are of good courage, and we would rather be away from the body and at home with the Lord."[32] Murphy does not cite other passages, but one that she might have added is Philippians 1:21, 23-24, "For to me to live is Christ and to die is gain. . . . My desire is to depart and be with Christ, for that is far better. But to remain in the flesh is more necessary on your account."

Murphy notes that some scholars consider that these passages "allude to or presuppose a conscious intermediate state between death and final resurrection," and she admits, "It is not clear what to make of these passages."[33] As a philosopher, she does not wish "to take sides with one or the other" exegetical position, but she does wish to suggest that the meaning of the passages is sufficiently contested as to preclude the conclusion that the New Testament authors aim "to teach *anything* about humans' metaphysical constitution."³⁴ Had they so wished, they would have done so more clearly and incontrovertibly. She appeals in particular to Joel Green's criticisms of the view that the Lukan passages refer to a disembodied conscious state prior to the resurrection. Trained both in New Testament scholarship and in neuroscience, Green aims to demonstrate the broad correspondence of the biblical portraits of the human person with the physicalism of contemporary neuroscience. Like Murphy, he takes up the case of Phineas Gage along with other neuroscientific research. He agrees with Murphy that this research has outdated the notion of the spiritual soul: "If the capacities traditionally allocated to the 'soul'—for example, consistency of memory, conscious-ness, spiritual experience, the capacity to make decisions on the basis of self-deliberation, planning and action on the basis of that decision, and taking responsibility for these decisions and actions—have a neural basis, then the concept of 'soul,' as traditionally understood in theology as a person's 'authentic self,' seems redundant."³⁵ Indeed, he wonders why theologians devoted so much attention to "soul" in the first place.³⁶

Green provides detailed exegesis of certain passages in the New Tes-tament that have been used to connect Christian eschatology to the spiri-tual soul. With respect to Luke 23:43, for example, he argues that the Second-Temple understandings of "Paradise" are too complex to allow us to assume that Luke's Jesus is referring to an intermediate state. Green explains that "[i]n the literature of Second Temple Judaism, Paradise could be used with reference simply to heaven, the divine abode and place of bliss, without temporal indicators. It might refer to an intermediate abode of the righteous, though most often it refers to the endtime dwelling of the righteous with God."³⁷ For Green, Luke's Jesus may simply mean that death immediately introduces the righteous person into the final consum-mation. There may be no "time" after death, and so the introduction to Paradise would be immediate.

Regarding 2 Corinthians 5:6-8, Green grants that many biblical scholars interpret the passage as indicative of a conscious interme-diate state. E. P. Sanders, for example, reads 2 Corinthians 5:2-4 as distinguishing "the inner person from its [bodily] clothing" and consid-ers Philippians 1:23 to be "clearly a case of anthropological dualism" because Paul "thinks that when he dies his true self will go to be with the Lord."³⁸ James D. G. Dunn similarly affirms that 2 Corinthians 5 allows for the possibility that the delay of the parousia means a period of waiting (with the Lord) after death, in addition to the temporal waiting that we now experience.[39] In his *Paradise Now and Not Yet*, Andrew Lincoln interprets 2 Corinthians 5:8 as implying an intermediate state: "Death before the parousia will therefore bring a fuller enjoyment of heavenly existence than believers can experience in this life, yet their enjoyment will not be complete until they possess the heavenly body for which God has prepared them."[40] Resurrection, not spiritual immortality, is what Paul longs for. Yet God does not abandon believers who die before the parousia: they go to be with Christ.

In Green's interpretation, the central point is that Paul does not want to be "naked" or "unclothed" (2 Cor 5:3-4). Paul wants to be "further clothed" by bodily resurrection (5:4). Rather than desiring to escape from bodiliness, he wants to receive the glorified body pledged by the Holy Spirit (5:5; 1 Cor 15). On this basis, Green concludes that 2 Corinthians 5:6-8 has to do with the resurrection body rather than with a "disembodied, human existence in an intermediate state."[41]

Rather surprisingly, Green does not discuss Matthew 10:28. Treating this verse in their three-volume commentary on Matthew's Gospel, W. D. Davies and Dale Allison observe, "ψυχήν is here the disembodied 'soul' which can survive bodily death and later be reunited with a resurrected body. The conception, whether due to the influence of Hellenism or whether a faithful continuation of OT thought, is 'dualistic.'"[42] Rudolph Schnackenburg offers another perspective on Matthew 10:28. Granted that the verse distinguishes between the body (which humans can kill) and the soul (which humans cannot kill), Schnackenburg argues that "soul" here simply indicates that human existence is not merely corporeal.[43] This is all that one needs to say, however, to arrive at the survival of the spiritual soul after the death of the body. Such survival implies neither a Cartesian or Platonic dualism, nor a denial that bodily resurrection is at the center of Jesus' eschatological promises.

Philippians 1:21-23 also merits attention. Stephen Fowl observes that this text, like 2 Corinthians 5:6-8, gestures toward what life after death will be. As Fowl points out, early Christian writings (specifically *1 Clement* and Polycarp's *Epistle to the Philippians*) teach that Paul, like other martyrs, was received at his death directly into Christ's presence. For Fowl this calls to mind the scene in the Book of Revelation where the Seer "saw under the altar the souls of those who had been slain for the word of God and for the witness they had borne" (Rev 6:9). When these souls cry out to the Lord for justice, "they were each given a white robe and told to rest a little longer, until the number of their fellow servants and their brethren should be complete, who were to be killed as they themselves had been" (Rev 6:11). Fowl recognizes that this scene may be metaphorical, and he does not assume that it necessarily reveals an intermediate state.[44]

Gordon Fee argues that interpretation of Philippians 1:21-23 requires taking into account the fact that Paul's eschatology has spatial and temporal dimensions. Spatially, Paul assumes that he will be with Christ (and thus in heaven) after he dies; temporally, for Paul "a person's death does not usher him or her into 'timeless' existence; the bodily resurrection still awaits one 'at the end.'"[45] Fee adds, however, that death may usher in a timeless existence that makes unnecessary further waiting for the parousia (this point, noted by Green, is similarly made by Ernest Best with regard to 2 Cor 5:6-8).[46] In Fee's view, Paul anticipates an intermediate state. Yet Fee holds that such a state may not in fact exist, because God alone knows whether life after death will involve the temporality required for a mode of existence to be distinguished as "intermediate."

Regarding 2 Corinthians 5:1-10, Green's emphasis on Paul's desire to be "further clothed" (5:4) with the glorified body hardly need conflict with Paul's suggestion that after death he will be "away from the body" yet "at home with the Lord" (5:8). In his treatment of 2 Corinthians 5, Green devotes most of his exegesis to 1 Corinthians 15, with a comparatively brief examination of 2 Corinthians 5:1-5. He does not directly discuss 2 Corinthians 5:6-8, even though 5:6-8 is where Paul suggests that he expects to be with Christ after death but prior to the resurrection of the body.

Green's discussion leads him to conclude that according to the New Testament, "belief in life-after-death requires embodiment—that is, re-embodiment."[47] The point is simple: "there is no part of us, no aspect of our personhood, that survives death."[48] But is the New Testament teaching so simple? Indeed, although Green in his conclusion emphatically denies that the New Testament allows for any state after death other than bodily resurrection, elsewhere he is more nuanced. He grants, for example, that "an intermediate state of some sort would certainly have had a place in popular conceptions of the afterlife among Luke's audience."[49] He admits that Jesus' reference to "Paradise" (Luke 23:43) could "refer to an intermediate abode of the righteous," as the term does in 1 Enoch, although he considers this possibility to be doubtful.[50] These nuances would be amplified, I think, by discussion of more of the relevant texts.[51]

Murphy affirms that "participation in the post-resurrection kingdom" will involve "personal transformation," and she notes that "a great deal of what lasts in the post-resurrection kingdom must be those relationships within the body of Christ that now make us the people we are."[52] She envisions our relationship with God in the postresurrection kingdom as involving the same knowing and loving that we now experience. Yet how can we have intimate knowledge and supreme love of God in the kingdom without sharing more profoundly in God's spiritual nature than mere neural pathways, however transformed, could allow us to do? Second Peter 1:4, with its promise that we will become "partakers in the divine nature," suggests that such participation will indeed characterize the eschatological Kingdom.[53] Other New Testament passages make a similar point, perhaps most notably Paul's assertion in 1 Corinthians 13:12 that "then I shall understand fully, even as I have been fully understood." Paul's relationship to God will then possess the supreme intimacy of "face to face" knowledge (1 Cor 13:12).

In response to Murphy's nonreductive physicalism, Terence Nichols remarks that if she were right, "then even in heaven we could not know God directly, through intuition; for that to happen, we would need a spiritual receptor, a faculty by which we could perceive the spiritual God. . . . Without such a faculty, we can know God only indirectly."[54] The vision of God, our supremely intimate sharing in the wisdom and love of the Trinity, is ruled out by nonreductive physicalism. Eternal life worthy of the name—the fulfillment of Jesus' promise that "[i]f a man loves me, he will keep my word, and my Father will love him, and we will come to him and make our home with him" (John 14:23)—requires the spiritual soul.

CONCLUSION

Gregory of Nyssa sensitively portrays the shocking transition that death brings about: "we see someone who was just now living and speaking, but all at once loses breath, voice, and movement, with all his natural faculties of perception quenched, with no ability to see or hear, or to use any other of the means by which perception receives its impressions."[55] For Murphy and Green, death brings an utter end to the human person, since humans are solely physical beings. God will then reconstitute the human person in resurrection. In her philosophical analysis, Murphy argues that advances in philosophy and science have made Aquinas' account of the spiritual soul at best redundant: everything that Aquinas attributed to the spiritual soul can be shown to have a neural correlate.

Aquinas, however, already recognized that physical processes are thoroughly involved in human cognition. He does not appeal to the spiritual soul as though it were another material principle. Rather, Aquinas posits the spiritual soul both for theological reasons and because otherwise one cannot account for conceptual abstraction from material particulars. If neural processes were all there is, then one would simply be substituting one material particular for another, rather than knowing the universal in the particular. Sanctification and divinization worthy of the name also mandate that we possess a spiritual soul. Otherwise, we face a profound reduction of the scope of human intimacy with God, since no matter how much our neural pathways are transformed, neural pathways do not possess much potential for intimate union with divine spirit.

As we have seen, Murphy argues that "the New Testament authors are not intending to teach *anything* about humans' metaphysical composition."[56] Although I agree that the New Testament authors are not developing philosophical views, it does seem to me that they include certain anthropological assumptions and claims in their writings. Jesus and Paul affirm that humans undergo bodily death without undergoing annihilation. When Jesus warns about caring for one's soul which humans cannot kill, and when Paul envisions a period of disembodied life with Christ after death, these passages uphold the place of reflection on the spiritual soul within a biblically guided eschatology. Far from being redundant, the doctrine of the soul allows for the New Testament's rich account of graced participation in the divine life, both now and in the life to come. Christian eschatology is right to affirm the doctrine not only philosophically but also biblically.

Joined to our exposition of meritorious works of love in chapter 5, this chapter's presentation of the spiritual soul and its capacity for knowing and loving has prepared us to explore the consummation of the eschatological community's passage from death to life, following in the footsteps of Christ by his gift of the Holy Spirit. Let us now turn to the bodily resurrection and beatific vision of the blessed, those who have desired "a better country, that is, a heavenly one" (Heb 11:16).

7

Bodily Resurrection and Beatific Vision

☙

Commenting on 1 Corinthians 13:12, Anthony Thiselton observes that Paul's phrase "now we see in a mirror dimly" employs a metaphor drawn from Platonic philosophical culture to describe indirect knowledge, while Paul's promise of a "face to face" encounter refers to "the perfection of uninterrupted personal intimacy with God."[1] Similarly, commenting on 1 John 3:2, "we shall be like him, because we shall see him as he is," Rudolph Schnackenburg explains that "becoming like God seems to be the consequence of glory, the radiant light of divine glory. Already in late Judaism the Messiah and those who participate in eschatological salvation were expected to share in this divine prerogative."[2] Schnackenburg concludes, "Likeness to God and seeing God together sum up the whole content of Christian hope."[3] If supreme intimacy with God constitutes Christian hope, however, what need is there for the resurrection of the body and (in N. T. Wright's words) "God's victorious transformation of the whole cosmos"?[4]

This final chapter asks whether an insistence on bodily resurrection and new creation can be joined with an equal insistence on the beatific vision. Jürgen Moltmann affirms that we "die into the eternally bounteous God and the wide space of his creative love," and he uses biblical images such as the New Jerusalem and the divine Shekinah to speak about the glory, beauty, and peace of the new creation.[5] Joseph Ratzinger envisions that the final consummation will bring about "the point of integration of all in all, where each thing becomes completely itself precisely by being completely in the other. In such integration, matter belongs to spirit in a wholly new and different way, and spirit is utterly one with matter."[6] On this view, bodily resurrection and beatific vision fit together within the context of "universal exchange and openness."[7] Ratzinger cautions that it is impossible to develop a concrete conception of what this integration will be like, but he would agree with Wright's view that the biblical images provide real insight into the world to come. Wright holds that not only can we expect to enjoy an "intimate fellowship" with God in Jesus Christ, but also we can anticipate that "the redeemed people of God in the new world will be the agents of his love going out in new ways, to accomplish new creative tasks, to celebrate and extend the glory of his love."[8] Wright, however, downplays the vision of God, and his insistence on "new creative tasks" threatens to bog us down in endless work.

In chapter 4, we examined three elements of the eschatological community: the apostolic teaching and fellowship (faith), the breaking of bread and the prayers (the Eucharist), and the sharing of possessions (almsgiving). Each of these elements is sustained by Jesus' royal and priestly work at the right hand of the Father, and each unites our passage to his by transforming our souls and enabling us to do meritorious works of love. In turn, the world to come, as depicted by Thomas Aquinas, fulfills in a transcendent and glorious manner these three elements of the eschatological community. Aquinas' approach has been well summarized by Carlo Leget: "Despite the apophatic and overflowing character of heaven, it may function as a magnifying mirror showing more clearly what is hard to see in earthly life. The relationship with God, which pertains to the most hidden core of the human being, is exposed in its full glory. Every element of eternal life points to this core, being the expression of it, either spiritually or materially."[9]

THE FULFILLMENT OF APOSTOLIC TEACHING AND FELLOWSHIP (FAITH)

Aquinas depicts the vision of God, which fulfills faith in a transcendent manner, as the fullness of interpersonal communion. Humans cannot be happy without "the vision of the divine essence," because "man is not perfectly happy, so long as something remains for him to desire and seek."[10] But don't humans generally desire and seek spatio-temporal goods? Aquinas asks whether human happiness can consist in wealth, honors, fame, power, health, pleasure, and/or any created spiritual good. Without discounting these goods, he concludes that "[i]t is impossible for any created good to constitute man's happiness. For happiness is the perfect good, which lulls the appetite altogether; else it would not be the last end, if something yet remained to be desired."[11] Human desire cannot rest in these limited goods; we seek communion with "the universal fount itself of good," God the Trinity, whom Aquinas describes as "the common object of happiness of all the blessed, as being the infinite and perfect good."[12] Friendship with the Father, Son, and Holy Spirit makes each of the blessed happy. The blessed enjoy God together rather than solely individually, because sharing happiness with friends belongs to the *bene esse* of happiness.[13]

Discussing the vision of God, Aquinas points out that this "vision" cannot be like the kinds of intelligible insights that we attain here and now. The vision of God cannot be a finite concept or judgment of the mind about God, nor can it be based upon knowing a likeness of God. Rather, it must be intimate knowing that locates us within the divine life itself. Only in this way could we "see him as he is" in his divinity (1 John 3:2). Since no created intellectual act comes anywhere near to being able to attain to the uncreated triune God, beatific knowing requires "the light of glory strengthening the intellect to see God."[14] God the Trinity radically elevates and transforms our rationality by making his glory present to us so that mere concepts of God are no longer needed: "God is present to the intellect seeing him not by way of a similitude, but by his essence."[15]

Seeking to evoke such knowing, which is of course utterly ineffable, Aquinas appeals to Psalm 36:9, "For with you is the fountain of life; in your light do we see light."[16] He also points to Ephesians 1:17-18, where Paul speaks of our eschatological inheritance as requiring the elevation of our minds and hearts to apprehend God. Paul urges believers to have "the eyes of your hearts enlightened, that you may know what is the hope to which he has called you, what are the riches of his glorious inheritance in the saints."[17] Another biblical passage to which Aquinas refers in the same vein is John 17:3, "And this is eternal life, that they know you the only true God, and Jesus Christ whom you have sent."[18]

Jesus reveals the glorious God of supreme love, supreme humility, who is also the all-powerful and all-knowing "I am" (John 8:58; Exod 3:14). In revealing God's glory, Jesus does not make it less transcendent. Rather, Jesus calls upon the Father to reveal to us in eternal life the glory of the divine Persons: "Father, I desire that they also, whom you have given me, may be with me where I am, to behold my glory which you have given me in your love for me before the foundation of the world" (John 17:24). To be with Jesus in the life to come means to "behold his glory" as Son and Word, in the Love and Gift of the Father. This is the transcendent fulfillment of faith. Our earthly understanding of human enterprise must give way to the "glory" that characterizes sharing in Trinitarian communion in "spirit and truth" (John 4:24).[19]

The "deiformity" that God gives to human rationality means that the vision of God cannot be compared to either practical or intellectual work here and now.[20] Eternal life flows from the light of glory rather than from the natural light of the intellect, and the light of glory unites the blessed with God's own life rather than giving a higher natural knowledge of God. It follows that the vision of God differs among the blessed depending on the extent to which they possessed, in this life, "faith working through love" (Gal 5:6). Aquinas observes that "he who possesses the more charity, will see God the more perfectly, and will be the more beatified."[21] The glory that God gives the communion of the blessed consists in adoptive sonship in the Son, the "riches of his glorious inheritance." Caught up in the Trinitarian life, the blessed, as a community of friends, "possess" God and "enjoy him as the ultimate fulfilment of desire."[22] In this respect Aquinas quotes the impassioned imagery of Song of Songs 3:4, "I held him, and would not let him go."[23] The beatific vision involves the whole Trinity making himself known to the blessed; nothing of the Trinity "is hidden from the seer," even though we cannot know God in the infinite mode in which he knows himself.[24]

Does the vision of God leave room for our accomplishing "new creative tasks"?[25] The answer has to do with what Aquinas means by the "deiformity" that eternal life works in us. As a sharing in the beatitude of the Trinity, eternal life moves on quite different lines from the ventures that occupy our earthly life. Richard Bauckham and Trevor Hart describe this well: "In eternity we shall no longer have goals towards which we must measure our temporal progress. In the worship whose only purpose is to please God and to enjoy God, we shall eternally lose

ourselves in the beauty and love of God and eternally enjoy the surprise
of finding ourselves in God."[26] Aquinas argues that the vision of God
will be an all-at-once, participatory "seeing" of the Father, Son, and Holy
Spirit: "What is seen in the Word is seen not successively, but at the same
time."[27] The blessed will share in God's own Trinitarian communion not
as onlookers, but as real participants, caught up into God's life rather
than being observers who watch God moment to moment. The blessed
will be supremely engaged and energized in enjoying God and each other
in God. By contrast, an everlasting duration of new cosmic projects, as
Wright seems to envision, fits more closely with Aquinas' understanding
of hell, where "true eternity does not exist, but rather time."[28]

To share in the Trinitarian life, however, is also to share in the Lord
of history "according to his purpose which he set forth in Christ as a
plan for the fulness of time, to unite all things in him, things in heaven
and things on earth" (Eph 1:9-10). Unlike a Platonic ascent to the realm
of forms where "true being dwells,"[29] the beatific vision is not abstracted
from history. Comparing the Creator to a craftsman, Aquinas states,
"Now the craftsman works through the word conceived in his mind,
and through the love of his will regarding some object. Hence also God
the Father made the creature through his Word, which is his Son; and
through his Love, which is the Holy Spirit."[30] In the beatific vision, the
blessed discover history in its divine roots: "the processions of the Persons are the type of the productions of creatures."[31] History is discovered
anew in the Trinitarian wisdom and love. Sharing in God as friends (or
sons or Bride) introduces the blessed to history in its Christological and
providential fullness. Within the Trinitarian life, the blessed discover
history redeemed (cf. Rev 22:3-5).[32]

The fulfillment of faith in vision thus allows for what would otherwise be impossible, namely a realistic hope for what Matthew Lamb
calls the final "harmony and beauty of the whole creation," inclu-
sive of the "countless histories of suffering."[33] As David Hart puts it,
through faith "we begin to see—more clearly the more we are able to
look upon the world with the eye of charity—that there is in all the
things of earth a hidden glory waiting to be revealed, more radiant
than a million suns, more beautiful than the most generous imagination or most ardent desire can now conceive."[34] This hidden glory is
the mystical reality of the Church. Hart adds that even now, despite
the sin and suffering under which all creation groans, this glory is "not

entirely hidden: veiled, rather, but shining in and through and upon all things."[35] Somewhat similarly, Wright describes Jesus' resurrection as a victory, a restoration of creation to what it always should have been, namely the kingdom of God.[36]

We might still ask, however, whether Aquinas' affirmation that humankind's ultimate destiny is the vision of God (and no lesser project) makes the kingdom of God fundamentally otherworldly rather than a place of transformed bodiliness. In answer, we can recall that God promises to "swallow up death for ever" and to "wipe away tears from all faces" (Isa 25:8).[37] Plato's mistake—an understandable one—lay in his inability to conceive of God sustaining human bodies in an incorruptible state, so that embodied persons are able to commune everlastingly with divine realities. Jesus' resurrection reveals God's plan for our bodiliness.[38] Indeed, no human intimacy with God can be fully human when it lacks bodily expression. Aquinas points out that the soul's separation from the body after death holds "the soul back from tending with all its might to the vision of the divine essence. For the soul desires to enjoy God in such a way that the enjoyment also may overflow into the body."[39] As Paul emphasizes, the body is meant "for the Lord, and the Lord for the body" (1 Cor 6:13). The body will be fully "for the Lord" in the resurrection.

In order for our bodies to be fully "for the Lord," our bodies must not only be incorruptible but also be fully translucent to interpersonal communion.[40] In the beatific vision, far more than now in the communion of faith, we will be able to follow Paul's command to "glorify God in your body" (1 Cor 6:20). In the beatific vision, interpersonal communion will govern entirely the way that our bodiliness manifests itself, as signaled already by Christ's transfiguration, when "his face shone like the sun, and his garments became white as light" (Matt 17:2).[41] Whereas in this life our bodiliness governs our days, in eternal life our participation in divine life—no longer an experience of "days" but rather "continuous day" (Zech 14:7)—will govern our bodiliness. Aquinas quotes Augustine's description of the body as now often turning the mind "'away from that vision of the highest heaven'" but as then glorying, *qua* body, in the "vision of the highest heaven."[42]

THE FULFILLMENT OF THE BREAKING OF BREAD
AND THE PRAYERS (THE EUCHARIST)

What will the new creation, with its glorious interplay of spiritual and bodily, be like? Wright states that "God's space and ours" will one day "be joined in a quite new way, open and visible to one another, married together forever."[43] Similarly, commenting on the eschatological imagery of Isaiah 65–66, he remarks, "It looks as though God intends to flood the universe with himself, as though the universe, the entire cosmos, was designed as a receptacle for his love. . . . [The world] is designed to be filled, flooded, drenched in God."[44] What would it mean for the world to be "drenched in God"?

In this regard, the images of a new temple and a new Jerusalem are used by Jesus in the Book of Revelation, when he instructs the Seer to write to the angel of the church in Sardis, "He who conquers, I will make him a pillar in the temple of my God; never shall he go out of it, and I will write on him the name of my God, and the name of the city of my God, the new Jerusalem which comes down from my God out of heaven, and my own new name" (Rev 3:12). The intimacy includes an actual participation in the power that Jesus receives from the Father, as we learn in Revelation 2:26-27. More than this—if more could be— Jesus promises that the redeemed will "sit with me on my throne, as I myself conquered and sat down with my Father on his throne" (Rev 3:21). This intimacy of God and his people is astounding: we will be caught up into the Trinitarian "throne." Knowing and loving God will move from the periphery to the center of our lives, in an unfathomably rich way. The intimacy is marital: the "holy city Jerusalem coming down out of heaven from God" (Rev 21:10) is "the Bride, the wife of the Lamb" (21:9). The Seer of the Book of Revelation finds that the "holy city Jerusalem" has "no temple" because "its temple is the Lord God the Almighty and the Lamb" (21:22). Similarly, there is no physical light in the "city," because "the glory of God is its light, and its lamp is the Lamb" (21:23). The entire city, the new creation, will have the Trinity as its temple and share in the divine glory.[45]

This transformation of creation into the temple of the Trinity requires the purification of the cosmos. With regard to this cleansing in preparation for cosmic worship, Aquinas quotes 2 Peter 3:10 and 12, "The day of the Lord will come like a thief, and then the heavens will pass away with a loud noise, and the elements will be dissolved with fire, and the earth and the works that are upon it will be burned up. . . . [T]he heavens will be kindled and dissolved, and the elements will melt with fire."[46] He connects this imagery with the psalmist's words about God's coming judgment: "before him is a devouring fire, round about him a mighty tempest" (Ps 50:3). The goal of this fire is the restoration of all creation to its original purity, so that creation might fully give praise to its Creator.[47] Ben Witherington similarly comments on 2 Peter 3 by remarking that the fire "strips bare and exposes the earth but does not cause it to dissolve or disappear."[48]

Like Christ's return, the fiery cleansing belongs to the transition from the cosmos as we know it to "a new heaven and a new earth" (Rev 21:1). Josef Pieper observes that this "process of transition from the temporal being of the historical world to direct participation—whatever its particular form—in God's 'eternity' lies wholly and utterly beyond our power of imagination."[49] The same point is made even more strongly by Joseph Ratzinger: "The cosmic imagery of the New Testament cannot be used as a source for the description of a future chain of cosmic events. All attempts of this kind are misplaced. Instead, these texts form part of a description of the mystery of the Parousia in the language of liturgical tradition. The New Testament conceals and reveals the unspeakable coming of Christ, using language borrowed from that sphere which is graciously enabled to express in this world the point of contact with God."[50] Aquinas grants that the cosmic imagery of the end time exceeds our understanding. Discussing Ezekiel 37's prophecy of the dry bones, for example, he invokes the principle of divine condescension: "Just as Moses divided the works of the six days into days, in order that the uncultured people might be able to understand, although all things were made together according to Augustine (*Gen. ad Lit.* iv), so Ezechiel expressed the various things that will happen in the resurrection, although they will all happen together in an instant."[51] Even so, Aquinas assumes that the biblical images offer valuable insight into the cosmic transition. He thus keeps well away from the claim of some theologians that we can no longer suppose that "the course of history must be definitely stopped by a cataclysm of universal dimensions. . . . Theology does not take an interest in any apocalyptic understanding of history (not even the one upheld by the historical Jesus)."[52]

Aquinas argues that the cleansing must include all corporeal elements that have been corrupted and/or have been in subjects who have committed sin. He explains that although "a corporeal thing cannot be the subject of the stain of sin, nevertheless, on account of sin corporeal things contract a certain unfittingness for being appointed to spiritual purposes."[53] He gives as an example our hesitation to perform sacred rites in "places where crimes have been committed," until those places have been cleansed.[54] The cleansing fire will burn "as the instrument of God's providence and power," purifying rather than consuming the corporeal elements.[55] Since all corporeal elements are to be cleansed, no one will escape death: all human bodies will be consumed by the fire.[56] Underscoring the unity of the material creation, Aquinas observes that "it is fitting that man, being a part of the world, be cleansed with the same fire as the world."[57] The fire will operate in a purgatorial manner, preparatory to the last judgment, on those who are good but not yet fully holy.[58]

Returning in glory to this liturgically renewed cosmos, Christ Jesus will bring about the resurrection of the dead, both the just and the wicked.[59] Aquinas recognizes that the scope of the resurrection is called into question by certain biblical passages, among them Daniel 12:2, "many of those who sleep in the dust of the earth shall awake" and even 1 Corinthians 15 and Romans 8, which connect the resurrection of the dead with configuration to Christ (which the wicked have rejected). Arguing that not only the just are raised from the dead, Aquinas points out that human nature itself involves a certain configuration to Christ: "Hence all will be conformed to him in the restoration of natural life, but not in the likeness of glory."[60]

Aquinas takes seriously the liturgical image of the "trumpet" that sounds to wake the dead: "For the Lord himself will descend from heaven with a cry of command, with the archangel's call, and with the sound of the trumpet of God" (1 Thess 4:15). Following Gregory the Great, Aquinas is willing to suppose that the "cry of command" and "sound of the trumpet" signify Christ's bodily appearing, "because as soon as he appears all nature will obey his command in restoring human bodies."[61] Yet Aquinas does not rule out the possibility that the bodily sign by which Christ works our bodily resurrection may be literally his voice of command.[62] The new creation will be called into being not only through the fire that purifies everything corrupt and stained in the old created order, but also through Christ's bodily sign, renewing the material creation from within the material creation. The role of the angels ("the archangel's call") will be to gather together the dispersed material elements so as to assist in the restoration of human bodies, although God alone reunites soul and body and glorifies the resurrected person. Aquinas opposes the view "that 'our body in that glory of the resurrection will be impalpable, and more subtle than wind and air: and that our Lord, after the hearts of the disciples who handled him were confirmed, brought back to subtlety whatever could be handled in him.'"[63]

In Revelation 20:4-5, the Seer has a vision in which the Christian martyrs "came to life, and reigned with Christ a thousand years. The rest of the dead did not come to life until the thousand years were ended." The Seer describes this as "the first resurrection" (20:5) and proclaims, "Blessed and holy is he who shares in the first resurrection!" (20:6). Indebted to Augustine, Aquinas interprets the "first resurrection" as the time of the Church, when humans "rise again from their sins to the gift of grace" and thereby "reign with Christ."[64] While thus rejecting millennialism, Aquinas holds that some, including the Virgin Mary, are raised prior to the general resurrection. Those who receive this privilege do so because by raising them God bears witness to Christ's resurrection.[65] No one can know the time of the end of the world and the general resurrection, despite numerous efforts to calculate when it must occur: "The falseness of these calculators is evident, as will likewise be the falseness of those who even now cease not to calculate."[66]

If Jesus judges each person at the moment of death—as indicated by Jesus' words to the good thief, "Today you will be with me in Paradise" (Luke 23:43)—will there also be a last judgment of all humans at his Second Coming? Citing John 12:48, "the word that I have spoken will be his judge on the last day," Aquinas observes that aspects of each person's life resonate "through the whole course of time," and so "all these things must be brought to judgment at the end of time."[67] Since individual persons exist within a web of relationships, all history must be judged as a unity, without thereby excluding an immediate judgment of each person after death. When Jesus, "filled with the truth of the Word of God, passes judgment on all things," the wise order of God's providence will be fully revealed.[68]

For Aquinas, then, Jesus' Second Coming brings all cosmic projects to their end; the purifying fire and last judgment definitively order all things to God. This consummation is the fulfillment of eucharistic communion: "all human affairs are ordered for the end of beatitude, which is everlasting salvation."[69] In the new order of creation, the blessed commune in the very life of the triune God. Wright at times comes close to this position, as when he describes love as "the food they eat in God's new world" and "the music God has written for all his creatures to sing."[70]

THE FULFILLMENT OF OUR SHARING ALL THINGS (ALMSGIVING)

In eternal life, we will share all material things and indeed our very selves without experiencing any lack or discomfort. Contemplating how this might be so, Aquinas begins by exploring the incorruptibility of the resurrected body, also strongly affirmed by Wright.[71] For Aquinas as for Wright, 1 Corinthians 15:42 is central: "What is sown is perishable, what is raised is imperishable." Aquinas also points to Philippians 3:20-21, "But our commonwealth is in heaven, and from it we await a Savior, the Lord Jesus Christ, who will change our lowly body to be like his glorious body, by the power which enables him even to subject all things to himself."[72] Resurrected persons receive their same body, now glorified.[73]

It would seem, however, that if our bodies are incorruptible, they will no longer experience sensation, since sensation comes about through a bodily alteration. In this regard, Aquinas highlights the permeability of the body to the soul in the state of glory. The glory of the soul overflows to the body so that the whole person experiences "unchangeable enjoyment of God."[74] Resurrected and glorified bodies will experience "spiritual alteration" of the senses, rather than material alteration.[75] All of the bodily senses will be supremely active with perfect sweetness, so that (for instance) vocal praise will not hurt the ears of the blessed, nor intense light their eyes.

Aquinas goes on to describe the resurrected and glorified body as "subtle," which he defines in terms of penetrative power (e.g., the sun's rays). In communing with each other, we will not crowd each other.[76] The body will remain palpable but will become more like the soul. The permeability of the glorified body to the soul also will produce agility in movement: "by the gift of agility it is subject to the soul as its mover, so that it is prompt and apt to obey the spirit in all the movements and actions of the soul."[77] In order to see the beauty of the whole new creation, the blessed will need to move, and they will enjoy bodily movement that is "agile" in the sense that it fully expresses the soul's movements of joy.[78] The beauty of the new creation will be enhanced, too, by what Aquinas calls the "clarity" of the resurrected bodies. Drawing upon both the transfiguration of Jesus and upon Jesus' promise that "the righteous will shine like the sun in the kingdom of their Father" (Matt 13:43), Aquinas supposes that the permeability of the body to the soul will give the body (while retaining its natural color) a brightness "resulting from the soul's glory," as when something is aglow from the sun's rays.[79]

When Christ comes and judges the entire created universe, he will come in his glorified flesh and "the divine justice will be made manifest in all things."[80] Yet even when the sins of the blessed are revealed they will not be put to shame, because of their repentance in Christ.[81] After this judgment, all things will manifest supreme beauty: "at the one same time, the world will be renewed, and man will be glorified."[82] In this "new heaven" and "new earth" (Rev 21:1), the universe itself will shine with God's glory, like a splendid robe bestowed upon the blessed.

In this glorified cosmos, the blessed will enjoy the "rooms" or "mansions" depicted by Jesus in John 14:2. These "rooms" will be larger or smaller depending upon the person's love: greater love means a greater capacity to share in the life of the Trinity.[83] When we use our skills and talents well in this life, we do so out of love of God and neighbor. Our earthly projects will be burned in divine "fire," so as to expose their hidden love: "[E]ach man's work will become manifest; for the Day will disclose it, because it will be revealed with fire, and the fire will test what sort of work each one has done. If the work which any man has built on the foundation survives, he will receive a reward" (1 Cor 3:13-14). The only true foundation is Jesus Christ and his love. In this way our skills and talents truly are, as Wright says, "enhanced and ennobled and given back to us to be exercised to his glory,"[84] in the communion of love. Aquinas states that each of the blessed becomes "a participator of the Godhead, and consequently endowed with regal power."[85] Aquinas also speaks of the "gifts" or "dowry" of "the Bride, the wife of the Lamb" (Rev 21:9). The person will be made fit for the delights of marriage with the Trinity.[86]

In rejoicing in God, the blessed rejoice in the works that God enabled them to do so that they could be as they are. Aquinas describes this secondary joy as an "aureole" or little "crown" given to the blessed in addition to "the essential reward [beatitude itself] which is called the *aurea*."[87] Quoting 2 Timothy 2:5, "An athlete is not crowned unless he competes according to the rules," Aquinas remarks that certain contests involve special rewards. Just as in earthly life difficult deeds receive rewards—"a crown to the conqueror, a prize to the runner"—so also the Church in the new creation displays the eternal rewards of difficult deeds.[88] Some earthly actions involve a more profound sharing of ourselves with God and neighbor, and the special beauty of these actions is not lost in the supreme sharing that is the new creation. Because of their configuration to Christ's life, Aquinas highlights consecrated virginity, martyrdom, and preaching/teaching about God.[89] He explains that "[w]here there is a notable kind of victory, a special crown is due."[90]

The Seer of the Book of Revelation describes one hundred and forty-four thousand redeemed virgins bearing the name of the Lamb and of the Father on their foreheads, who alone can "sing a new song before the throne" (14:3). Likewise, the Seer depicts "Babylon the great," the opposite of the new Jerusalem, as "drunk with the blood of the saints and the blood of the martyrs of Jesus" (17:6). In the Seer's vision the martyrs share profoundly in Christ's sacrificial death: "I saw under the altar the souls of those who had been slain for the word of God and for the witness they had borne" (6:9). Aquinas compares the martyrs' victory to that of consecrated virgins, although the martyrs' victory is greater: "[J]ust as a special crown, which we call an aureole, is due to the most perfect victory whereby we triumph over the concupiscences of the flesh, in a word to virginity, so too an aureole is due to the most perfect victory that is won against external assaults."[91] By freely accepting death out of love for Christ, the martyrs show that even death must bow before Christ's victory. Christ gives humans strength, in other words, not only to face internal enemies (first and foremost concupiscence), but also to face external enemies with love.

Why include teachers and preachers among those envisioned as receiving a special "crown"? Articulating an evident objection to his view, Aquinas notes that "exaltation in the life to come corresponds to humiliation in the present life, because *he that humbleth himself shall be exalted* (Matt 23:12). But there is no humiliation in teaching and preaching, in fact they are occasions of pride."[92] Indeed, as Aquinas points out, the pride of teachers is the subject of the medieval gloss on Matthew 4:5, "Then the devil took him." The gloss warns that "the devil deceives many who are puffed up with the honor of the master's chair."[93] Aquinas replies that when rightly employed, the position of the teacher and preacher profits others by sharing the truth that nourishes the life of charity. In this regard Aquinas quotes Paul, "For though we live in the world we are not carrying on a worldly war, for the weapons of our warfare are not worldly but have divine power to destroy strongholds. We destroy arguments and every proud obstacle to the knowledge of God, and take every thought captive to obey Christ" (2 Cor 10:4-5).[94] When preached and taught, the Gospel reveals its power to unite humans in the divine life.

Although Christians have often failed to act with love, Wright points out that many Christians have manifested Christ's lordship in self-giving love. Among those whose witness has led to a more just social order, he names St. Francis, William Wilberforce, Desmond Tutu, Pope John Paul II, and Mother Teresa.[95] These well-known Christians give us a taste of the powerful influence of the kingdom of God in the world, and so do the many lesser-known believers who live out "the personal and intimate life of resurrection to which each of us is called."[96] Wright emphasizes, therefore, that faith in the resurrection is not only about the future; it has to do with the "patterns of new creation" that, as Wright points out, have been "woven into history" by Christ's faithful followers.[97]

In this light, why does not the theological tradition assign an "aureole" that directly corresponds to the virtue of justice, or one directly corresponding to poverty, obedience, or the many other virtuous acts? Aquinas answers that what Wright calls the "patterns of new creation" are best discerned not primarily by listing particular works of virtue, but by identifying the basic conflicts that humans experience after the Fall and that prevent us from sharing ourselves and our goods. Arguably, these basic conflicts—against the flesh (concupiscence), against the world (power), and against the devil (idolatry)—are to be found at the heart of all injustice in the world. To lead a life of preeminent holiness means to attain "exceptional victories" in these areas, in configuration to Christ's own pattern of life.[98]

Wright warns us to "[f]orget those images about lounging around playing harps."[99] This image, of course, comes from the Book of Revelation, where the "twenty-four elders fell down before the Lamb, each holding a harp" (5:8) and where holiness sounds "like the sound of harpers playing on their harps" (14:2). The image of the harp reminds us that eternal life is less like a continuation of earthly projects than like a symphony of Trinitarian truth and love in which we participate liturgically, as a temple of living stones formed by charity. The "harps" make manifest this liturgical consummation of all earthly work: "I saw what appeared to be a sea of glass mingled with fire, and those who had conquered the beast and its image and the number of its name, standing beside the sea of glass with harps of God in their hands. And they sing the song of Moses, the servant of God, and the song of the Lamb" (15:2-3).

Wright's concern is that this image might make the new creation seem boring. Our earthly labors seem the most real thing, and we wonder how we will live without them. Eternal life, however, involves plunging into the deepest reality, the Trinitarian life. Our earthly labors are not thereby negated. On the contrary, the self-giving love that in this life configures our labors to Christ, and that furthers his kingdom, also fuels the beauty and joy of the new creation. The body will shine with glory in accordance with the person's degree of self-giving love: "in the glorified body the glory of the soul will be known, even as through a crystal is known the color of a body contained in a crystal vessel."[100] The body's permeability to the soul displays not dualism but a glorious unity—even while the body retains its bodiliness, so that "the clarity of glory will overflow from the soul into the body according to the mode of the body."[101]

It is in this way that the new creation will be "more solid, more real, than the present one" (in C. S. Lewis' insight adopted by Wright).[102] To participate more deeply in the Trinitarian life is to become "more solid, more real," because created existence is a finite participation in God. To live fully in "the Lord God the Almighty and the Lamb" (Rev 21:22), so as to "worship him" and "see his face" (22:3-4), is the perfection of all our works of love.

CONCLUSION

As Wright observes, faith in Christ's resurrection is utterly opposed to "a hope that will cut the nerve of, and the need for, any attempt to make things better in the present world of space, time, and matter."[103] For Wright, this hinges upon a strong sense of the eschatological renewal of space, time, and matter. He emphasizes "hope for God's renewal of all things, for his overcoming of corruption, decay, and death, for his filling of the whole cosmos with his love and grace, his power and glory."[104] Aquinas has in view the same reality—the purification of the cosmos, the end of death and corruption, the transformation of the cosmos into the perfect temple of God the Trinity's love and glory. Eternal life will be marked by supreme knowing and loving, cosmic worship, and the beauty and joy of sharing all things.

This glorious fulfillment means that time, space, and matter will not continue as they are now. Not only will matter become incorruptible, but also the entire material creation will be purified and reconfigured in order to reflect fully the love of God. When the material cosmos is transformed into a temple of the Trinity, Aquinas does not think that it will look the same: plants, animals, and so forth will give way to material beauty of another kind, once generation and corruption are no more.[105] The spatial layout of the cosmos will become more "real" by participating fully in the hierarchy of love whose head is Christ Jesus. Bodily movements will gain a share in the glory of divine eternity, as in the subtlety and agility Christ's glorified body. Everything will be attuned to the vision of God, as God shares himself with us and we share with each other in him.

Aquinas' attention to the biblical images and promises enables him to imagine a new creation in which the Trinitarian life radically suffuses everything. The consummation of the Church's faith occurs in the radical intimacy of beatific vision, in which we are not onlookers but real participants in the Trinitarian life. The consummation of the Church's eucharistic worship takes place through the purification of the cosmos and its reconfiguration so as to manifest fully the hierarchy of love as the temple of the Trinity. The consummation of our sharing of possessions, our giving of ourselves and all that we have, appears in the glorification of our bodies so that we can fully share with each other the beauty and joy of the whole new creation.

In this life we have glimpses of the divine glory, but surely nothing like its full manifestation in the new creation. There will be no work to do other than to plunge, in the unity of body and soul, into God's glory ("face to face"). Knowing and loving God the Trinity, sharing in his eternal and ineffable triune wisdom and love, will be our task—and our bodies and the entire cosmos will be taken up into it, so that we are fully in "God the Almighty and the Lamb" (Rev 21:22) by the Holy Spirit. The redeemed human race, with the purified and reconfigured cosmos and the angels of God, will be married to God as his Bride.

Will this new creation be so beautiful and glorious, so reconfigured, as to lose its connection with the world that we now experience? Aquinas suggests that our historical experience will on the contrary be far more real in eternal life, because its hidden springs will be exposed and its defects purified. Just as in the new creation Christ will bear his scars (and the martyrs the signs of their conquests), so also the blessed who see the face of God will shine, not only spiritually but also bodily, with the beauty of the difficult victories that they achieved in this life by God's grace.[106] The power of Christ's resurrection appears most clearly in this life when the truth about God is spread, when humans freely give up their lives in bearing witness to Christ, and when lust for earthly pleasures no longer dominates. Not only these, but every other graced action on earth finds its consummation in the radical permeability or transparency to God the Trinity—our happiness or "beatitude"—that constitutes the eternal life won for us by Christ in accord with God's "purpose which he set forth in Christ as a plan for the fulness of time, to unite all things in him, things in heaven and things on earth" (Eph 1:9-10).

In sum, the vision of God fulfills our embodied life on earth and is profoundly united to bodily resurrection and the new creation of the cosmos. At the right hand of the Father, Jesus pours forth his Holy Spirit so as to bring about this consummation. When it is accomplished, we will be fully "rooted and grounded in love" and will "have power to comprehend with all the saints what is the breadth and length and height and depth, and to know the love of Christ which surpasses knowledge" so that we will "be filled with all the fulness of God" (Eph 3:17-19). God will be "all in all" (Eph 1:23).

Conclusion

No study of resurrection and eternal life can ignore the contemporary Western crisis of faith.[1] When we lack a relationship with the living God, literally nothing seems to await us after death; life becomes a thin veneer covering eternal annihilation.[2] In this situation, agnosticism passes for hope, as expressed by a recent writer: "I believe that after I have quaffed the cup containing the wine of life, emptied it to the last dregs, then I will not fear to turn to that other cup, the one whose contents can be designated only by X, an unknown, and a thing about which we can gain no knowledge at all until we drink for ourselves."[3] Even Karl Rahner, from a Christian perspective, can say only that the "fuller life which is to endure for ever is still concealed—in that silent future which we are going to meet."[4]

Christian faith, however, enables us to say more about the life to come than that it is the unknowable "silent future." Eternal life is not "a thing about which we can gain no knowledge at all until we drink for ourselves." We can instead anticipate being, at the moment of death, in the intermediate state with a conscious awareness of Christ's presence and that of others. For Christians, eternal life is not utterly unknown here and now: the saints, with whom we are in communion in Christ, are already enjoying the vision of God, and the new creation has already begun in Jesus Christ and his mother Mary.[5] All are actively preparing for the consummation of all things through the Second Coming of Jesus, the resurrection of the dead, and the last judgment. Death ushers those who love God not into destruction, radical loneliness, or alienation, but into a deeper and richer interpersonal communion.

The God who redeems us so gloriously is the same God who created us. Christians discover, therefore, that there is no need to choose between valuing the spiritual gifts that God has given us and valuing the bodily gifts. Thus when Gregory of Nyssa expresses fear of misfortune and death, his sister Macrina encourages him, "if you have some fondness for this body, and you are sorry to be unyoked from what you love, do not be in despair about this."[6] Macrina assures him that in the resurrection, he will receive his own body, "woven again from the same elements, not indeed with its present coarse and heavy texture, but with the thread respun into something subtler and lighter."[7] The purpose of this refinement is "so that the beloved body may be with you and be restored to you again in better and even more lovable beauty."[8] Far from denigrating the body, the revelation of our soul's created and graced "immensity" calls us to enjoy, in our risen flesh, "the immeasurable riches of his grace" (Eph 2:7).[9]

By contrast, Richard Dawkins argues that "[b]eing dead will be no different from being unborn—I shall be just as I was in the time of William the Conqueror or the dinosaurs or the trilobites."[10] He supposes that the annihilation of an "I," someone who knows and loves, is no different from nonexistence per se. The devaluation of persons implied by this perspective is striking. Here the gift of life has no Giver and no enduring value. If our own annihilation is nothing serious, how can the annihilation of anyone else be of much concern?[11] Against this devaluation of persons, it is love of persons—rooted in affirmation of divine generosity—that best attunes us to faith in resurrection and eternal life.[12] Thus Augustine and Søren Kierkegaard call attention to the First Letter of John, with its testimony that "he who does not love his brother whom he has seen, cannot love God whom he has not seen" (1 John 4:20) and its insistence that "God gave us eternal life, and this life is in his Son" (5:11).

Plato also deserves some credit here. Although the *Timaeus* subordinates the creator to the eternal forms, Plato rightly intuits that the creator "was good, and the good can never have any jealousy of anything. And being free from jealousy, he desired that all things should be like himself as they could be."[13] The creator delights in sharing his goodness, and he creates humans to commune in this goodness. This insight provides a foretaste of Christian eschatology, rooted in the beauty and bounty of creation. It is no wonder that Socrates says of the true philosopher, "Such a one, as soon as he beholds the beauty of this world, is reminded of true beauty, and his wings begin to grow; then is he fain to lift his wings and fly upward."[14] This ascent can take the unfortunate form of a rejection of this world, as when Socrates calls the body a "prison house," but it need not do so.[15] The lover of beauty can love this world's beauty even more by discerning its source in the gifting God. Indeed, only by renouncing this world as our ultimate end can we fully affirm the goodness of the world and of our existence in the world.[16]

We can say something, then, about Christ's passage and ours, and about our final destiny in Christ. It is important that we bear witness to these realities, especially in a culture that increasingly embraces despair. But at the same time, we do not thereby presume to tie up the many loose ends. Faith is not yet sight; hope is not yet attainment. God's works go too far beyond what we can conceptualize, and we still have to "work out [our] salvation with fear and trembling" (Phil 2:12). In the darkness of his sufferings, Job begs to be protected, remembered, and desired by God: "Oh that you would hide me in Sheol, that you would conceal me until your wrath be past, that you would appoint me a set time, and remember me! . . . You would call, and I would answer you; you would long for the work of your hands" (Job 14:13, 15). God's beautiful answer to Job is Christ Jesus, whom we receive in the church through the Holy Spirit.[17] In Jesus, God protects, remembers, calls, and longs for us.

Notes

INTRODUCTION

1   Richard B. Hays, "'Why Do You Stand Looking Up toward Heaven?' New Testament Eschatology at the Turn of the Millennium," *Modern Theology* 16 (2000): 133. See also Pope Benedict XVI, *Light of the World: The Pope, the Church, and the Signs of the Times: A Conversation with Peter Seewald*, trans. Michael J. Miller and Adrian J. Walker (San Francisco: Ignatius Press, 2010), 179: "Our preaching, our proclamation, really is one-sided, in that it is largely directed toward the creation of a better world, while hardly anyone talks any more about the other, truly better world."

2   Hays, "'Why Do You Stand Looking Up toward Heaven?,'" 133.

3   Anthony Godzieba, e.g., thinks that "current Roman Catholic eschatology is in disarray. The problems are rooted not only in the fact that the *eschata* are fundamentally mysteries that lay beyond any humanly achieved certainty. There are also major questions concerning the relative appropriateness of the images, language, and categories to be used for liturgical and personal prayer, for preaching, and for theological reflection upon eternal life. Crafting a contemporary eschatology has been made more difficult due to the demise of theology's traditional dualistic anthropology and by the fact that the theological discussion of 'personal identity' has lagged behind the contemporary philosophical discussions of subjectivity and alterity." Godzieba, "Bodies and Persons, Resurrected and Postmodern: Towards a Relational Eschatology," in *Theology and Conversation: Towards a Relational Theology*, ed. J. Haers and P. De Mey (Leuven: Leuven University Press, 2003), 211. Godzieba expresses concern that the 1970 revisions of the funeral liturgy removed references to "soul," and he seeks to provide a postmodern, nondualist account of "soul" as symbolizing "the intersubjectively sharable incarnated depth of the self" (224).

4   For the development of Christian eschatology under the influence of Greek philosophical culture, see Brian E. Daley, S.J., *The Hope of the Early Church: A Handbook of Patristic Eschatology* (Cambridge: Cambridge University Press, 1991); Daley, "A Hope for Worms: Early Christian Hope," in *Resurrection: Theological and Scientific Assessments*, ed. Ted Peters, Robert John Russell, and Michael Welker (Grand Rapids: Eerdmans, 2002), 136–64. See also more specialized studies such as Charalambos Apostolopoulos, *Phaedo Christianus: Studien zur Verbindung und Abwägung des Verhältnisses zwischen dem platonischen "Phaidon" und dem Dialog Gregors von Nyssa "Über die Seele und die Auferstehung"* (Frankfurt: Lang, 1986).

5   Seeking to move beyond the academic enclosure of Aquinas' *sacra doctrina* within "historical theology," I engage Aquinas in a constructive and selective manner, rather than attempting to write historical theology. Aquinas' eschatology largely corresponds with that of the *Catechism of the Catholic Church*.

6   This emphasis on contemporary biblical scholarship will be contested by some scholars. For Peter Phan, e.g., developments in "interreligious dialogue, liberation theology, feminist thought, ecological theology, the new physics, and process philosophy" mean that "Christian eschatology has entered a new era in which another framework is required for interpreting both the *eschaton* and the *eschata*." Phan, "Contemporary Context and Issues in Eschatology," *Theological Studies* 55 (1994): 536. Given that the fundamental interpretive framework for eschatology must always be divine revelation, my contention is that an eschatology that is "adequate for our times" (536) need not thereby be one indebted primarily to the intellectual trends of our times.

7   Joseph Ratzinger, *Eschatology: Death and Eternal Life*, trans. Michael Waldstein and Aidan Nichols, O.P., 2nd ed. (Washington, D.C.: Catholic University of America Press, 2007), 171. Ratzinger adds, "This complicating factor in the theological appropriation of Scripture is in any case something demanded by the structure of the Bible's own affirmations. As in the case of the topic of immortality, what the New Testament offers to reflection is a beginning, not an end. Through christology, it gives a new focus to both of these questions. Yet this new center is itself in search of suitable anthropological means of expression. The Bible itself forbids Biblicism" (171).

8   Alexander Schmemann, *Great Lent: Journey to Pascha*, rev. ed. (Crestwood, N.Y.: St. Vladimir's Seminary Press, 1974), 12. See also Schmemann, *For the Life of the World: Sacraments and Orthodoxy*, 2nd ed. (Crestwood, N.Y.: St. Vladimir's Seminary Press, 1973), 106: "I know that in Christ this great Passage, the *Pascha* of the world has begun, that the light of the 'world to come' comes to us in the joy and peace of the Holy Spirit." Along these lines, see Georges Florovsky, "Eschatology in the Patristic Age: An Introduction," *Studia Patristica* 2 (1957): 235–40; Jean Daniélou, S.J., *The Lord of History: Reflections on the Inner Meaning of History*, trans. Nigel Abercrombie (London: Longmans, Green, 1958), 214–15; Raniero Cantalamessa, O.F.M. Cap., *Easter: Meditations on the Resurrection*, trans. Demetrio S. Yocum (Collegeville, Minn.: Liturgical Press, 2006), 33. The subtitle of the original Italian edition of Cantalamessa's book is *Un passaggio a cio che non passa*.

9   I should note that although I affirm the bodily assumption of the Virgin Mary into heaven, an account of this mystery of faith is beyond the scope of this book. On

the Virgin Mary's Assumption see esp. Pope John Paul II, *Redemptoris Mater*, with introduction and commentary by Joseph Ratzinger and Hans Urs von Balthasar, published as *Mary: God's Yes to Man* (San Francisco: Ignatius Press, 1988).

10   See my *Sacrifice and Community: Jewish Offering and Christian Eucharist* (Oxford: Blackwell, 2005); Levering, *Christ and the Catholic Priesthood: Ecclesial Hierarchy and the Pattern of the Trinity* (Chicago: Hillenbrand Books, 2010). See also Terence McGuckin, "The Eschatology of the Cross," *New Blackfriars* 75 (1994): 364–77.

11   Regarding those who freely reject Jesus' love, I argue in my *Predestination: Biblical and Theological Paths* (Oxford: Oxford University Press, 2011) that the hell of the damned exists: some angels and humans are everlastingly lost. In this earlier book, I have said what I have to say about the hell of the damned, and so I do not repeat it here. For further discussion of this topic see, e.g., Carlo Leget, *Living with God: Thomas Aquinas on the Relation between Life on Earth and "Life" after Death* (Leuven: Peeters, 1997), 233–44; John Saward, *Sweet and Blessed Country: The Christian Hope for Heaven* (Oxford: Oxford University Press, 2005), 98–108.

12   Christoph Schönborn, O.P., *From Death to Life: The Christian Journey*, trans. Brian McNeil, C.R.V. (San Francisco: Ignatius Press, 1995), 14. Schönborn's book, in its retrieval of the Fathers and its focus on resurrection and eternal life, inspires my own.

13   Thomas Aquinas, *Summa theologiae* III, q. 57, a. 1. Here and throughout this book I use the 1920 translation by the English Dominican Fathers, reprinted as Thomas Aquinas, *Summa Theologica*, 5 vols. (Westminster, Md.: Christian Classics, 1981).

14   See Douglas Farrow, "Eucharist, Eschatology and Ethics," in *The Future as God's Gift: Explorations in Christian Eschatology*, ed. David Fergusson and Marcel Sarot (Edinburgh: T&T Clark, 2000), 200; cf. 213. Farrow warns against "the platonizing tendency" in Christian eschatology (202), by which he means the tendency to move away from the covenantal/priestly particularity of Jesus (and of the Eucharist). See also Oscar Cullman's point that "[i]t is, then, the *present* Lordship of Christ, inaugurated by His resurrection and exaltation to the right hand of God, that is the centre of the faith of primitive Christianity." Cullmann, *The Earliest Christian Confessions*, trans. J. K. S. Reid (London: Lutterworth Press, 1949), 58.

15   Richard Bauckham and Trevor Hart, *Hope against Hope: Christian Eschatology at the Turn of the Millennium* (Grand Rapids: Eerdmans, 1999), 169. Without much comment, Bauckham and Hart accept the view that Platonic philosophy, with its emphasis on the immortal soul and on contemplation of the eternal forms, compromised patristic and medieval eschatology by promoting "a more purely intellectualist and individualist understanding of the vision" as opposed to "a more holistic understanding of human destiny" (170–71; cf. 128–29, 178–79).

16   See Richard B. Hays, *The Conversion of the Imagination: Paul as Interpreter of Israel's Scripture* (Grand Rapids: Eerdmans, 2005), esp. the first essay in this collection, "The Conversion of the Imagination: Scripture and Eschatology in 1 Corinthians," 1–24. Cf. Garrett Green, "Imagining the Future," in Fergusson and Sarot, *The Future as God's Gift*, 73–87.

17   Pope Benedict XVI, "Intervention at the Fourteenth General Congregation of the Synod (14 October 2008)," in *Insegnamenti* IV, 2 (2008): 493–94.

18 Pope Benedict XVI, Post-Synodal Apostolic Exhortation *Verbum Domini* (Vatican City: Libreria Editrice Vaticana, 2010), §47.

19 For the text of the Apostles' Creed, see the *Catechism of the Catholic Church*, 2nd ed. (Vatican City: Libreria Editrice Vaticana, 1997), 49.

20 In strongly affirming that Scripture should be "the soul of theological studies," I am not advocating a "*sola scriptura*" approach to catechesis or to theology. With *Dei Verbum*, I affirm that "Sacred Tradition and sacred Scripture, then, are bound closely together, and communicate one with the other. For both of them, flowing out from the same divine well-spring, come together in some fashion to form one thing, and move towards the same goal. Sacred Scripture is the speech of God as it is put down in writing under the breath of the Holy Spirit. And Tradition transmits in its entirety the Word of God which has been entrusted to the apostles by Christ the Lord and the Holy Spirit. It transmits it to the successors of the apostles so that, enlightened by the Spirit of truth, they may faithfully preserve, expound and spread it abroad by their preaching. Thus it comes about that the Church does not draw her certainty about all revealed truths from the holy Scriptures alone. . . . Sacred Tradition and sacred Scripture make up a single sacred deposit of the Word of God, which is entrusted to the Church. By adhering to it the entire holy people, united to its pastors, remains always faithful to the teaching of the apostles, to the brotherhood, to the breaking of bread and the prayers (cf. Acts 2:42)." See the Dogmatic Constitution on Divine Revelation, *Dei Verbum*, §§9–10, in *Vatican Council II: The Conciliar and Post Conciliar Documents*, vol. 1, new rev. ed., ed. Austin Flannery, O.P. (Northport, N.Y.: Costello, 1998), 755.

21 Plato, *Symposium*, trans. Michael Joyce, in Plato, *The Collected Dialogues*, ed. Edith Hamilton and Huntington Cairns (Princeton: Princeton University Press, 1961), 211e, 563.

22 N. T. Wright, *Surprised by Hope: Rethinking Heaven, the Resurrection, and the Mission of the Church* (New York: HarperCollins, 2008), 153. For similar views, see C. Kavin Rowe, *World Upside Down: Reading Acts in the Graeco-Roman Age* (Oxford: Oxford University Press, 2009), 122–23; Murray J. Harris, "Resurrection and Immortality in the Pauline Corpus," in *Life in the Face of Death: The Resurrection Message of the New Testament*, ed. Richard N. Longenecker (Grand Rapids: Eerdmans, 1998), 147–70, esp. 165–68.

23 N. T. Wright, *The Resurrection of the Son of God* (Minneapolis: Fortress, 2003), 49–50. See also Wright, *The Challenge of Jesus: Rediscovering Who Jesus Was and Is* (Downers Grove, Ill.: InterVarsity, 1999), 123. For ways of conceiving early Christianity's inculturation, see Paul L. Gavrilyuk, "Harnack's Hellenized Christianity or Florovsky's 'Sacred Hellenism': Questioning Two Metanarratives of Early Christian Engagement with Late Antique Culture," *St. Vladimir's Theological Quarterly* 54 (2010): 323–44. See also Wayne Meeks, "Judaism, Hellenism and the Birth of Christianity," in *Paul beyond the Judaism/Hellenism Divide*, ed. Troels Engberg-Pedersen (Louisville, Ky.: Westminster John Knox, 2001), 17–28.

24 See Oscar Cullmann, *Immortality of the Soul or Resurrection of the Dead? The Witness of the New Testament* (New York: Macmillan, 1958), 15–17. Cullmann holds that the soul becomes immortal only through faith in Jesus' resurrection. Influentially, Martin Werner argued that the early Church de-eschatologized and Hellenized

the Gospel: see Werner, *Die Entstehung des christlichen Dogmas* (Bern: P. Haupt, 1941). See also Karl Barth, *The Resurrection of the Dead*, trans. H. J. Stenning (Eugene, Ore.: Wipf & Stock, 2003), 207. For resurrection and immortality as found in late Second-Temple Jewish literature, suggesting that any simple contrast between Hebrew and Greek perspectives is a false one, see Maurice Gilbert, "Immortalité? Résurrection? Faut-il choisir? Témoignage du judaïsme ancient," in *Le judaïsme à l'aube de l'ère chrétienne*, ed. Philippe Abadie and Jean-Pierre Lemonon (Paris: Cerf, 2001), 271–97; James Barr, *The Garden of Eden and the Hope of Immortality* (London: SCM Press, 1992), chap. 5.

25 Martin Heidegger, "Einleitung in die Phaenomenologie der Religion," in Heidegger, *Phänomenologie des religiösen Lebens* (Frankfurt: Klostermann, 1995), 104.

26 Tertullian, "The Prescription against Heretics," trans. Peter Holmes, in *Latin Christianity: Its Founder, Tertullian*, ed. A. Cleveland Coxe, Ante-Nicene Fathers, vol. 3 (Peabody, Mass.: Hendrickson, 1994), 7.10, 246. For Tertullian's use of philosophy in his theology of resurrection, see Claudia Setzer, *Resurrection of the Body in Early Judaism and Early Christianity: Doctrine, Community, and Self-Definition* (Leiden: Brill, 2004), 136–37.

27 Jürgen Moltmann, *History and the Triune God: Contributions to Trinitarian Theology*, trans. John Bowden (New York: Crossroad, 1991), 95. For a helpful response to what he calls the "Theory of Theology's Fall into Hellenistic Philosophy" in light of the numerous proponents of this theory (including Moltmann), see Paul L. Gavrilyuk, *The Suffering of the Impassible God: The Dialectics of Patristic Thought* (Oxford: Oxford University Press, 2004), esp. 1–46 and 176–79. According to Moltmann, "Thomas replaces the biblical history of promise with a finalistic [teleological] metaphysics. He replaces the hope which seeks the fulfilment of the promise with the natural striving for happiness which according to Augustine can come to fulfilment only in God himself. The 'coming God,' *ho erchomenos, deus adventurus*, is replaced by the 'unmoved Mover' who draws all creatures to him by virtue of *eros*. The eschatological promise of the 'new heaven and new earth'— 'Behold, I make all things new' (Rev. 21.5)—is replaced by the *visio Dei beatifica in patria*, i.e. heaven, the bliss of the pure spirits in the world beyond" (Moltmann, *History and the Triune God*, 95).

28 Hans Urs von Balthasar, "Some Points of Eschatology," in Balthasar, *The Word Made Flesh*, trans. A. V. Littledale with Alexander Dru, vol. 1 of *Explorations in Theology* (San Francisco: Ignatius Press, 1989), 261n9. See also, along similar lines (and with important nuances), Balthasar, "The Fathers, the Scholastics, and Ourselves," trans. Edward T. Oakes, S.J., *Communio* 24 (1997): 72–80, 394–96. At the same time, Balthasar was deeply indebted to the Fathers and praised Gregory of Nyssa, among the most Platonic Fathers, for knowing "better than anyone how to transpose ideas inwardly from the spiritual heritage of ancient Greece into a Christian mode." See Hans Urs von Balthasar, *Presence and Thought: An Essay on the Religious Philosophy of Gregory of Nyssa*, trans. Mark Sebanc (San Francisco: Ignatius Press, 1995), 15. David Bentley Hart similarly gives pride of place to Gregory of Nyssa, even while admitting that Gregory's eschatology can (mistakenly) seem to be "a barely regenerate Platonism." Hart, *The Beauty of the Infinite: The Aesthetics of Christian Truth* (Grand Rapids: Eerdmans, 2003), 402.

29 For surveys of recent eschatology, with particular attention to Wolfhart Pannenberg and Jürgen Moltmann, see Hans Schwarz, *Eschatology* (Grand Rapids: Eerdmans, 2000), 107–72, 341–46; Christoph Schwöbel, "Last Things First? The Century of Eschatology in Retrospect," in Fergusson and Sarot, *The Future as God's Gift*, 217–41; Stephen Williams, "Thirty Years of Hope: A Generation of Writing on Eschatology," in *Eschatology in Bible and Theology: Evangelical Essays at the Dawn of a New Millennium*, ed. Kent E. Brower and Mark W. Elliott (Downers Grove, Ill.: InterVarsity, 1997), 243–62. I discuss the eschatologies of Bulgakov, Barth, and Balthasar in my *Predestination*, chap. 5; more controversially, on the relationship of Barth to Hegel, see Adam Eitel, "The Resurrection of Jesus Christ: Karl Barth and the Historicization of God's Being," *International Journal of Systematic Theology* 10 (2008): 36–53. For Karl Rahner's views see Peter C. Phan, "Eschatology," in *The Cambridge Companion to Karl Rahner*, ed. Declan Marmion and Mary E. Hines (Cambridge: Cambridge University Press, 2005), 174–92; Phan, *Eternity in Time: A Study of Karl Rahner's Eschatology* (London: Associated University Presses, 1988).

30 R. R. Reno, *Genesis* (Grand Rapids: Brazos Press, 2010), 27. For Reno, Christian Platonism is acceptable except for when it encourages the dichotomy of "perfect, eternal, unchanging, spiritual versus imperfect, temporal, changeable, and bodily" (64).

31 Ratzinger, *Eschatology*, xxv.

32 Ratzinger, *Eschatology*, xxv.

33 Ratzinger, *Eschatology*, 78; cf. 140–59 on the soul. Along the same lines see Stephen Finlan, "Second Peter's Notion of Divine Participation," in *Theōsis: Deification in Christian Theology*, ed. Stephen Finlan and Vladimir Kharlamov (Eugene, Ore.: Pickwick, 2006), 33; Josef Pieper, *Death and Immortality*, trans. Richard and Clara Winston (South Bend, Ind.: St. Augustine's Press, 1999), 95–105. See also Romano Guardini, *The Death of Socrates: An Interpretation of the Platonic Dialogues: Euthyphro, Apology, Crito and Phaedo*, trans. Basil Wrighton (New York: Meridian Books, 1962), 102, 106–7.

34 Joseph Ratzinger, "Faith, Reason and the University: Memories and Reflections (The Regensburg Lecture)," §22, app. 1 in James V. Schall, S.J., *The Regensburg Lecture* (South Bend, Ind.: St. Augustine's Press, 2007), §22, 136; cf. §29, 138.

35 This paragraph comes in part from my "God and Greek Philosophy in Contemporary Biblical Scholarship," *Journal of Theological Interpretation* 4 (2010): 169–85.

36 Jaroslav Pelikan, *Christianity and Classical Culture: The Metamorphosis of Natural Theology in the Christian Encounter with Hellenism* (New Haven: Yale University Press, 1993), ix, 3.

37 Martin Hengel, *Judaism and Hellenism: Studies in Their Encounter in Palestine during the Early Hellenistic Period* (Eugene, Ore.: Wipf & Stock, 2003), 149. For a survey of the pioneering work in this field, largely done by Jewish scholars, see Yaacov Shavit, *Athens in Jerusalem: Classical Antiquity and Hellenism in the Making of the Modern Secular Jew*, trans. Chaya Naor and Niki Werner (London: Littman Library of Jewish Civilization, 1997), 281–336. Shavit is interested in "the structural similarity between the complex intercultural relations that existed between Judaism and the Hellenistic civilization in the ancient world and those that exist

between Jews and Western culture in the modern age," granted that "the character of European culture is not identical with that of Hellenistic culture" (299–300). See also Shaye J. D. Cohen's "Hellenism in Unexpected Places," in *Hellenism in the Land of Israel*, ed. John J. Collins and Gregory E. Sterling (Notre Dame: University of Notre Dame Press, 2001), 216–43.

38 See Richard J. Bauckham, *Jude, 2 Peter* (Nashville: Thomas Nelson, 1996), 180–82.

39 See Richard J. Bauckham, *Jesus and the God of Israel: God Crucified and Other Studies on the New Testament's Christology of Divine Identity* (Grand Rapids: Eerdmans, 2009), 246, 249.

40 See Ben Witherington III, *Jesus the Sage: The Pilgrimage of Wisdom* (Minneapolis: Fortress, 2000). See also James Barr, *Biblical Faith and Natural Theology* (Oxford: Oxford University Press, 1993), 58–80; as well as the word study by Ralph Marcus, "Divine Names and Attributes in Hellenistic Jewish Literature," *Proceedings of the American Academy for Jewish Research* 3 (1931–32): 43–120.

41 N. T. Wright, "Reflected Glory: 2 Corinthians 3.18," in Wright, *The Climax of the Covenant: Christ and the Law in Pauline Theology* (Minneapolis: Fortress, 1992), 190; for a similar account see M. David Litwa, "2 Corinthians 3:18 and Its Implications for *Theosis*," *Journal of Theological Interpretation* 2 (2008): 117–33, esp. 128–32. For a quite different perspective on glory, see Carey C. Newman, "Resurrection as Glory: Divine Presence and Christian Origins," in *The Resurrection: An Interdisciplinary Symposium on the Resurrection of Jesus*, ed. Stephen T. Davis, Daniel Kendall, S.J., and Gerald O'Collins, S.J. (Oxford: Oxford University Press, 1997), 59–89; cf. Newman, *Paul's Glory-Christology: Tradition and Rhetoric* (Leiden: Brill, 1991). See also Ben C. Blackwell, "Immortal Glory and the Problem of Death in Romans 3.23," *Journal for the Study of the New Testament* 32 (2010): 285–308.

42 Wright, *Surprised by Hope*, 161. Wright's teacher, G. B. Caird, makes a similar point: "Too often evangelical Christianity has treated the souls of men as brands plucked from the burning and the world in general as a grim vale of soul-making. It has been content to see the splendour of the created universe, together with all the brilliant achievements of human labour, skill, and thought, as nothing more than the expendable backdrop for the drama of redemption. One of the reasons why men of our generation have turned against conventional Christianity is that they think it involves writing off the solid joys of this present life for the doubtful acquisition of some less substantial treasure. . . . The whole point of the resurrection of the body is that the life of the world to come is to be lived on a renewed earth. . . . Everything of real worth in the old heaven and earth, including the achievements of man's inventive, artistic, and intellectual prowess, will find a place in the eternal order." Caird, "The Christological Basis of Christian Hope," in Caird et al., *The Christian Hope* (London: SPCK, 1970), 22–24. Cf. Jacob Neusner's point that for rabbinic Judaism, the redeemed people of God "lives in the material world of marketplace and farm, and engages in the material and physical transactions of farming and love." Neusner, *Rabbinic Judaism: The Theological System* (Boston: Brill Academic, 2002), 256. See also Jane Idleman Smith and Yvonne Yazbeck Haddad, *The Islamic Understanding of Death and Resurrection* (Oxford: Oxford University Press, 2002), esp. 89.

43   Cf. Grace M. Jantzen, "Do We Need Immortality?," *Modern Theology* 1 (1984): 25–44, and the response by Charles Taliaferro, "Why We Need Immortality," *Modern Theology* 6 (1990): 367–77.

CHAPTER I

1   For a rich theology of death, see Adrienne von Speyr's short book *The Mystery of Death*, trans. Graham Harrison (San Francisco: Ignatius Press, 1988). See also Richard Schenk, O.P., *"And Jesus Wept*: Notes towards a Theology of Mourning," in *Reading John with St. Thomas Aquinas: Theological Exegesis and Speculative Theology*, ed. Michael Dauphinais and Matthew Levering (Washington, D.C.: Catholic University of America Press, 2005), 212–37.

2   See, e.g., Kevin J. Madigan and Jon D. Levenson, *Resurrection: The Power of God for Christians and Jews* (New Haven: Yale University Press, 2008), 106; cf. 7, 59, 65. On this point see also Ratzinger, *Eschatology*, 120–23; Pope Benedict XVI, *Spe Salvi* (Vatican City: Libreria Editrice Vaticana, 2007), §45.

3   Wright, *Surprised by Hope*, 5. See also the *Catechism of the Catholic Church*, §632. The Catechism clarifies that "Jesus did not descend into hell to deliver the damned, nor to destroy the hell of damnation, but to free the just who had gone before him" (§633). For discussion of contemporary Catholic theology with regard to the intermediate state, see Angelo Scola, "Jesus Christ, Our Resurrection and Life: On the Question of Eschatology," trans. Margaret Harper McCarthy, *Communio* 24 (1997): 311–25; Martin F. Connell, *"Descensus Christi ad Inferos:* Christ's Descent to the Dead," *Theological Studies* 62 (2001): 262–82.

4   Schmemann, *For the Life of the World*, 106.

5   Wright, *The Resurrection of the Son of God*; see also Wright, *The New Testament and the People of God* (Minneapolis: Fortress, 1992), 286, 321, 324. On the question of whether this view of the intermediate state is strengthened by accounts of near-death experiences, see the tentatively positive appraisals of Jerry L. Walls, *Heaven: The Logic of Eternal Joy* (Oxford: Oxford University Press, 2002), 133–60; Terence Nichols, *Death and Afterlife: A Theological Introduction* (Grand Rapids: Brazos Press, 2010), 91–112. On near-death experiences, angels and demons, and heaven and hell, citing numerous Fathers of the Church, see also Seraphim Rose, *The Soul after Death: Contemporary "After-Death" Experiences in Light of the Orthodox Teaching on the Afterlife* (Platina, Calif.: St. Herman of Alaska Brotherhood, 2009), although he is too quick to blame Catholic and Protestant rationalism (e.g., in his insistence that heaven is truly, rather than metaphorically, "up" and hell "down"). For St. Symeon the Younger, the Stylite, to whom Rose is much indebted, see David Hester, "The Eschatology of the Sermons of Symeon the Younger the Stylite," *St. Vladimir's Theological Quarterly* 34 (1990): 329–42.

6   Wright, *The Resurrection of the Son of God*, 41; cf. 151. For an argument that Mark 12:24-27 requires the intermediate state, see Bradley R. Trick, "Death, Covenants, and the Proof of Resurrection in Mark 12:18-27," *Novum Testamentum* 49 (2007): 232–56.

7   Wright, *Surprised by Hope*, 162. Wright is aware of the view that after death we no longer experience temporal progression but instead immediately experience resurrection. This view, he thinks, is contradicted by biblical revelation. See also the

discussion of Wright's views in Markus Bockmuehl, "Did St. Paul Go to Heaven When He Died?," in *Jesus, Paul and the People of God: A Theological Dialogue with N. T. Wright*, ed. Nicholas Perrin and Richard B. Hays (Downers Grove, Ill.: InterVarsity, 2011), 211–31 and Wright's clarification in his "Response to Markus Bockmuehl," 231–34.

8   Wright, *Surprised by Hope*, 171; cf. 177–83 on humans who "after death . . . become at last, by their own effective choice, *beings that once were human but now are not*, creatures that have ceased to bear the divine image at all" (182). Cf. Plato, *Timaeus* 91d–92b, trans. Benjamin Jowett, in Plato, *The Collected Dialogues*, 1210–11: "The race of birds was created out of innocent light-minded men who, although their minds were directed toward heaven, imagined, in their simplicity, that the clearest demonstration of the things above was to be obtained by sight; these were remodeled and transformed into birds, and they grew feathers instead of hair. The race of wild pedestrian animals, again, came from those who had no philosophy in any of their thoughts, and never considered at all about the nature of the heavens, because they had ceased to use the courses of the head, but followed the guidance of those parts of the soul which are in the breast. In consequence of these habits of theirs they had their front legs and their heads resting upon the earth to which they were drawn by natural affinity, and the crowns of their heads were elongated and of all sorts of shapes, into which the courses of the soul were crushed by reason of disuse. And this was the reason why they were created quadrupeds and polypods. God gave the more senseless of them the more support that they might be more attracted to the earth. And the most foolish of them, who trail their bodies entirely upon the ground and have no longer any need of feet, he made without feet to crawl upon the earth. The fourth class were the inhabitants of the water; these were made out of the most entirely senseless and ignorant of all, whom the transformers did not think any longer worthy of pure respiration, because they possessed a soul which was made impure by all sorts of transgression, and instead of the subtle and pure medium of air, they gave them the deep and muddy sea to be their element of respiration. And hence arose the race of fishes and oysters, and other aquatic animals, which have received the most remote habitations as a punishment of their outlandish ignorance."

9   Wright, *Surprised by Hope*, 171.

10 Wright, *Surprised by Hope*, 172.

11 Wright, *Surprised by Hope*, 172.

12 John Calvin, *Institutes of the Christian Religion*, trans. Henry Beveridge (Grand Rapids: Eerdmans, 1989), III.xxv.6, 267. Calvin warns against trying to discover "whether or not they already enjoy celestial glory" (III.xxv.6, 267).

13 Wright, *Surprised by Hope*, 28; see Wright, *The Resurrection of the Son of God*, 174–75 and elsewhere. Cf. Jürgen Moltmann, "Is There Life after Death?," in *The End of the World and the Ends of God: Science and Theology on Eschatology*, ed. John Polkinghorne and Michael Welker (Harrisburg, Pa.: Trinity Press International, 2000), 244, 252–53. Similarly rejecting the spiritual soul, Wolfhart Pannenberg holds that what remains after death is "the communion with Christ and with the eternal God, who continues to affirm his communion with us. Since the dead are not lost from the presence of God, however, it is conceivable that their life—as it stands

as a whole in the presence of God's eternity—may become present once more to themselves, if God so decides. What happens in the moment of death, then, is that we are no longer present to ourselves, nor to other creatures, although we remain present to God. It is this inextinguishable presence to God's eternity that provides the condition of the possibility that the same life of ours can come alive again, if God so wills and at the time of his discretion. It will not be another life, but the same life; not in the sequence of separate instants of time, but our life as a whole, as it stands in the presence of God's eternity." Pannenberg, "Constructive and Critical Functions of Christian Eschatology," *Harvard Theological Review* 77 (1984): 131. But if death obliterates us as we are in ourselves, it is difficult to see how "we remain present to God," since the "we" in question—the ones who are supposedly "present"—are not simply God's eternal idea of us.

14 Wright, *Surprised by Hope*, 28.

15 Wright, *Surprised by Hope*, 160, 161; cf. 152, 155.

16 Wright, *The Resurrection of the Son of God*, 203. Wright is here summarizing the position held by late Second-Temple Jews regarding the dead in the intermediate state. In *Surprised by Hope* he avoids giving an ontological account of how the dead in the intermediate state can be conscious. See also Cullmann, *Immortality of the Soul or Resurrection of the Dead?*, 17. For further examples, see John W. Cooper, *Body, Soul, and Life Everlasting: Biblical Anthropology and the Monism-Dualism Debate*, 2nd ed. (Grand Rapids: Eerdmans, 2000), 159–64.

17 Wright, *Surprised by Hope*, 169.

18 Wright, *Surprised by Hope*, 169.

19 Wright, *Surprised by Hope*, 169.

20 For the quite different view of John Wesley, see Edgardo A. Colón-Emeric, *Wesley, Aquinas, and Christian Perfection: An Ecumenical Dialogue* (Waco, Tex.: Baylor University Press, 2009), 53–55, 156–57. See also Brett Salkeld's succinct account of Augustine's view in his *Can Catholics and Evangelicals Agree about Purgatory and the Last Judgment?* (Mahwah, N.J.: Paulist Press, 2011), 41–42; cf. Konde Ntedika, *L'évolution de la doctrine du purgatoire chez Saint Augustin* (Paris: Études Augustiniennes, 1966).

21 Cf. Saward, *Sweet and Blessed Country*, 49–51.

22 Wright, *Surprised by Hope*, 173. Wright insists that the doctrine of purgatory is a "mythology" that should be "abhorrent to anyone with even a faint understanding of Paul" (170–71). For problems elided by Wright's position, see esp. Walls, *Heaven*, 51–62.

23 Wright, *Surprised by Hope*, 173.

24 See Wright, *The Resurrection of the Son of God*, 87–90; cf. Johannes Pedersen, *Israel: Its Life and Culture* (Atlanta: Scholars Press, 1991), 460–70. Karl Rahner holds that for the dead "everything is, as it were, encompassed by an infinite remoteness. . . . One is, as it were, engulfed in an infinite loneliness, left utterly to one's self, and at the same time alien to one's self." Rahner, "Hidden Victory," in *Theological Investigations*, vol. 7, trans. David Bourke (New York: Herder, 1971), 153. For similar views of the realm of death (specifically with regard to Jesus' entrance into it), see the German Catholic Bishops' Conference, *The Church's Confession of Faith: A Catholic Catechism for Adults* (San Francisco: Ignatius Press, 1987), 162–63. See

also Ratzinger, *Eschatology*, 93; Ratzinger, *Introduction to Christianity*, trans. J. R. Foster (San Francisco: Ignatius Press, 2004), 293–301.

25 Wright, *Surprised by Hope*, 240.

26 See Hans Urs von Balthasar, *Mysterium Paschale: The Mystery of Easter*, trans. Aidan Nichols, O.P. (Grand Rapids: Eerdmans, 1993), 165–67; Balthasar, "The Descent into Hell," in Balthasar,, *Spirit and Institution*, trans. Edward T. Oakes, S.J., vol. 4 of *Explorations in Theology* (San Francisco: Ignatius Press, 1995), 401–14; Balthasar, *The Action*, trans. Graham Harrison, vol. 4 of *Theo-Drama: Theological Dramatic Theory* (San Francisco: Ignatius Press, 1994), 325–61. Geoffrey Wainwright notes that in Balthasar's thought *Mysterium Paschale* offers, "as we now know in retrospect, a compromise that would eventually give way to the even more radical idea that in his descent into hell Jesus underwent—vicariously of course—*the full fate of the damned*." Wainwright, "Eschatology," in *The Cambridge Companion to Hans Urs von Balthasar*, ed. Edward T. Oakes, S.J., and David Moss (Cambridge: Cambridge University Press, 2004), 117. Drawing heavily on Balthasar but holding that Christ does not experience damnation, Regis Martin likewise argues that the bitterest alienation in hell (Sheol) is necessary to complete the kenosis of the cross. See Regis Martin, *The Suffering of Love: Christ's Descent into the Hell of Human Hopelessness* (Petersham, Mass.: St. Bede's, 1995), 112–13 and elsewhere. See also the appreciative summaries of Balthasar's view in Edward T. Oakes, S.J., *Pattern of Redemption: The Theology of Hans Urs von Balthasar* (New York: Continuum, 1994), 237–46; Aidan Nichols, O.P., *No Bloodless Myth: A Guide through Balthasar's Dramatics* (Washington, D.C.: Catholic University of America Press, 2000), 159–71, 207–24. For critical reflection on Balthasar's position, see, e.g., René Lafontaine, "'Arrivés a Jésus, ils le trouvèrent mort' (Jo. xix, 39): Hans Urs von Balthasar, théologien du samedi saint," *Revue Thomiste* 86 (1986): 635–43; Raymond E. Brown, S.S., *The Death of the Messiah*, vol. 2 (New York: Doubleday, 1994), 1286–87. The fullest study is Alyssa Lyra Pitstick, *Light in Darkness: Hans Urs von Balthasar and the Catholic Doctrine of Christ's Descent into Hell* (Grand Rapids: Eerdmans, 2007), although Pitstick unfortunately suggests that Balthasar deliberately entered into heresy on this point.

27 Hans Urs von Balthasar, *The Last Act*, trans. Graham Harrison, vol. 5 of *Theo-Drama: Theological Dramatic Theory* (San Francisco: Ignatius Press, 1998), 256.

28 Balthasar, *The Last Act*, 267. The internal quotations are from Adrienne von Speyr, *The Birth of the Church*, vol. 4 of *Johannes* (San Francisco: Ignatius Press, 1994), 211–12.

29 Balthasar, *The Last Act*, 268.

30 Balthasar, *Mysterium Paschale*, 180–81. By contrast, Karl Barth does not view Christ's "descent into hell" as describing his experience of Holy Saturday. For discussion see David Edward Lauber, "Towards a Theology of Holy Saturday: Karl Barth and Hans Urs von Balthasar on the descensus ad inferna" (Ph.D. diss., Princeton Theological Seminary, 1999), 128.

31 See esp. the careful analysis by Andrew Hofer, O.P., "Balthasar's Eschatology on the Intermediate State: The Question of Knowability," *Logos* 12 (2009): 148–72.

32 Ben Witherington III, *A Socio-Rhetorical Commentary on 1-2 Peter*, vol. 2 of *Letters and Homilies for Hellenized Christians* (Downers Grove, Ill.: IVP Academic, 2007),

188. Cf. George W. E. Nickelsburg, *1 Enoch: A Commentary on the Book of 1 Enoch* (Minneapolis: Fortress, 2001).

33 Joel B. Green, *1 Peter* (Grand Rapids: Eerdmans, 2007), 128.

34 Clement of Alexandria, *The Stromata, or Miscellanies*, in *Fathers of the Second Century*, ed. A. Cleveland Coxe, *Ante-Nicene Fathers*, vol. 2 (Peabody, Mass.: Hendrickson, 1994), VI.6, 490–91. For discussion see Larry W. Hurtado, *Lord Jesus Christ: Devotion to Jesus in Earliest Christianity* (Grand Rapids: Eerdmans, 2003), 633–35; Jean Daniélou, S.J., *The Theology of Jewish Christianity*, trans. and ed. J. A. Baker (London: Darton, Longman, & Todd, 1964), 233–48.

35 Athanasius, Letter LIX, *To Epictetus*, in *Athanasius: Select Works and Letters*, ed. Archibald Robinson, trans. John Henry Newman, *Nicene and Post-Nicene Fathers*, vol. 4 (Peabody, Mass.: Hendrickson, 1994), 572.

36 John of Damascus, *The Orthodox Faith* III.29, in John of Damascus, *Writings*, trans. Frederic H. Chase Jr. (Washington, D.C.: Catholic University of America Press, 1958), 334.

37 Hilarion Alfeyev, *Christ the Conqueror of Hell: The Descent into Hades from an Orthodox Perspective* (Crestwood, N.Y.: St. Vladimir's Seminary Press, 2009).

38 Alfeyev, *Christ the Conqueror of Hell*, 203. The same conclusion regarding the doctrine of the descent into hell in the patristic period is reached by Rémi Gounelle, *La descente du Christ aux Enfers: Institutionnalisation d'une croyance* (Paris: Institut d'Études augustiniennes, 2000); see also Ralph V. Turner, "*Descendit ad inferos*: Medieval Views on Christ's Descent into Hell and the Salvation of the Ancient Just," *Journal of the History of Ideas* 27 (1966): 173–94. By contrast, Wayne Grudem argues that Christ's "descent into hell" is "a late intruder into the Apostles' Creed that never really belonged there in the first place and that, on historical and Scriptural grounds, deserves to be removed." Grudem, "He Did Not Descend into Hell: A Plea for Following Scripture Instead of the Apostles' Creed," *Journal of the Evangelical Theological Society* 34 (1991): 103.

39 Alfeyev, *Christ the Conqueror of Hell*, 208.

40 Alfeyev, *Christ the Conqueror of Hell*, 211.

41 Here Metropolitan Hilarion cites with approbation Sergius Bulgakov's *The Lamb of God*, trans. Boris Jakim (Grand Rapids: Eerdmans, 2008).

42 Alfeyev, *Christ the Conqueror of Hell*, 217. He cites in this regard Daniélou's *The Theology of Jewish Christianity*.

43 See Thomas Aquinas, *Summa theologiae* II–II, q. 2, a. 7, ad 3 (drawing upon Hebrews 11:6). Aquinas follows Augustine in arguing that the missions of the Word and Holy Spirit produced faith and charity in persons who lived prior to Christ. See Augustine, Letter 164, in *The Confessions and Letters of Augustine*, ed. Philip Schaff, trans. J. G. Cunningham, *Nicene and Post-Nicene Fathers*, vol. 1 (Peabody, Mass.: Hendrickson, 1994), 515–21.

44 Aquinas recognizes that the Nicene Creed does not include Christ's descent into hell, but he does not know the history of the Apostles' Creed, which he attributes to the apostles. See II–II, q. 1, a. 9, obj. 4 and ad 4.

45 Augustine, Letter 164, 515.

46 When Jesus' body and soul were rent asunder in the terrible crucible of death, Jesus was a dead man but not, strictly speaking, a "man," since to be a human means to

be a body-soul unity: see III, q. 50, a. 4. It is important to note that the Word of God remained united to both Jesus' soul or body: see III, q. 50, aa. 2–3.

47 Aquinas cites Hebrews 11:33 in III, q. 49, a. 5, ad 1. With medieval theology of the communion of saints in view, Joseph Ratzinger states, "The Christian lives in the presence of the saints as his own proper ambience, and so lives 'eschatologically'" (*Eschatology*, 9). For further reflection on the medieval ambience of the communion of saints, in light of the Reformation critique, see Carlos Eire, *A Very Brief History of Eternity* (Princeton: Princeton University Press, 2010), chaps. 3 and 4. For an effort to find a middle ground, see Michael Perham, *The Communion of Saints: An Examination of the Place of the Christian Dead in the Belief, Worship, and Calendars of the Church* (London: SPCK, 1980).

48 III, q. 49, a. 5, ad 1.

49 III, q. 52, a. 5, ad 2.

50 III, q. 52, a. 2. As Aquinas says elsewhere (indebted to Augustine), "Directly Christ died his soul went down into hell, and bestowed the fruits of his Passion on the saints detained there; although they did not go out as long as Christ remained in hell, because his presence was part of the fulness of their glory" (III, q. 52, a. 5, ad 3).

51 III, q. 52, a. 1. For historical-critical discussion see Alan Cooper, "Ps 24:7-10: Mythology and Exegesis," *Journal of Biblical Literature* 102 (1983): 37–60. Cooper argues that Psalm 24:7-10 "is a fragment or remnant of a descent myth—a myth in which a high god, forsaking his ordinary domain, descends to the netherworld, where he must confront the demonic forces of the infernal realm" (43). In an appendix to his article, Cooper reviews the function of Psalm 24:7-10 in early Christian writings, with a focus on Christ's descent into hell according to the *Gospel of Nicodemus*. Translated by E. Hennecke in *New Testament Apocrypha*, ed. W. Schneemelcher, vol. 1 (Philadelphia: Westminster, 1963), 444–49, 470–81.

52 III, q. 52, a. 1. Cf. Marianne Meye Thompson, *Colossians and Philemon* (Grand Rapids: Eerdmans, 2005), 58–60. Thompson observes, "Just as the principalities and powers proved to have no final authority over the one who is their head, so those who share in his death also share in his life and hence also in his victory. They find themselves in the kingdom of God's beloved Son, subject to his rule and supremacy, not to the rule and supremacy of darkness" (60).

53 Hurtado, *Lord Jesus Christ*, 632–33.

54 III, q. 52, a. 5, ad 1.

55 III, q. 52, a. 5, ad 1.

56 III, q. 52, a. 5, ad 1.

57 III, q. 52, a. 4, ad 3. See Joseph A. Fitzmyer, S.J., *The Gospel According to Luke (X–XXIV)* (Garden City, N.Y.: Doubleday, 1985), 1510–11: "Greek *paradeisos* is used in the LXX to translate *gan*, 'garden' (Gen 2:8, 'a garden in Eden'; Gen 13:10, 'the garden of God'). Cf. Philo, *De opif. mund.* 153-155, etc.; Josephus, *Ant.* 1.1,3 §37, etc. From the Genesis use it developed in time an eschatological nuance, a place of expected bliss (e.g. Ezek 31:8), and even more specifically as the mythical place or abode of the righteous after death (*T. Levi* 18:10-11; *Ps. Sol.* 14:3; *1 Enoch* 17–19; 60:8; 61:12). This last sense could be what is intended in the Lucan passage." Fitzmyer goes on, however, to dissociate Luke 23:43 from any relation

to the "credal 'descent into hell'" (1511) on the grounds that Luke did not envision this. Since I agree with Wright that the New Testament affirms a conscious intermediate state, Aquinas' connection of Luke 23:43 with Christ's entrance into the intermediate state seems quite plausible.

58 III, q. 52, a. 2.
59 III, q. 52, a. 8.
60 III, q. 52, a. 8. For discussion of purgatory, see Pope Benedict XVI, *Spe Salvi* (Vatican City: Libreria Editrice Vaticana, 2007), §§46–48. See also Ratzinger, *Eschatology*, 218–33; Benedict Ashley, O.P., *Theologies of the Body: Humanist and Christian* (Braintree, Mass.: Pope John Center, 1985), 608–9; Nichols, *Death and Afterlife*, 171–76. For further historical context, emphasizing the influence of the Venerable Bede's appropriation of patristic views but lacking a theological understanding of purification, see Isabel Moreira, *Heaven's Purge: Purgatory in Late Antiquity* (Oxford: Oxford University Press, 2010). See also Claude Carozzi, *Le voyage de l'âme dans l'au-delà d'après le littérature latine (Ve–XIIIe siècle)* (Palais Farnèse: École Français de Rome, 1994). For the Orthodox understanding of purification (but not purgatory) after death, see Rose, *The Soul after Death*, 175–93, 196–213.
61 III, q. 52, a. 2.
62 III, q. 52, a. 4, ad 1.
63 Kallistos Ware, *The Orthodox Way*, rev. ed. (Crestwood, N.Y.: St. Vladimir's Seminary Press, 2002), 136.
64 Cited in III, q. 54, a. 2, *sed contra*.
65 See III, q. 46, a. 6; III, q. 50, esp. aa. 1 and 6.
66 See Calvin, *Institutes* II.xvi.8–11, 441–44. For discussion see Lauber, *Towards a Theology of Holy Saturday*, 53–54; Grudem, "He Did Not Descend into Hell," 106.

CHAPTER 2

1 See Christopher R. Seitz, "'In Accordance with the Scriptures': Creed, Scripture, and 'Historical Jesus,'" in Seitz, *Word without End: The Old Testament as Abiding Theological Witness* (Grand Rapids: Eerdmans, 1998), 57. Seitz concludes, "To say that Jesus died and rose again in accordance with the scriptures reminds the church of its status as adopted into the promises of God begun with Israel" (60).
2 See Jon D. Levenson, *Resurrection and the Restoration of Israel: The Ultimate Victory of the God of Life* (New Haven: Yale University Press, 2006), 30, 35–81; Philip S. Johnston, *Shades of Sheol: Death and Afterlife in the Old Testament* (Downers Grove, Ill.: InterVarsity, 2002), 69–97. Late Second-Temple literature at times envisions Sheol as containing separate abodes for those enjoying reward and those undergoing punishment: see Richard Bauckham, *The Fate of the Dead: Studies on the Jewish and Christian Apocalypses* (Leiden: Brill, 1998), 86–90.
3 Levenson, *Resurrection and the Restoration of Israel*, 92. See also Levenson, *Sinai and Zion: An Entry into the Jewish Bible* (San Francisco: Harper & Row, 1985).
4 Levenson, *Resurrection and the Restoration of Israel*, 95. Cf. Levenson, *Sinai and Zion*, 137–42; Madigan and Levenson, *Resurrection*, 81–106.
5 Levenson, *Resurrection and the Restoration of Israel*, 140. On Israel as God's firstborn son, see also Levenson, *The Death and Resurrection of the Beloved Son: The*

Transformation of Child Sacrifice in Judaism and Christianity (New Haven: Yale University Press, 1993), 37–42.

6   See Levenson, *Resurrection and the Restoration of Israel*, 143.

7   See Levenson, *Resurrection and the Restoration of Israel*, 161.

8   Levenson, *Resurrection and the Restoration of Israel*, 180; cf. Madigan and Levenson, *Resurrection*, 146–65. For similar emphases regarding the development of the Old Testament doctrine of resurrection, see James L. Crenshaw, "Love Is Stronger Than Death: Intimations of Life beyond the Grave," in *Resurrection: The Origin and Future of a Biblical Doctrine*, ed. James H. Charlesworth et al. (New York: T&T Clark, 2006), 53–78; Ratzinger, *Eschatology*, 80–90.

9   Levenson, *Resurrection and the Restoration of Israel*, 189.

10 Levenson, *Resurrection and the Restoration of Israel*, 189, citing *b. Ber.* 17a. For different reasons, David Novak likewise holds that the world to come will be radically different from the present time: see Novak, "Law and Eschatology: A Jewish-Christian Intersection," in *The Last Things: Biblical and Theological Perspectives on Eschatology*, ed. Carl E. Braaten and Robert W. Jenson (Grand Rapids: Eerdmans, 2002), 112. By contrast, in his summary of Rabbinic Jewish doctrine, Jacob Neusner takes a more this-worldly view: when the Messiah gathers all Israelites into the Holy Land, Israel will forever study Torah, "eat and drink, sing and dance, and enjoy God, who will be lord of the dance" (*Rabbinic Judaism*, 260).

11 See Levenson, *Resurrection and the Restoration of Israel*, 191; Madigan and Levenson, *Resurrection*, 171–200.

12 Levenson, *Resurrection and the Restoration of Israel*, 196. Among scholars who contend that the experience of martyrdom under Antiochus IV produced Jewish resurrection belief, Levenson names George W. E. Nickelsburg, John Day, and Alan F. Segal: see Nickelsburg, *Resurrection, Immortality, and Eternal Life in Intertestamental Judaism* (Cambridge, Mass.: Harvard University Press, 1972), 19; Day, "The Development of Belief in Life after Death in Ancient Israel," in *After the Exile: Essays in Honour of Rex Mason*, ed. John Barton and David J. Reimer (Macon, Ga.: Mercer University Press, 1996), 231–57; and Segal, *Life after Death: A History of Afterlife in the Religions of the West* (New York: Doubleday, 2004), 265–72. Levenson argues against this position in *Resurrection and the Restoration of Israel*, 191–200. Regarding Zoroastrianism, he grants that there was a Persian influence upon Second-Temple Judaism but concludes that "at most the force of Zoroastrian eschatology nudged Judaism along in its movement toward a belief in the future resurrection of the dead. If Jewish apocalyptic is the mother of the expectation of a general resurrection, then Zoroastrian theology (which probably influenced the development of apocalyptic in Jewish circles) is at best the grandmother" (*Resurrection and the Restoration of Israel*, 215–16).

13 For a similar argument, see Richard Bauckham, "Life, Death, and the Afterlife in Second Temple Judaism," in Bauckham, *The Jewish World around the New Testament* (Grand Rapids: Baker Academic, 2010), 245–56. Bauckham comments, "The Old Testament God—the Creator, the Source of life, the Lord of life—undoubtedly *could* raise the dead. That he *would* do so became clear once death was perceived as contradicting God's righteousness and God's love. The Old Testament God could be trusted to vindicate the righteous and to be faithful in his love for his own. If

these purposes could be fully attained only beyond death, then he could be trusted to raise the dead. In this way it was precisely faith in the Old Testament God which led to the hope of resurrection as a virtually necessary implication" (249). In this vein see also Walter Brueggemann, "Faith at the *Nullpunkt*," in Polkinghorne and Welker, *The End of the World and the Ends of God*, 143–54; J. Gerald Janzen, "Resurrection and Hermeneutics: On Exodus 3:6 in Mark 12:26," *Journal for the Study of the New Testament* 23 (1985): 43–58; Richard B. Hays, "Reading Scripture in Light of the Resurrection," in *The Art of Reading Scripture*, ed. Ellen F. Davis and Richard B. Hays (Grand Rapids: Eerdmans, 2003), 227–29.

14 See Levenson, *Resurrection and the Restoration of Israel*, 227–29. For a comprehensive and appreciative engagement with Levenson's book, see Justin Edward Gillespie, *The Development of Belief in the Resurrection within the Old Testament: A Critical Confrontation of Past and Present Proposals* (Rome: Pontificia Universitas Sanctae Crucis, 2009), 257–405. On the near-sacrifice of Isaac see Levenson's *The Death and Resurrection of the Beloved Son* and my *Sacrifice and Community*, 33–37, 46–49.

15 Craig A. Evans offers an extensive defense of Wright's view on this point: see Evans, "Jesus and the Continuing Exile of Israel," in *Jesus and the Restoration of Israel: A Critical Assessment of N. T. Wright's "Jesus and the Victory of God*," ed. Carey C. Newman (Downers Grove, Ill.: InterVarsity, 1999), 77–100; see also in Wright's favor the essays in James M. Scott, ed., *Exile: Old Testament, Jewish and Christian Conceptions* (Leiden: Brill, 1997). Steven M. Bryan criticizes Wright's position by arguing that Second-Temple texts envision an "incomplete restoration" rather than an "ongoing exile": see Bryan, *Jesus and Israel's Traditions of Judgement and Restoration* (Cambridge: Cambridge University Press, 2002), 16. See also the criticisms of Wright's view in Luke Timothy Johnson, "A Historiographical Response to Wright's Jesus," in Newman, *Jesus and the Restoration of Israel*, 210–12.

16 See Wright, *The New Testament and the People of God*, 247, 279, 285, 299–300, and elsewhere. Also helpful is Donald E. Gowan, *Eschatology in the Old Testament*, 2nd ed. (New York: T&T Clark, 2000). For discussion of Wright's views see Greg K. Beale, "The Eschatological Conception of New Testament Theology," in Brower and Elliott, *Eschatology in Bible and Theology*, 26–28.

17 The following three paragraphs rely on N. T. Wright, *Jesus and the Victory of God* (Minneapolis: Fortress, 1996). For a survey of Jesus' mission that draws much more than does Wright on the Gospel of John (and on its incarnational and sacramental portrait of divine love), see Gerald O'Collins, S.J., *Jesus: A Portrait* (London: Darton, Longman & Todd, 2008).

18 Cf. Ben Witherington III, *Jesus, Paul, and the End of the World: A Comparative Study in New Testament Eschatology* (Downers Grove, Ill.: InterVarsity, 1992).

19 In this regard see also Timothy C. Gray, *The Temple in the Gospel of Mark: A Study in Its Narrative Role* (Tübingen: Mohr Siebeck, 2008); Crispin H. T. Fletcher-Louis, "The Destruction of the Temple and the Relativization of the Old Covenant: Mark 13:31 and Matthew 5:18," in Brower and Elliott, *Eschatology in Bible and Theology*, 145–69.

20 Wright argues that Jesus' confrontation with the Pharisees was largely about whether or not to resist Rome through violence. On this topic, I find persuasive

the criticisms put forward by Johnson, "A Historiographical Response to Wright's Jesus," 213–15.

21 See Wright, *The Resurrection of the Son of God*, 689. For the same view see Raymond E. Brown, S.S., *The Virginal Conception and Bodily Resurrection of Jesus* (New York: Paulist Press, 1973), 76, 127; Richard B. Hays, *The Moral Vision of the New Testament: Community, Cross, New Creation: A Contemporary Introduction to New Testament Ethics* (New York: HarperCollins, 1996), 165–66. See also Michael R. Licona's *The Resurrection of Jesus: A New Historiographical Approach* (Downers Grove, Ill.: IVP Academic, 2010), esp. chap. 5. On the empty tomb see Carolyn Osiek, "The Women at the Tomb: What Were They Doing There?," *Ex Auditu* 9 (1993): 97–107.

22 Wright, *The Resurrection of the Son of God*, 582; cf. 562.

23 Wright, *The Resurrection of the Son of God*, 690–91.

24 Wright, *The Resurrection of the Son of God*, 605–10. See also Robert H. Gundry, "The Essential Physicality of Jesus' Resurrection According to the New Testament," in *Jesus of Nazareth: Lord and Christ*, ed. Joel B. Green and Michael Turner (Grand Rapids: Eerdmans, 1994), 204–19; Brown, *The Virginal Conception and Bodily Resurrection of Jesus*, 87–92, 127–28. For the view that the resurrection narratives "were originally narrated in the tradition of angelophanies or divine epiphanies," see George W. E. Nickelsburg, *Resurrection, Immortality, and Eternal Life in Intertestamental Judaism and Early Christianity*, 2nd ed. (Cambridge, Mass.: Harvard University Press, 2006), 247; cf. Gerd Lüdemann, *The Resurrection of Jesus: History, Experience, Theology*, trans. John Bowden (Minneapolis: Fortress, 1994), 33–109.

25 See Wright, *The Resurrection of the Son of God*, 602–4, 610. For scholarly assessment of Wright's *The Resurrection of the Son of God*, see Markus Bockmuehl, "Compleat History of the Resurrection: A Dialogue with N. T. Wright," *Journal for the Study of the New Testament* 26 (2004): 489–504; Gijsbert van den Brink, "How to Speak with Intellectual and Theological Decency on the Resurrection of Christ? A Comparison of Swinburne and Wright," *Scottish Journal of Theology* 61 (2008): 408–19; Michael Welker, "Wright on the Resurrection," *Scottish Journal of Theology* 60 (2007): 458–75; George Hunsinger, "The Daybreak of the New Creation: Christ's Resurrection in Recent Theology," *Scottish Journal of Theology* 57 (2004): 163–80. See also Wright's "An Incompleat (but Grateful) Response to the Review by Markus Bockmuehl of *The Resurrection of the Son of God*," *Journal for the Study of the New Testament* 26 (2004): 505–10.

26 Dale C. Allison Jr., *The Historical Christ and the Theological Jesus* (Grand Rapids: Eerdmans, 2009), 117. For similar views, see, e.g., Segal, *Life after Death*, 448–51, 709, 725; Henry J. Cadbury, "Intimations of Immortality in the Thought of Jesus," in *Immortality and Resurrection*, ed. Krister Stendahl (New York: Macmillan, 1965), 115–49; John Shelby Spong, *Eternal Life: A New Vision: Beyond Religion, Beyond Theism, Beyond Heaven and Hell* (New York: HarperCollins, 2009), 177, 212; Geza Vermes, *The Resurrection: History and Myth* (New York: Doubleday, 2008), 151–52; Marcus J. Borg, "An Appreciative Disagreement," in Newman, *Jesus and the Restoration of Israel*, 241.

27 Allison, *The Historical Christ and the Theological Jesus*, 111.

28 See also Dale C. Allison Jr., *Resurrecting Jesus: The Earliest Christian Tradition and Its Interpreters* (New York: T&T Clark, 2005). For the conjecture that the disciples' mental state caused them to experience his "presence" in visions, see David Friedrich Strauss, *The Life of Jesus Critically Examined*, trans. George Eliot (Philadelphia: Fortress, 1972); Gerd Lüdemann, *The Resurrection of Jesus*, esp. 81–84, 97–100; John Hick, *The Metaphor of God Incarnate* (London: SCM Press, 1993), 38; Michael Goulder, "Did Jesus of Nazareth Rise from the Dead?," in *Resurrection: Essays in Honour of Leslie Houlden*, ed. Stephen Barton and Graham Stanton (London: SPCK, 1994), 58–68. See Gerald O'Collins, S.J.'s response to this conjecture in his "The Resurrection: The State of the Questions," in Davis, Kendall, and O'Collins, *The Resurrection*, 10–13, as well as in the same volume Peter F. Carnley's defense of Hick's view: Carnley, "Response," 29–40. For further criticisms of this conjecture see Robert H. Gundry, "Trimming the Debate," in *Jesus' Resurrection: Fact or Figment? A Debate between William Lane Craig and Gerd Lüdemann*, ed. Paul Copan and Ronald K. Tacelli (Downers Grove, Ill.: InterVarsity, 2000), 108–11; Gerald O'Collins, S.J., *Jesus Risen: An Historical, Fundamental and Systematic Examination of Christ's Resurrection* (New York: Paulist Press, 1987), 107–9; Wolfhart Pannenberg, *Jesus: God and Man*, trans. L. L. Wilkins and D. A. Priebe (London: SCM Press, 1968), 95–98.

29 James D. G. Dunn, *Jesus Remembered*, vol. 1 of *Christianity in the Making* (Grand Rapids: Eerdmans, 2003), 874. The same point regarding the term "resurrection" is made by Craig A. Evans, "In Appreciation of the Dominical and Thomistic Traditions: The Contribution of J. D. Crossan and N. T. Wright to Jesus Research," in *The Resurrection of Jesus: John Dominic Crossan and N. T. Wright in Dialogue*, ed. Robert B. Stewart (Minneapolis: Fortress, 2006), 56–57, a volume that also sets forth Crossan's theory that Jesus was not properly buried.

30 Dunn, *Christianity in the Making*, 874. Dunn affirms that the apostolic testimony to Jesus' resurrection can and should be subjected to historical investigation, although Dunn insists more strongly than does Wright on the role of faith. For criticism of Wright regarding the role of faith, see Bockmuehl, "Compleat History of the Resurrection," 502–3; Hunsinger, "Daybreak of the New Creation," 172–76. Hunsinger goes further than Bockmuehl (or Dunn) by arguing that historical investigation is inappropriate to the event. See the defense of Wright's position offered by Van den Brink, "How to Speak with Intellectual and Theological Decency," 417–19. For the issues involved here, see also Bockmuehl, "Resurrection," in *The Cambridge Companion to Jesus*, ed. Markus Bockmuehl (Cambridge: Cambridge University Press, 2001), 102–18. For earlier efforts to deny the applicability of historical investigation to the Resurrection—often in response to Pannenberg's *Jesus: God and Man*—see Willi Marxsen, "The Resurrection of Jesus as a Historical and Theological Problem," in *The Significance of the Message of the Resurrection for Faith in Jesus Christ*, ed. C. F. D. Moule (London: SCM Press, 1968), 15–50; G. E. Michalson Jr., "Pannenberg on the Resurrection and Historical Method," *Scottish Journal of Theology* 33 (1980): 345–59; Peter Carnley, *The Structure of Resurrection Belief* (Oxford: Oxford University Press, 1987); and Sarah Coakley, "Is the Resurrection a 'Historical' Event? Some Muddles and Mysteries," in *The Resurrection of Jesus Christ*, ed. Paul Avis (London: Darton, Longman & Todd, 1993), 85–115; as

well as Wright's response to this line of thought in Wright, *The Resurrection of the Son of God*, 5–6, 15–18.

31 Dunn, *Christianity in the Making*, 876. Against attempts such as Marxsen's to explain the resurrection in terms of something that happened to the first believers as opposed to something that happened to Jesus, see David Fergusson, "Interpreting the Resurrection," *Scottish Journal of Theology* 38 (1985): 287–305.

32 See Otto Hermann Pesch, *Thomas von Aquin: Grenze und Größe mittelalterlicher Theologie* (Mainz: Matthias-Grünewald-Verlag, 1988), 330; cf. Yves Congar, O.P., "Le moment 'économique' et le moment 'ontologique' dans la Sacra Doctrina (Révélation, Théologie, Somme théologique)," in *Mélanges offerts à M.-D. Chenu* (Paris, 1967), 179. The development of Aquinas' thought on the causality of Christ's Resurrection is traced by Nicholas Crotty, C.P., "The Redemptive Role of Christ's Resurrection," *Thomist* 25 (1962): 54–106 and, more recently, by Jean-Pierre Torrell, O.P., "La causalité salvifique de la resurrection du Christ selon saint Thomas," *Revue Thomiste* 96 (1996): 179–208. Torrell has shown the significance of Christ's resurrection for Aquinas' *Summa theologiae*: see Torrell, *Spiritual Master*, vol. 2 of *Saint Thomas Aquinas*, trans. Robert Royal (Washington, D.C.: Catholic University of America Press, 2003), 131–35; along these lines see also Brian V. Johnstone, "The Debate on the Structure of the *Summa theologiae* of St. Thomas Aquinas from Chenu (1939) to Metz (1998)," in *Aquinas as Authority*, ed. Paul van Geest, Harm Goris, and Carlo Leget (Leuven: Peeters, 2002), 187–200. See also Pim Valkenberg's "Aquinas and Christ's Resurrection: The Influence of the *Lectura super Ioannem* 20-21 on the *Summa theologiae*," in Dauphinais and Levering, *Reading John with St. Thomas Aquinas*, 277–89. For historical analysis of Aquinas' theology of resurrection in its medieval context, see Hermann J. Weber, *Die Lehre von der Auferstehung der Toten in den Haupttraktaten der scholastischen Theologie von Alexander von Hales zu Duns Skotus* (Freiburg: Herder, 1973); Francis Ruello, "'La resurrection des corps sera l'oeuvre du Christ': Raison et Foi au Moyen Âge," *Les Quatre Fleuves* 15–16 (1982): 93–112; Caroline Walker Bynum, *The Resurrection of the Body in Western Christianity, 200–1336* (New York: Columbia University Press, 1995), 232–42, 256–71.

33 Wright, *Jesus and the Victory of God*, 662. In response to Wright, C. Stephen Evans points out, "For Christians there is no reason to think that the historical accounts about Jesus produced by this method, legitimate and valuable as they may be for pragmatic and apologetic purposes, give us our best access to the historical events in first-century Palestine as they actually occurred." Evans, "Methodological Naturalism in Historical Biblical Scholarship," in Newman, *Jesus and the Restoration of Israel*, 204.

34 For the view that historical-critical research and Christian faith are inevitably at odds, see Michael Legaspi, *The Death of Scripture and the Rise of Biblical Studies* (Oxford: Oxford University Press, 2010). Legaspi explains that "the scriptural Bible and the academic Bible are fundamentally different creations oriented toward rival interpretive communities. Though in some ways homologous, they can and should function independently if each is to retain its integrity. . . . A rational, irenic study of the Bible supported by state resources and disciplined by academic standards cultivated across a range of fields has produced, in a relatively

short time, an astonishing amount of useful information. It has become clear, though, that academic criticism in its contemporary form cannot offer a coherent, intellectually compelling account of what this information is actually *for*" (169). Cf. Jonathan Sheehan, *The Enlightenment Bible: Translation, Scholarship, Culture* (Princeton: Princeton University Press, 2005). The relationship between historical research and biblical exegesis is fruitfully explored in Joseph Ratzinger/Pope Benedict XVI's foreword to his *Jesus of Nazareth: From the Baptism in the Jordan to the Transfiguration*, trans. Adrian J. Walker (New York: Doubleday, 2007), xi–xxiv.

35 III, q. 53, a. 1, *sed contra.*

36 III, q. 53, a. 1.

37 Oliver O'Donovan comments that "in his resurrection the moral order was publicly and cosmically vindicated." O'Donovan, *Resurrection and Moral Order: An Outline for Evangelical Ethics*, 2nd ed. (Grand Rapids: Eerdmans, 1994), 148. See also Joel B. Green, "'Witnesses of His Resurrection': Resurrection, Salvation, Discipleship, and Mission in the Acts of the Apostles," in Longenecker, *Life in the Face of Death*, 237: "Jesus had represented the coming of the kingdom as the coming of God's reign of justice, which means the deconstruction of worldly powers and worldly systems of valuation. In raising Jesus from the dead, God verified the truth of Jesus' message. . . . In the resurrection, God has provided for Jesus' ministry an unassailable sanction, so that Jesus' message of salvation-as-reversal and his career as the one whose humiliation has been overturned in exaltation might become paradigmatic for the redemptive experience of those who follow him."

38 III, q. 53, a. 1.

39 III, q. 53, a. 1.

40 III, q. 53, a. 1. For Aquinas' treatment of 1 Corinthians 15 in his Commentary on 1 Corinthians, see Bynum, *The Resurrection of the Body*, 232–36. With regard to 1 Corinthians 15:44, "It is sown a physical body, it is raised a spiritual body," Aquinas holds that the principle of resurrection is the divine power, not something intrinsic to the dynamism of the human body; on this point see Bauckham and Hart, *Hope against Hope*, 124. For the centrality of resurrection in Paul, see J. R. Daniel Kirk, *Unlocking Romans: Resurrection and the Justification of God* (Grand Rapids: Eerdmans, 2008); G. Walter Hansen, "Resurrection and the Christian Life in Paul's Letters," in Longenecker, *Life in the Face of Death*, 203–24.

41 Commenting on 1 Corinthians 15:20-23 from a contemporary exegetical perspective, Daniel G. Powers notes three ways in which Paul here describes the resurrection of believers as "taking place through participation in Christ's resurrection." Powers, *Salvation through Participation: An Examination of the Notion of the Believers' Corporate Unity with Christ in Early Christian Soteriology* (Leuven: Peeters, 2001), 155. First, the risen Christ is the first-fruits; second, unity with Adam in death is paralleled with unity with Christ in resurrection life; third, phrases such as "in Christ" emphasize "the paramount importance of one's unity with Christ in order to share in the eschatological resurrection" (155). Aquinas considers that Jesus' resurrection is the cause of the resurrection of all the dead, not only of believers. Only believers, however, rise to eternal life with God. For a thorough discussion of resurrection in the Corinthian correspondence, see Wright, *The Resurrection of the Son of God*, 277–371.

42 See also Acts 2:24-28, where Peter applies to Jesus Psalm 16:8-11, with its refer-
    ence to the impossibility of God abandoning the righteous person to Sheol.

43 III, q. 53, a. 1. For a theologically astute introduction to Job 19:25, a passage that
    is obscure in the Hebrew, see J. Gerald Janzen, *Job* (Atlanta: John Knox, 1985),
    131–50. Wright is less insightful: see Wright, *The Resurrection of the Son of God*,
    96–99.

44 For the relationship in Romans 6 of Jesus' resurrection to ours, see Powers, *Sal-
    vation through Participation*, 156–62. For exegetical analysis of resurrection in
    Romans 6 in the context of Paul's theology of the Law, see esp. Kirk, *Unlocking
    Romans*, 107–20. For Romans 6 as describing a foretaste of resurrection life, see
    Madigan and Levenson, *Resurrection*, 239–40, drawing particularly upon Cyril
    of Jerusalem, *Lectures on the Christian Sacraments*, trans. R. W. Church, ed. F. L.
    Cross (Crestwood, N.Y.: St. Vladimir's Seminary Press, 1977).

45 See Kirk, *Unlocking Romans*, 76–80; Morna D. Hooker, "Raised for Our Acquittal
    (Rom 4:25)," in *Resurrection in the New Testament*, ed. R. Bieringer, V. Koperski,
    and B. Lataire (Leuven: Leuven University Press, 2002), 323–41. For theological
    reflections on Romans 4 see Joseph Ratzinger, *Faith and the Future* (San Francisco:
    Ignatius Press, 2009), 37–60.

46 For love as an ordering theme in interpreting Jesus' resurrection, see Gerald
    O'Collins, S.J., "Christ's Resurrection as Mystery of Love," *Heythrop Journal* 25
    (1984): 39–50.

47 Levenson, *Resurrection and the Restoration of Israel*, 217.

48 III, q. 53, a. 2, obj. 2 and *sed contra*. Raymond Brown comments, "It is true that
    as I Cor 15:4 now stands, the resurrection itself is dated to the third day, but that
    may be a simplification. As we have noted, there is no other NT evidence that the
    early Christians tried to date exactly this eschatological event. What they did date
    was the discovery of the empty tomb on the first day of the week, which happened
    to be the third day after the burial. Since the empty tomb story became the setting
    and vehicle of the kerygmatic formula 'Jesus was raised,' it is not unlikely that the
    dating 'on the third day' really reflects the events surrounding the empty tomb"
    (Brown, *The Virginal Conception and Bodily Resurrection of Jesus*, 124). Cf. Michael
    Welker's view that the "third day" simply means that Jesus was fully dead: see
    Welker, "Wright on the Resurrection," 474.

49 III, q. 53, a. 2, ad 3. The figures of the Law already enabled people who had faith
    in what those figures signified to be united to Christ in the Spirit. The New Law
    fulfills the Old, and the New Law itself will be fulfilled by the state of glory.

50 Ratzinger, *Jesus of Nazareth*, 250.

51 III, q. 54, a. 4, ad 1.

52 In this vein, Aquinas quotes John 10:18 in III, q. 54, a. 4, *sed contra*. See the theo-
    logical reflections on this image from the Gospel of John in Ratzinger, *Jesus of
    Nazareth*, 272–86.

53 On the shepherd image and messianic suffering, see Wright, *Jesus and the Victory
    of God*, 533–34; Michael F. Bird, *Are You the One Who Is to Come? The Historical
    Jesus and the Messianic Question* (Grand Rapids: Baker Academic, 2009), 133–36.
    Wright treats the scars not for their symbolic power but with respect to the (trans)
    physicality of the risen Jesus: see Wright, *The Resurrection of the Son of God*, 605,

658. On the eschatological significance of Jesus' bodily scars, see, e.g., Beth Felker Jones, *Marks of His Wounds: Gender Politics and Bodily Resurrection* (Oxford: Oxford University Press, 2007), 109–11.

54   See III, q. 55, a. 2. For discussion see Leo J. Elders, S.V.D., "La Résurrection du Christ dans la théologie de saint Thomas d'Aquin," *Nova et Vetera* (French ed.) 74 (1999): 26.

55   See III, q. 55, a. 5, ad 3; III, q. 55, a. 1. For background see Thomas Marschler, *Auferstehung und Himmelfahrt Christi in der Scholastichen Theologie bis zu Thomas von Aquin* (Münster: Aschendorff, 2003), 449–68. See also O'Collins, "The Resurrection," 9; O'Collins, *Interpreting the Resurrection* (Mahwah, N.J.: Paulist Press, 1988), 5–21; David J. Norman, O.F.M., "Doubt and the Resurrection of Jesus," *Theological Studies* 69 (2008): 786–811.

56   Michael Welker remarks that "many biblical texts try to express this complicated identity of the resurrected Christ with the pre-Easter Jesus by, on the one hand, highlighting the *palpability* of the presence of the resurrected Christ and by, on the other hand, emphasizing that this presence is the presence of an *appearance*" (Welker, "Resurrection and Eternal Life," 282; cf. 284). Welker fears that Wright leaves too much room for conceiving of Jesus' Resurrection as though it were a resuscitation: see Welker, "Wright on the Resurrection," 463–65. But Welker's formulation is also problematic: "He, Jesus of Nazareth, is risen. In his stubborn yet enormously rich individuality, and thus 'bodily', he is present 'again'. But this does not mean that his biological body is 'alive again', but rather his entire life which was borne by the biological and mental-spiritual body, but which now seeks and finds a new body for those and in those who witness to him, a new body to be the bearer of his earthly, historical existence" ("Wright on the Resurrection," 471).

57   III, q. 55, a. 3. For discussion see Elders, "La Résurrection du Christ," 26–29.

58   See III, q. 55, a. 4.

59   III, q. 55, a. 4; cf. Janet E. Smith, "'Come and See,'" in Dauphinais and Levering, *Reading John with St. Thomas Aquinas*, 194–211. See also Anthony J. Kelly, *The Resurrection Effect: Transforming Christian Life and Thought* (Maryknoll, N.Y.: Orbis Books, 2008), 114–15, 127, 175; Michael Welker, "Resurrection and Eternal Life: The Canonic Memory of the Resurrected Christ, His Reality, and His Glory," in Polkinghorne and Welker, *The End of the World and the Ends of God*, 286–88.

60   III, q. 55, a. 6. Cf. Ashley, *Theologies of the Body*, 591.

61   III, q. 53, a. 1, ad 1.

62   I–II, q. 98, a. 3. See Luke Timothy Johnson, *Hebrews: A Commentary* (Louisville, Ky.: Westminster John Knox, 2006), 82–84, 87.

63   III, q. 55, a. 5.

64   Cited in III, q. 55, a. 5.

65   Cf. Wright, *The Resurrection of the Son of God*, 605–6.

66   See III, q. 55, a. 6, ad 4; cf. ad 2.

67   Cited in III, q. 54, a. 2.

68   III, q. 57, a. 4. See Marschler, *Auferstehung und Himmelfahrt Christi*, 653–54.

69   III, q. 56, a. 1.

70   See Holtz, "La valeur sotériologique," 612–14, 630–32; Elders, "La Résurrection du Christ," 29–31. See also Scott Brodeur, *The Holy Spirit's Agency in the*

Resurrection of the Dead: An Exegetico-Theological Study of 1 Corinthians 15,44b-49 and Romans 8,9-13 (Rome: Editrice Pontificia Università Gregoriana, 1996).

CHAPTER 3

1   Wright, *Surprised by Hope*, 113. See Daniélou, *The Lord of History*, 204; Yves Congar, O.P., *Jesus Christ*, trans. Luke O'Neill (New York: Herder & Herder, 1966), 152–53, 179–89. For assessment and critique of some historical-critical reconstructions of Jesus' ascension (e.g., the supposition that a mythological ascension narrative arose from visions of an exalted Jesus that were later redescribed as embodied resurrection appearances), see Pierre Benoit, *Jesus and the Gospel*, vol. 1, trans. Benet Weatherhead (New York: Herder & Herder, 1973), 209–53; cf. Gerhard Lohfink, *Die Himmelfahrt Jesu: Untersuchungen zu den Himmelfahrts- und Erhöhungstexten bei Lukas* (Munich: Kösel-Verlag, 1971). In Wright's view, Jesus is utterly alone in "God's new world," whereas for Catholics the whole Church (head and members) is already present in God's new world, even if not in its perfection: through Mary's bodily assumption, the new Eden is not a lonely place for the new Adam. See the *Catechism of the Catholic Church*, §§963–72; Hans Urs von Balthasar, *Mary for Today*, trans. Robert Nowell (San Francisco: Ignatius Press, 1988), 29–32.

2   Wright, *Surprised by Hope*, 153.

3   Benoit, *Jesus and the Gospels*, 252.

4   For the necessity of conceiving this "place" eschatologically, rather than in this-worldly spatial or even sacramental terms, see Douglas Farrow, *Ascension Theology* (New York: T&T Clark, 2011), 47–49.

5   See Giorgio Buccellati, "Ascension, Parousia, and the Sacred Heart: Structural Correlations," *Communio* 25 (1998): 72: "It was this contrast, this paradox, this scandal, that confronted the Sanhedrin: their contemporary Jesus, a mortal like them, was in his human specificity 'at the right sides of God,' i.e., physically linked with the One who is above all physical limitation."

6   Douglas Farrow, *Ascension and Ecclesia: On the Significance of the Doctrine of the Ascension for Ecclesiology and Christian Cosmology* (Grand Rapids: Eerdmans, 1999), 25. Farrow comments that "it is indeed the ascension towards which the biblical story constantly strives, esp. in its messianic dimensions, not the resurrection in and of itself" (26–27). On this point see also Vermes, *The Resurrection*, 137.

7   See Wright, *Jesus and the Victory of God*, 551, 644–45.

8   See Green, "'Witnesses of His Resurrection,'" 231–32.

9   For discussion of Hebrews see Farrow, *Ascension and Ecclesia*, 33–35; cf. Farrow, "Melchizedek and Modernity," in *The Epistle to the Hebrews and Christian Theology*, ed. Richard Bauckham et al. (Grand Rapids: Eerdmans, 2009), 284–91.

10 James D. G. Dunn, *Did the First Christians Worship Jesus? The New Testament Evidence* (Louisville, Ky.: Westminster John Knox, 2010), 103. For discussion see Martin Hengel, "'Sit at My Right Hand!' The Enthronement of Christ at the Right Hand of God and Psalm 110:1," in Hengel, *Studies in Early Christology* (Edinburgh: T&T Clark, 1995), 119–225. Hengel draws particularly on Christopher Markschies, "'Sessio ad dexteram.' Bemerkungen zu einem altchristlichen Bekenntnismotiv in der christologischen Diskussion altkirchlicher Theologen," in

Le Trône de Dieu, ed. M. Philonenko (Tübingen: 1993), and Ferdinand Hahn, *The Titles of Jesus in Christology*, trans. H. Knight and G. Ogg (Cleveland: World, 1969). See also David M. Hay, *Glory at the Right Hand: Psalm 110 in Early Christianity* (Nashville: Abingdon, 1973); Donald Juel, *Messianic Exegesis: Christological Interpretation of the Old Testament in Early Christianity* (Philadelphia: Fortress, 1988), 135–50.

11 Mark S. Smith, *The Early History of God: Yahweh and the Other Deities in Ancient Israel*, 2nd ed. (Grand Rapids: Eerdmans, 2002), 185. See also William G. Dever, *Did God Have a Wife? Archaeology and Folk Religion in Ancient Israel* (Grand Rapids: Eerdmans, 2005), which argues that most pre-exilic Israelites also worshipped the goddess Asherah in addition to YHWH. For Smith's assessment of the status of Asherah, see his Preface to the Second Edition, xxx–xxxvi; see also Benjamin D. Sommer, *The Bodies of God and the World of Ancient Israel* (Cambridge: Cambridge University Press, 2009), 150, 155–59. Sommer concludes that "at least at an early stage of Israelite history and at least in the north, the goddess Asherah was worshipped alongside Yhwh" (159).

12 Smith, *The Early History of God*, 185. Smith holds that "[t]exts dating to the Exile or shortly beforehand are the first to attest to unambiguous expressions of Israelite monotheism" (191); he has in view particularly Second Isaiah.

13 Smith, *The Early History of God*, 204.

14 Smith, *The Origins of Biblical Monotheism*, 86.

15 Sommer, *The Bodies of God and the World of Ancient Israel*, 1. From a similar perspective David H. Aaron observes, "I find no evidence that God-related idioms have special linguistic status in Tanakh. Nowhere in Tanakh are we informed that literal statements about the deity are impossible because of transcendence or any other divine characteristic." Aaron, *Biblical Ambiguities: Metaphor, Semantics, and Divine Imagery* (Leiden: Brill, 2002), 11. Aaron goes on to say that "theology, in the sense that it would come to be known in Judaism and Christianity, was quite specifically a creation of the late Hellenistic era" (17–18; cf. 186–92).

16 Sommer, *The Bodies of God and the World of Ancient Israel*, 5.

17 Sommer, *The Bodies of God and the World of Ancient Israel*, 8.

18 See Smith, *The Origins of Biblical Monotheism*, 150. Smith comments, "As a result of the editing of later monotheists, only scattered references to a number of other deities who belong to the middle levels of the pantheon have survived. Indeed, the Bible hardly provides an objective or complete picture of Israel's religion, because of significant editorial selection. Fortunately, biblical criticisms of polytheism preserve some vestiges of information about polytheism into the late monarchic period" (155). For Smith's views on the development of monotheism, see also 163 and 170, as well as his chapter on "Monotheism in Isaiah 40–55" (chap. 10). See also Michael Mach, "Concepts of Jewish Monotheism during the Hellenistic Period," in *The Jewish Roots of Christological Monotheism*, ed. Carey C. Newman, James R. Davila, and Gladys S. Lewis (Leiden: Brill, 1999), 21–42.

19 See Sommer, *The Bodies of God and the World of Ancient Israel*, 168; cf. Yehezkel Kaufmann, *The Religion of Israel: From Its Beginnings to the Babylonian Exile*, trans. and abridged Moshe Greenberg (Chicago: University of Chicago Press, 1960).

20 Israelite "monotheism," Sommer adds, also maintained a consistent opposition to

portraying YHWH in pictorial or sculpted form: see *The Bodies of God and the World of Ancient Israel*, 150. For questions in this regard, see Tryggve N. D. Mettinger, *No Graven Image? Israelite Aniconism in Its Ancient Near Eastern Context* (Stockholm: Almqvist & Wiksell International, 1995).

21 In my view, the possibility that Old Testament authors and/or redactors are using anthropomorphic language metaphorically is much greater than is admitted by Smith and esp. by Sommer, but this is a discussion for another book.

22 Bauckham remarks, "Jewish monotheism was a historical phenomenon, whose ways of portraying God and his uniqueness were often fashioned out of older or non-Jewish materials that lacked the typically sharp Second Temple Jewish understanding of divine uniqueness" (*Jesus and the God of Israel*, 157, cf. 108–11).

23 *Jesus and the God of Israel*, 157. He adds, "This is not to say that there are no traces remaining in Second Temple Jewish literature of the notions that God is the most eminent example of the species 'deity' or that God is the chief of a divine hierarchy" (157). The important text that Bauckham originally published as *God Crucified: Monotheism and Christology in the New Testament* (Grand Rapids: Eerdmans, 1998) is reprinted in *Jesus and the God of Israel*, 1–59. For a similarly helpful argument about Jesus' inclusion in the divine identity, see C. Kavin Rowe, *Early Narrative Christology: The Lord in the Gospel of Luke* (New York: Walter de Gruyter, 2006).

24 See Hengel, "'Sit at My Right Hand!,'" 124–28.

25 Farrow, *Ascension and Ecclesia*, 113. Drawing appreciatively on John Damascene's *The Orthodox Faith*, Farrow emphasizes nonetheless that "the ecclesiastical tradition consistently sided with Irenaeus [in favor of an embodied ascension] when the chips were down" (*Ascension and Ecclesia*, 113). For the same point see Farrow's *Ascension Theology*, chap. 3.

26 *Summa theologiae* I, q. 3, a. 1, obj. 2–4.

27 I, q. 3, a. 1.

28 I, q. 3, a. 1, ad 3.

29 I, q. 1, a. 10. See also Aquinas, *De potentia*, q. 4, a. 1, trans. English Dominican Fathers (Eugene, Ore.: Wipf and Stock, 2004).

30 See I, q. 1, a. 10.

31 See I, q. 1, a. 9; cf. III, q. 1, a. 1, *sed contra*; III, q. 60, a. 4; III, q. 61, a. 1.

32 I, q. 1, a. 9.

33 I, q. 1, a. 8, ad 2. Aquinas cites 2 Corinthians 10:5 in a similar discussion in his Commentary on Boethius' *De Trinitate*, q. 2, a. 3.

34 III, q. 58, a. 1, obj. 1.

35 III, q. 58, a. 1, obj. 2.

36 III, q. 58, a. 1, obj. 3.

37 III, q. 58, a. 1, obj. 3: "sedere et stare videntur oppositionem habere."

38 John of Damascus, *The Orthodox Faith* IV.2, 336, quoted in III, q. 58, a. 1, ad 1.

39 John of Damascus, *The Orthodox Faith* I.4, 170; cf. 171 as well as Gregory of Nazianzus, *Sermon* 28.8 (PG 36.36AB). Damascene does not claim to comprehend the essence of this God: "The Divinity, then, is limitless and incomprehensible, and this His limitlessness and incomprehensibility is all that can be understood about Him" (*The Orthodox Faith*, 172).

40 See Farrow, *Ascension Theology*, 45.

41 I, q. 58, a. 1.
42 Augustine, *On the Psalms*, trans. Scholastica Hebgin and Felicitas Corrigan (Westminster, Md.: Newman Press, 1960), Discourse on Psalm 15, 162.
43 III, q. 58, a. 1.
44 III, q. 58, a. 1.
45 Discussing Psalm 110:1 along with Psalm 2:7, "You are my son, today I have begotten you," Jon Levenson argues that the point is that "Davidic kingship is an earthly manifestation of divine kingship" (Levenson, *Sinai and Zion*, 155). According to Levenson, YHWH promises in Psalm 110:1 to bring all nations into subjection to the Davidic king in Jerusalem. The political power of the Davidic king will be perfect and enduring. Just as the Davidic king is subject to YHWH, so also all other kings will be subject to the Davidic king. Through the mediation of the Davidic king in Jerusalem, therefore, God will rule over all nations.
46 See III, q. 58, a. 1, ad 2.
47 See III, q. 58, a. 1, ad 3, citing *Hom.* xxix *in Evang.*
48 Thomas Aquinas, *Commentary on the Epistle to the Hebrews*, trans. Chrysostom Baer, O.Praem. (South Bend, Ind.: St. Augustine's Press, 2006), chap. 1, lect. 2, §41, 22–23.
49 Aquinas, *Commentary on the Epistle to the Hebrews*, chap. 1, lect. 2, §42, 23.
50 See also Darrell L. Bock, *Acts* (Grand Rapids: Baker Academic, 2007), 312.
51 Bauckham, *Jesus and the God of Israel*, 249.
52 John of Damascus, *The Orthodox Faith* IV.2, 336. This passage serves as the *sed contra* of III, q. 58, a. 2.
53 III, q. 58, a. 2, ad 1. For discussion of Trinitarian appropriation see Gilles Emery, O.P., *The Trinitarian Theology of St. Thomas Aquinas*, trans. Francesca Aran Murphy (Oxford: Oxford University Press, 2007), chap. 13.
54 Irenaeus, *Against Heresies* IV.20.9, in *The Apostolic Fathers with Justin Martyr and Irenaeus*, ed. Alexander Roberts and James Donaldson, rev. A. Cleveland Coxe, Ante-Nicene Fathers, vol. 1 (Peabody, Mass.: Hendrickson, 1994), 487.
55 *Discourse IV Against the Arians*, in Athanasius, *Select Works and Letters*, ed. Archibald Robertson, trans. John Henry Newman, *Nicene and Post-Nicene Fathers*, vol. 4 (Peabody, Mass.: Hendrickson, 1994), 443. Schönborn notes that *Discourse IV*'s opponent, Marcellus of Ancyra, held that "everything that is said about Christ's sitting at the right hand of God refers to Christ as a man" with the consequence that the Son's humanity will no longer be needed at the end of time (*From Death to Life*, 29). For discussion see Markus Vinzent, *Pseudo-Athanasius, Contra Arianos IV. Eine Schrift gegen Asterius von Kappadokien, Eusebius von Cäsarea, Markell von Ankyra und Photin von Sirmium* (Leiden: Brill, 1996).
56 *Discourse IV Against the Arians*, 444.
57 III, q. 58, a. 2.
58 III, q. 58, a. 3, obj. 3. On the *Glossa ordinaria*, see chaps. 2–6 in Karlfried Froehlich, *Biblical Interpretation from the Church Fathers to the Reformation* (Burlington, Vt.: Ashgate, 2010).
59 III, q. 58, a. 3, obj. 3.
60 As Farrow puts it in his *Ascension Theology*, "As the incarnate one, our saviour, Jesus is always at the right hand of God; indeed, he *is* the right hand of God. Yet his

entry into the new creation is also his entry into the full dispensation of the divine power he mediates as saviour, and from this perspective his ascension is rightly spoken of as an exaltation *to* God's right hand" (46).

61 III, q. 58, a. 2.

62 III, q. 58, a. 2.

63 III, q. 58, a. 2.

64 See I, q. 42, aa. 3 and 4, to which Aquinas refers in III, q. 58, a. 2.

65 See I, q. 42, a. 4, *sed contra*.

66 Aquinas, *Commentary on the Epistle to the Hebrews*, chap. 1, lect. 2, §43, 23.

67 Aquinas, *Commentary on the Epistle to the Hebrews*, chap. 1, lect. 2, §43, 23.

68 See also III, q. 2, aa. 10–12 on the grace of union.

69 III, q. 58, a. 2, ad 2.

70 III, q. 58, a. 2, ad 2.

71 See Morna D. Hooker, *The Gospel According to Saint Mark* (London: A. & C. Black, 1991), 391.

72 III, q. 58, a. 3.

73 See III, q. 7, a. 1. For further discussion see my *Christ's Fulfillment of Torah and Temple: Salvation According to Thomas Aquinas* (Notre Dame: University of Notre Dame Press, 2002), 34–41; Torrell, *Spiritual Master*, chap. 7. See also III, q. 7, a. 13, where Aquinas explains that in Jesus the "grace of union" is prior, though not in time, to the habitual grace that comes about through the mission of the Holy Spirit.

74 Cf. II–II, q. 2, a. 7, ad 3.

75 III, q. 8, a. 1. See Daniel A. Keating, "Justification, Sanctification and Divinization in Thomas Aquinas," in *Aquinas on Doctrine: A Critical Introduction*, ed. Thomas G. Weinandy, O.F.M. Cap., Daniel A. Keating, and John P. Yocum (New York: T&T Clark, 2004), 139–58; Torrell, *Spiritual Master*, chap. 6.

76 III, q. 7, a. 1; III, q. 8, a. 5. Yves Congar observes that "every gift of grace which is made to men passes through the understanding and love of the Christ-man, and is perfectly in agreement with the divine Will: the Son knows the Father and always does His will" (Congar, *Jesus Christ*, 150). For the same point, in response to Jacques Dupuis, see Gilles Emery, O.P., "Missions invisibles et missions visibles: le Christ et son Esprit," *Revue Thomiste* 106 (2006): 51–99.

77 Aquinas cites Philippians 2:8-9 in III, q. 49, a. 6, *sed contra*.

78 III, q. 49, a. 6.

79 III, q. 49, a. 6.

80 III, q. 49, a. 6. See Marschler, *Auferstehung und Himmelfahrt Christi*, 268–85.

81 III, q. 49, a. 6.

82 Farrow observes with concern that Augustine at times (though not in the *City of God*) makes the revelation of Jesus' divine sonship the central purpose of Jesus' ascension: see Farrow, *Ascension and Ecclesia*, 119–20. Farrow defends Augustine more robustly in his *Ascension Theology*, 38–39.

83 III, q. 58, a. 3.

84 III, q. 57, a. 6.

85 III, q. 57, a. 6; III, q. 58, a. 3, ad 3. Aquinas quotes the phrase "the mightier gifts of God" from the Gloss on Romans 8:34.

86 III, q. 57, a. 6.

87 Farrow, *Ascension and Ecclesia*, 28.

88 III, q. 57, a. 6.

89 Aquinas quotes Ephesians 2:6 in III, q. 58, a. 4, obj. 1.

90 III, q. 58, a. 4, obj. 3.

91 Judith Kovacs and Christopher Rowland, *Revelation: The Apocalypse of Jesus Christ* (Oxford: Blackwell, 2004).

92 M. Robert Mulholland Jr., *Revelation: Holy Living in an Unholy World* (Grand Rapids: Zondervan, 1990), 138.

93 Ben Witherington III, *Revelation* (Cambridge: Cambridge University Press, 2003), 108.

94 Aquinas quotes Hebrews 1:13 in III, q. 58, a. 4, *sed contra*.

95 III, q. 58, a. 4.

96 III, q. 58, a. 4, ad 2. In this vein see the lengthy quotations from Augustine and John Chrysostom found in Schönborn, *From Death to Life*, 37–40. Regarding Christ's sitting at the right hand of the Father, Schönborn emphasizes that "[t]his article of faith is in a sense the most ecclesiological of the christological articles" (37).

97 I, q. 12, a. 5. See A. N. Williams, *The Ground of Union: Deification in Aquinas and Palamas* (Oxford: Oxford University Press, 1999), 65–101.

98 See I, q. 12, aa. 5–6.

99 III, q. 59, aa. 1 (*sed contra*) and 2.

100 See III, q. 59, aa. 2–4, 6. See Jean-Pierre Torrell, O.P., "Le sacerdoce du Christ dans la *Somme de théologie*," *Revue Thomiste* 99 (1999): 75–100.

101 III, q. 58, a. 4, ad 3.

102 III, q. 59, a. 6, *sed contra*. See the commentary on this verse by John Chrysostom and Severian of Gabala in *1 Corinthians: Interpreted by Early Christian Commentators*, trans. and ed. Judith L. Kovacs (Grand Rapids: Eerdmans, 2005), 93–94. For brief contemporary commentary see Richard B. Hays, *First Corinthians* (Louisville, Ky.: John Knox, 1997), 94. Hays emphasizes Paul's lesson for the present life of the Corinthian believers.

103 III, q. 59, a. 4.

104 W. D. Davies and Dale C. Allison Jr., *Commentary on Matthew XIX–XXVIII*, vol. 3 of *A Critical and Exegetical Commentary on the Gospel According to Saint Matthew* (New York: T&T Clark, 1997), 57–58.

105 Suppl., q. 90, a. 1; q. 89, a. 1. Aquinas follows Augustine's view that the twelve thrones should not be interpreted literally, although neither should the judgment be understood in a disembodied manner: Suppl., q. 89, a. 2, ad 1.

106 III, q. 59, a. 5, ad 3. For a rich discussion of this point, see Bryan Kromholtz, O.P., *On the Last Day: The Time of the Resurrection of the Dead According to Thomas Aquinas* (Fribourg: Fribourg University Press, 2010).

107 See III, q. 58, a. 1, ad 2.

108 See III, q. 58, a. 3; III, q. 58, a. 4, ad 1.

109 See Farrow, *Ascension and Ecclesia*, 119–20.

110 Jean Daniélou, S.J., *Etudes d'exégèse judéo-chrétienne* (Paris: 1966), 48, cited in Schönborn, *From Death to Life*, 37.

CHAPTER 4

1 Dogmatic Constitution on the Church, *Lumen Gentium*, §48, in *Vatican Council II*, vol. 1, 407–8. Cf. "The Kingdom of God and the Heavenly-Earthly Church: The Church in Transition according to *Lumen Gentium*," chap. 3 in Schönborn, *From Death to Life*: Schönborn observes, "In terms of her Head and of her goal, she is a *heavenly* Church. Since she is an earthly Church, she knows that she is a *pilgrim* Church, stretching out to reach her goal. . . . It is only when we contemplate the Church in her earthly-heavenly transitional existence that we have the *whole* Church in view" (65–66).

2 *Lumen Gentium*, §12, 363.

3 *Lumen Gentium*, §§3 and 48, 351 and 408; cf. §3 and 7, 351 and 355.

4 I *Lumen Gentium*, §§4 and 7, 352 and 356. Cf. Henri de Lubac, S.J.'s classic works, *The Splendor of the Church*, trans. Michael Mason (San Francisco: Ignatius Press, 1986) and *The Motherhood of the Church*, trans. Sergia Englund, O.C.D. (San Francisco: Ignatius Press, 1982).

5 *Lumen Gentium*, §8, 358. In her *God and the Art of Happiness* (Grand Rapids: Eerdmans, 2010), Ellen Charry raises the question of whether Christian life on earth can or should be a happy one. I think that happiness in this life is best attainable through the elements of Christian life that I emphasize in this chapter, namely sharing in the apostolic teaching and fellowship, eucharistic worship, and charitable almsgiving. For a richer account than I can provide here, see Servais Pinckaers, O.P., *The Pursuit of Happiness—God's Way: Living the Beatitudes*, trans. Mary Thomas Noble, O.P. (New York: Alba House, 1998). See also Schönborn, *From Death to Life*, 123.

6 Larry W. Hurtado, *At the Origins of Christian Worship: The Context and Character of Earliest Christian Devotion* (Grand Rapids: Eerdmans, 1999), 115. For similar views of the Kingdom of God and "imperial Christianity," see Benedict T. Viviano, O.P., *The Kingdom of God in History* (Eugene, Ore.: Wipf & Stock, 2002); Walter Rauschenbusch, *Christianity and the Social Crisis*, ed. Paul B. Raushenbush (New York: HarperCollins, 2007), chap. 4. Cf. Stanley Hauerwas, *Against the Nations: War and Survival in a Liberal Society* (Notre Dame: University of Notre Dame Press, 1992), 112. For historical context regarding Christian apocalyptic expectations, showing that they certainly did not disappear, see Kevin L. Hughes, *Constructing Antichrist: Paul, Biblical Commentary, and the Development of Doctrine in the Middle Ages* (Washington, D.C.: Catholic University of America Press, 2005). See also Jean-Jacques Rousseau's political critique of Christianity, well summarized in Schönborn, *From Death to Life*, 101–4.

7 Wright, *The New Testament and the People of God*, 286.

8 Wright, *The New Testament and the People of God*, 321.

9 John Howard Yoder, "The Restitution of the Church: An Alternative Perspective on Christian History," in Yoder, *The Jewish-Christian Schism Revisited*, ed. Michael G. Cartwright and Peter Ochs (Grand Rapids: Eerdmans, 2003), 137. For a critique of Yoder as regards "Constantinian" Christianity, see Peter J. Leithart, *Defending Constantine: The Twilight of an Empire and the Dawn of Christendom* (Downers Grove, Ill.: IVP Academic, 2010).

10 See, e.g., Richard A. Horsley and Neil Asher Silberman, *The Message and the Kingdom: How Jesus and Paul Ignited a Revolution and Transformed the Ancient World* (Minneapolis: Fortress, 2002), 228; cf. Richard A. Horsley, *Covenant Economics: A Biblical Vision of Justice for All* (Louisville, Ky.: Westminster John Knox, 2009). For valuable alternatives to Horsley and Silberman's interpretation of the Book of Acts, see Rowe, *World Upside Down*; Green, "'Witnesses of His Resurrection.'" For a critical reading of Horsley's view of Jesus see Markus Bockmuehl, "Resistance and Redemption in the Jesus Tradition," in *Redemption and Resistance: The Messianic Hopes of Jews and Christians in Antiquity*, ed. Markus Bockmuehl and James Carleton Paget (New York: T&T Clark, 2007), 65–77. See also the adoption of Horsley's approach, with a focus on the resurrection as belonging to "anti-imperial polemic," in Setzer, *Resurrection of the Body*, 146.

11 Hurtado, *At the Origins of Christian Worship*, 115. These three elements also correspond to what Walter Brueggemann identifies as the three aspects of God's covenant according to Deuteronomy: Torah-based power, the centrality of the Passover, and the jubilee cancellation of debt. See Walter Brueggemann, "Always in the Shadow of the Empire," in *The Church as Counterculture*, ed. Michael L. Budde and Robert W. Brimlow (Albany: State University of New York Press, 2000), 49. As Barry Harvey says, the church's "interests are ultimately vested not in institutions that are condemned to pass away, but in the world to come." Barry Harvey, *Can These Bones Live? A Catholic Baptist Engagement with Ecclesiology, Hermeneutics, and Social Theory* (Grand Rapids: Brazos Press, 2008), 21.

12 For Aquinas' understanding of community in the context of medieval canon law and natural law, see Alasdair MacIntyre, "Natural Law as Subversive: The Case of Aquinas," in MacIntyre, *Ethics and Politics: Selected Essays*, vol. 2 (Cambridge: Cambridge University Press, 2006), 41–63.

13 For theological discussion of the relationship of the kingdom of God to the church, see *Lumen Gentium*, §5, 352–53; Schönborn, *From Death to Life*, 75–97, 110–11; Joseph Ratzinger, *Jesus of Nazareth: From the Baptism in the Jordan to the Transfiguration*, trans. Adrian J. Walker (New York: Doubleday, 2007), chap. 3. See also, for the point that the kingdom of God as proclaimed by Jesus is both politically relevant and irreducible to a political program, Allen Verhey, *The Great Reversal: Ethics and the New Testament* (Grand Rapids: Eerdmans, 1984), 30–33.

14 For Jesus' eschatological understanding of his ministry in Israel, through the lens of contemporary historical research, see Wright, *Jesus and the Victory of God*. See also, for the apostolic appropriation of Jesus' eschatological perspective, Verhey, *The Great Reversal*, esp. 41–48, 86–89, 113–21.

15 See Luke Timothy Johnson, *The Acts of the Apostles* (Collegeville, Minn.: Liturgical Press, 1992), 50: "Luke exploits the text [Joel 2:30] primarily to show that the gift of the Spirit is eschatological in that it inaugurates the new age, but is not yet the climax or the end. . . . As in Jesus' eschatological discourse in Luke 21:5-36, there is a distinction between the time of witnessing with signs and wonders, and the cosmic events that will precede the coming of the Lord." In Joel's prophecy, after warning his people about the approaching day of the Lord, the day of judgment, the Lord God pleads with his people to repent and believe in the mercy of God. If and when they do so, God promises that "[y]ou shall know that I am in the midst

of Israel, and that I, the Lord, am your God and there is none else. . . . And it shall come to pass afterward, that I will pour out my spirit on all flesh" (Joel 2:27-28). After this, the "great and terrible day of the Lord comes," and only those "who call upon the name of the Lord shall be delivered" (Joel 2:31-32). The day of the Lord will accomplish the full restoration of Israel and the judgment of all the nations (Joel 3:1-2).

16   Darrell L. Bock comments on this passage, "Community life is summarized as involving four key areas: apostolic teaching, fellowship, the breaking of bread together, and prayer. The newly formed community functions by believers devot-ing themselves . . . to these activities. The expression 'devoting themselves' has the idea of persistence or persevering in something" (Bock, *Acts*, 149). Regarding "the breaking of bread," Bock is unsure "whether the phrase refers to the Lord's Supper . . . or is a reference to taking some meals together, of which the Lord's Supper was a part" (Bock, *Acts* [Grand Rapids: Baker Academic, 2007], 150).

17   Luke Timothy Johnson points out that "[a]lthough Luke consistently speaks about possessions, he does not speak about possessions consistently." Johnson, *Sharing Possessions: Mandate and Symbol of Faith* (Philadelphia: Fortress, 1981), 13). After surveying the relevant texts of Luke, Johnson concludes that Jesus called some of his disciples to radical poverty, but not all. All followers of Jesus are called to almsgiving, but not all are called to give away all their possessions. Johnson observes that in Acts 2:44-45 and 4:32-35 there is a "complete pooling of property" and a "relinquishment of private ownership," but he finds that "on the strength of the textual evidence itself, the practice seems to have been less than absolute. Peter, after all, has a house to flee to when he escapes from prison (12:12), and if the Christians were 'breaking bread in their homes' (2:46), some houses obviously were retained in possession. Likewise in Acts 11 the Antiochean church, which takes up a collection to assist the church in Jerusalem, has both private possessions and distinctions in wealth among its members. See also Martin Hengel, *Property and Riches in the Early Church: Aspects of a Social History of Early Christianity*, trans. John Bowden (Philadelphia: Fortress, 1974), 31–34. Hengel emphasizes that the community described in Acts 2:44-45 expected the imminent return of Jesus.

18   For discussion see Robert W. Wall, *The Acts of the Apostles: Introduction, Commen-tary, and Reflections* in *The New Interpreter's Bible*, vol. 10, ed. Leander E. Keck (Nashville: Abingdon Press, 2002), 81–82. Earlier, Wall suggests that Oscar Cull-man may be right in connecting the Peter of Acts and the Peter of the Petrine letters, esp. as regards "the most important christological vocabulary of 1 Peter (1 Pet 2:21-25)" and "the apocalyptic eschatology of 2 Peter 3": Wall, *The Acts of the Apostles*, 63; see Oscar Cullmann, *Peter: Disciple, Apostle, Martyr* (Waco, Tex.: Baylor University Press, 2011), 33–69.

19   Luke Timothy Johnson argues that the distinction between "Hebrews" and "Hel-lenists" here contrasts Jews who primarily speak Aramaic with Jews who primarily speak Greek: see Johnson, *The Acts of the Apostles*, 105.

20   On Stephen see Johnson, *The Acts of the Apostles*, 111–12, 139–40, 142–43.

21   See Johnson, *The Acts of the Apostles*, 260.

22   See Johnson, *The Acts of the Apostles*, 266–67.

23   For Second-Temple parallels see Johnson, *The Acts of the Apostles*, 363.

24　Johnson reflects on what he calls "the idolatrous impulse" that equates human worth with what humans do for themselves, rather than grounding human worth on God's free gifting: see Johnson, *Sharing Possessions*, 85–88. Drawing upon the Torah's commandments about possessions and the prophetic critique of oppressors of the poor, Johnson states that "possessions symbolize our self-disposition toward God and other people in the world" (108). Sharing possessions shows that we recognize that all belongs to God, all is his gift.

25　Ben Witherington III notes that "Jesus is sifting Peter to the core to see whether he has the courage and perseverance to assume a shepherding role. Here Peter is being portrayed as a sage who teaches disciples, just as Jesus has been earlier in John 10." Witherington, *John's Wisdom: A Commentary on the Fourth Gospel* (Louisville, Ky.: Westminster John Knox, 1995), 356.

26　See Witherington, *John's Wisdom*, 251, 270, 343.

27　See Andreas J. Köstenberger and Scott R. Swain, *Father, Son and Spirit: The Trinity in John's Gospel* (Downers Grove, Ill.: InterVarsity, 2008); Ben Witherington III and Laura M. Ice, *The Shadow of the Almighty: Father, Son, and Spirit in Biblical Perspective* (Grand Rapids: Eerdmans, 2002).

28　Witherington argues, mistakenly in my view, against a eucharistic reading of John 6 in any strong sense: "While the passage has implications for seeing the sacraments as *signs* that point away from themselves and do not in themselves provide eternal life any more than the eating of the physical bread and fish by the five thousand provide eternal life, it is not about the sacraments, but rather about receiving Jesus. 'It is the spirit that gives life; the flesh is useless' (v. 63)" (*John's Wisdom*, 163). For a similar rejection of a eucharistic interpretation, see Leon Morris, *The Gospel According to John*, rev. ed. (Grand Rapids: Eerdmans, 1995), 331–37. For a eucharistic interpretation of John 6, indebted particularly to Raymond Brown, see Jerome Kodell, O.S.B., *The Eucharist in the New Testament* (Collegeville, Minn.: Liturgical Press, 1988), 123–26.

29　See Morris, *The Gospel According to John*, 599.

30　For overviews of Paul's eschatology, see esp. Andrew T. Lincoln, *Paradise Now and Not Yet: Studies in the Role of the Heavenly Dimension in Paul's Thought with Special Reference to His Eschatology* (Cambridge: Cambridge University Press, 1981); Witherington, *Jesus, Paul, and the End of the World*.

31　See Powers, *Salvation through Participation*, 165–66.

32　For discussion see Timothy B. Savage, *Power through Weakness: Paul's Understanding of the Christian Ministry in 2 Corinthians* (Cambridge: Cambridge University Press, 1996); Frank J. Matera, *II Corinthians: A Commentary* (Louisville, Ky.: Westminster John Knox, 2003), 38. Hans Urs von Balthasar addresses both the letters and contemporary ecclesiology in his *Paul Struggles with His Congregation: The Pastoral Message of the Letters to the Corinthians*, trans. Brigitte L. Bojarska (San Francisco: Ignatius Press, 1992).

33　For discussion of 1 Corinthians 11:17-34 see Powers, *Salvation through Participation*, 179–90; Hays, *First Corinthians*, 192–203. Hays links the "remembrance" (1 Cor 11:24-25) to Exodus 12:14, according to which "Passover is to be 'a day of remembrance for you,' a day in which Israel recalls God's deliverance of his people from bondage" (199). For Hays, however, this "remembrance" does not indicate a sacramental making-present, which I find surprising given that the Passover "remembrance" enacts Israel's liturgical participation in a past event. Compare Carol Meyers' reading of Exodus 12:14, in which Meyers argues that the text "indicates that the whole congregation, past, present, and future . . . is involved throughout. A festival including an entire group has the effect of unifying a population and giving people a corporate identity, connecting everyone with the shared past it commemorates" (*Exodus* [Cambridge: Cambridge University Press, 2005], 95). See also Anthony C. Thiselton, *The First Epistle to the Corinthians: A Commentary on the Greek Text* (Grand Rapids: Eerdmans, 2000), 878–82.

34 See Thiselton's wide-ranging discussion of this verse (he translates κοινωνία as "communal participation"): Thiselton, *The First Epistle to the Corinthians*, 761–67. See also Kevin Madigan and Jon Levenson's observation that "the Eucharist as practiced in ancient Christianity was also strongly associated with, and expected to supply the believer a foretaste of, the resurrected life. The Eucharist, in particular, was imagined as a meal, a feast, one that anticipated the eschatological banquet" (Madigan and Levenson, *Resurrection*, 243, cf. 244–45). Given the context of the Last Supper, the eschatological meal should not of course be separated from its sacrificial component. On this point, see my *Sacrifice and Community*.

35 For the intensity of this participation, see Gorman's emphasis on "co-crucifixion" and "theosis" in his *Inhabiting the Cruciform God*, although Gorman surprisingly neglects Paul's sacramental discourse.

36 For discussion see Powers, *Salvation through Participation*, 170–78. In his *Among the Gentiles: Greco-Roman Religion and Christianity* (New Haven: Yale University Press, 2009), Luke Timothy Johnson sharply criticizes Paul's equation of Greco-Roman worship practices with demon worship. I think that Johnson underestimates the deleterious nature of worshipping false gods, a point that Israel's prophets applied not only to the Gentiles but also to Israel, from the Golden Calf (Exodus 32) onward. On this, see Hays, *First Corinthians*, 163–72, esp. 170. Johnson's point that Christian rhetoric could and did result in violence is well taken nonetheless. See also Guy G. Strousma, *The End of Sacrifice: Religious Transformations in Late Antiquity*, trans. Susan Emanuel (Chicago: University of Chicago, 2009).

37 On the difference between Paul and Acts 2:44-45, see Hengel, *Property and Riches in the Early Church*, 35–41.

38 For the importance of this passage in the Christian tradition, see, e.g., Cyril of Alexandria, *On the Unity of Christ*, trans. John Anthony McGuckin (Crestwood, N.Y.: St. Vladimir's Seminary Press, 1995), 59; Francis of Assisi, "Second Version of the Letter to the Faithful," in *Francis and Clare: The Complete Works*, trans. Regis J. Armstrong, O.F.M. Cap., and Ignatius C. Brady, O.F.M. (New York: Paulist Press, 1982), 67. Cf. Michael J. Gorman, *Inhabiting the Cruciform God: Kenosis, Justification, and Theosis in Paul's Narrative Soteriology* (Grand Rapids: Eerdmans, 2009), 89, building esp. on his interpretation of Philippians 2:6-11.

39 See Jan Lambrecht, S.J., *Second Corinthians* (Collegeville, Minn.: Liturgical Press, 1999), 141–43, 147, 151; as well as Verhey, *The Great Reversal*, 118–20.

40 See I–II, q. 106, a. 1, ad 3; I–II, q. 106, a. 3, ad 2; II–II, q. 2, a. 7, ad 3. For further discussion see Emery, "Missions invisibles et missions visibles," esp. 58–63. See

also Avery Dulles, S.J., "Who Can Be Saved?," in Dulles, *Church and Society: The Laurence J. McGinley Lectures, 1988–2007* (New York: Fordham University Press, 2008), 526, 531.

41 See I–II, q. 106, a. 1.

42 I–II, q. 106, a. 3.

43 See I–II, q. 106, a. 4, obj. 2 and ad 2.

44 I–II, q. 106, a. 1; cf. ad 1.

45 See II–II, q. 3, a. 2. See Romanus Cessario, O.P., *Christian Faith and the Theological Life* (Washington, D.C.: Catholic University of America Press, 1996), 121–24. On the relationship of resurrection faith and evangelization in the Book of Acts, see Green, "'Witnesses of His Resurrection,'" 238–42.

46 I–II, q. 106, a. 4. In this article Aquinas points out that Jesus is "the immediate cause of our being brought to the last end." For this reason, against Joachim of Fiore and his followers, Aquinas observes that it would be absurd to suppose that "the Gospel of Christ is not the Gospel of the kingdom" or that "another Gospel, that of the Holy Spirit, is to come." See I–II, q. 106, a. 4, obj. 4 and ad 4; cf. Henri de Lubac, S.J., *De Joachim à Schelling*, vol. 1 of *La postérité spirituelle de Joachim de Flore* (Paris: Éditions Lethielleux, 1979), 143–56.

47 II–II, q. 1, a. 7. In Aquinas' view, those closest in time to Jesus have greater knowledge than that possessed by any later persons: see II–II, q. 1, a. 7, ad 4. This conclusion about the preeminence of the apostles does not deny the development of doctrine in the Church, which Aquinas explains in terms of the creedal affirmations that the Church develops over time so as to refute the errors about God and salvation that inevitably arise (see II–II, q. 1, a. 9).

48 Quoted in II–II, q. 2, a. 6, ad 3. Similarly, the Apostle Paul can dare to say to the Corinthians, "Be imitators of me, as I am of Christ" (1 Cor 11:1; cf. 1 Cor 4:16). Cf. J. Brian Tucker, *You Belong to Christ: Paul and the Formation of Social Identity in 1 Corinthians 1–4* (Eugene, Ore.: Pickwick, 2010), 257–67.

49 II–II, q. 2, a. 6, ad 3. When a person "holds what he chooses to hold, and rejects what he chooses to reject," by contrast, the receptivity that characterizes faith's relationship to God is broken (II–II, q. 5, a. 3).

50 II–II, q. 1, a. 2, ad 2; cf. II–II, q. 1, a. 1. See Cessario, *Christian Faith and the Theological Life*, 51: "Because knowledge in faith initiates a relationship between the one who believes and the very Persons of the blessed Trinity, the virtue of faith is properly referred to as a 'supernatural virtue.'" Cessario goes on to define the virtue of faith according to Aquinas: "The virtue of faith is an infused *habitus* that enables the human person to attain the transcendent God who is the First Truth" (57–58). On the role of propositions in faith, see Cessario, *Christian Faith and the Theological Life*, 57, 75–76.

51 II–II, q. 4, a. 1.

52 II–II, q. 4, a. 1.

53 See II–II, q. 4, a. 3. Cf. Cessario, *Christian Faith and the Theological Life*, 74, 141–46.

54 III, q. 79, a. 1.

55 III, q. 79, a. 2. See Anscar Vonier, O.S.B., *A Key to the Doctrine of the Eucharist* (Bethesda, Md.: Zaccheus Press, 2003), 171. The eschatological significance of the

Eucharist has been demonstrated by Geoffrey Wainwright, *Eucharist and Eschatology* (Peterborough: Epworth Press, 2003). Wainwright does not discuss Aquinas in detail, but he remarks upon the eschatological conclusion of Aquinas' sequence of the Mass of Corpus Christi (*Eucharist and Eschatology*, 65).

56   III, q. 79, a. 1. Cf. Wainwright, *Eucharist and Eschatology*, chap. 2, esp. 72–74. Wainwright comments that "the eucharist is the meal at which the messiah feeds his people as a sign of the feasting in the coming kingdom" (117).

57   III, q. 79, a. 1.

58   Quoted by Aquinas in III, q. 79, a. 1.

59   III, q. 79, a. 1., quoting Augustine's Tractate 26 on the Gospel of John. Cf. Wainwright, *Eucharist and Eschatology*, 183. Augustine takes this insight from Cyprian: see Cyprian, Epistle 69, *Patrologia Latina* 3:1142B. For discussion see Guitmund of Aversa, *Of the Truth of the Body and Blood of Christ in the Eucharist*, trans. Mark G. Vaillancourt (Washington, D.C.: Catholic University of America Press, 2009), II.36, 154.

60   II–II, q. 24, a. 8.

61   II–II, q. 24, a. 8.

62   See i II–II, q. 24, a. 8, *sed contra*. See Wainwright's comments on the "already" and "not yet" of eschatology in relation to the Eucharist: Wainwright, *Eucharist and Eschatology*, 182–83, 189.

63   III, q. 79, a. 2, ad 1.

64   III, q. 79, a. 2, ad 1.

65   See Peter J. Leithart, *1 & 2 Kings* (Grand Rapids: Brazos Press, 2006), 141. Leithart comments that Elijah "is a Moses, desiring to die for the sake of Israel (as the apostle Paul was as well). At the broom tree in the wilderness he is refreshed. He lies down (a symbolic death), but the angel raises him up and feeds him (a symbolic resurrection)" (141).

66   For further discussion see my *Sacrifice and Community*, 94, 106–13.

67   III, q. 61, a. 1, ad 2.

68   III, q. 61, a. 1.

69   III, q. 61, a. 1.

70   III, q. 61, a. 1.

71   III, q. 65, a. 1; cf. III, q. 73, a. 1.

72   Torrell, *Spiritual Master*, 139. See also Bernhard Blankenhorn, O.P., "The Instrumental Causality of the Sacraments: Thomas Aquinas and Louis-Marie Chauvet," *Nova et Vetera* 4 (2006): 255–93, esp. 288–89. For an extension of Aquinas' position see Thomas G. Weinandy, O.F.M. Cap., "The Human Acts of Christ and the Acts That Are the Sacraments," in *Ressourcement Thomism: Sacred Doctrine, the Sacraments, and the Moral Life*, ed. Reinhard Hütter and Matthew Levering (Washington, D.C.: Catholic University of America Press, 2010), 150–68.

73   III, q. 65, a. 3.

74   III, q. 73, a. 3.

75   III, q. 73, a. 4. Since the priest acts *in persona Christi* in the Eucharist, whose sacramental celebration "is an image representing Christ's Passion," it is Christ Jesus who builds up the Church through the Eucharist (see III, q. 83, a. 1 and ad 3). Douglas Farrow rightly cautions that it is not "the function of the *church* to build

up Christ," against the view encouraged by Teilhard de Chardin's Cosmic Christ (*Ascension Theology*, 55). Farrow goes on to say, "the eucharist is left behind as a witness to the world of what actually happens in the ascension, namely, that the entire cosmos is fundamentally reordered to God in Christ. . . . [T]he eucharist is left behind as the means of participation in the offering that Christ in his ascension presents to the Father—himself and the people whose redemption he has won—and in all the benefits that flow from the Father's reception of that offering" (65–66). See also Pope Benedict XVI, *Sacramentum Caritatis* (Vatican City: Libreria Editrice Vaticana, 2007), §11, quoted in Farrow, *Ascension Theology*, 75: "The substantial conversion of bread and wine into the body and blood introduces within creation the principle of a radical change, a sort of 'nuclear fission', to use an image familiar to us today, which penetrates to the heart of all being, a change meant to set off a process which transforms reality, a process leading ultimately to the transfiguration of the entire world, to the point where God will be all in all."

76 See III, q. 73, a. 6.

77 Cf. N. T. Wright, *The Letter to the Romans: Introduction, Commentary, and Reflections*, in Keck, *The New Interpreter's Bible*, vol. 10, 531–36, 546–47.

78 III, q. 79, a. 1, ad 2.

79 For background see Hengel, *Property and Riches in the Early Church*, esp. chap. 1.

80 II–II, q. 31, a. 2, *sed contra*.

81 II–II, q. 31, a. 2.

82 See II–II, q. 31, a. 2, ad 1.

83 II–II, q. 31, a. 3, obj. 1.

84 See II–II, q. 26, aa. 7–8.

85 II–II, q. 31, a. 3.

86 II–II, q. 32, a. 9. See Terence M. O'Connor, O.S.M., *The Obligation of Almsgiving in Common Necessity According to St. Thomas* (Lake Bluff, Ill.: Pontifical Institutum "Angelicum" de Urbe, 1959), 57–59, emphasizing the role of prudence.

87 II–II, q. 183, a. 2.

88 See II–II, q. 184, a. 2.

89 See II–II, q. 184, a. 3, ad 1; II–II, q. 119, a. 2, ad 3: "those who give all their possessions with the intention of following Christ, and banish from their minds all solicitude for temporal things, are not prodigal but perfectly liberal." See also Gary A. Anderson's *Sin: A History* (New Haven: Yale University Press, 2009), 167–81. In his *Sharing Possessions*, Luke Timothy Johnson argues, mistakenly in my view, that "'In the *Rule of Benedict*, as in the Qumran writings, there is no ideology of friendship, or even an ideal of spiritual unity, underlying the community of possessions. . . . In this context, in addition to the other functions it always has in a closed community (setting boundaries, effecting social control), the community of goods serves to strengthen by theological legitimation the hand of authority and accentuate the utter dependence of the individual monk under the abbot" (*Sharing Possessions*, 130). Johnson supposes that patristic and medieval construals of the "state of perfection" have a "slender, superficial, selective, and suspect" biblical basis (131) and lead to abuse of power and "spiritual immaturity, irresponsibility, and alienation" (132). For a better perspective see Hans Urs von Balthasar, *The Christian State of Life*, trans. Sr. Mary Frances McCarthy (San Francisco: Ignatius Press, 1983).

90 II–II, q. 32, a. 6, obj. 3; II–II, q. 32, a. 10, obj. 3. Aquinas notes approvingly the Gloss on 2 Corinthians 8:13, which reads, "he says this, not because it would be better to give in abundance, but because he fears for the weak, and he admonishes them so to give that they lack not for themselves" (II–II, q. 32, a. 10, ad 3).

91 See *Contra impugnantes*, chap. 6, ad 7. For the controversy raging during the period that Aquinas composed this work, see Mark Johnson, introduction to Thomas Aquinas, *St. Thomas Aquinas and the Mendicant Controversies: Three Translations*, trans. John Proctor, O.P. (Leesburg, Va.: Alethes Press, 2007), vii–xxxiv. See also Christopher A. Franks, *He Became Poor: The Poverty of Christ and Aquinas's Economic Teachings* (Grand Rapids: Eerdmans, 2009), 133–48.

92 II–II, q. 117, a. 1, ad 2. He comments that "liberality depends not on the quantity given, but on the heart of the giver" (II–II, q. 117, a. 2, ad 1). See O'Connor, *The Obligation of Almsgiving*, 13–15, 39–45.

93 See Pope Benedict XVI, "On the Encyclical *God Is Love*," in *Where Are the Helpers? Charity and Spirituality*, ed. Paul Josef Cardinal Cordes, trans. Anthony J. Figueiredo with James D. Mixson (Notre Dame: University of Notre Dame Press, 2010), 9–13.

94 II–II, q. 32, a. 1, *sed contra*. See O'Connor, *The Obligation of Almsgiving*, 50–56, 60–73.

95 II–II, q. 32, a. 1, obj. 3. On the necessary connection between the church's faith, eucharistic worship, and almsgiving, see Manfred Lütz, "The Church, Love, and Power," in Cordes, *Where Are the Helpers?*, 139–62.

96 II–II, q. 30, a. 4. See Guy Mansini, O.S.B., "Mercy 'Twice Blest,'" in *John Paul II and St. Thomas Aquinas*, ed. Michael Dauphinais and Matthew Levering (Naples, Fla.: Sapientia Press, 2006), 75–100; O'Connor, *The Obligation of Almsgiving*, 30–33.

97 III, q. 46, a. 1, ad 3.

98 I, q. 38, a. 2.

99 II–II, q. 117, a. 6. See O'Connor, *The Obligation of Almsgiving*, 34–37, 78.

100 II–II, q. 118, a. 1.

101 II–II, q. 118, a. 1, ad 2.

102 II–II, q. 119, a. 2, obj. 1.

103 II–II, q. 119, a. 2.

104 II–II, q. 32, a. 10, ad 2. The reference is to Ambrose, *De Officiis* I.30.

105 II–II, q. 32, a. 10, *sed contra*.

106 II–II, q. 32, a. 9, ad 2.

107 II–II, q. 32, a. 5, *sed contra*.

108 II–II, q. 32, a. 3, ad 1.

109 II–II, q. 184, a. 7, ad 2.

110 II–II, q. 185, a. 7, ad 3.

111 II–II, q. 185, a. 6, ad 1.

112 Bauckham and Hart, *Hope against Hope*, 7. Bauckham and Hart note that "the scientist myth of unambiguous progress through scientific and technological domination of nature is still the ideological context in which many practising scientists think" (19). For the current state of this scientist myth, see Jeffrey Sachs' recent *Common Wealth: Economics for a Crowded Planet* (New York: Penguin

Books, 2008). Sachs argues that in order to avert the coming apocalypse, namely the destruction of the earth's ecosystems, the world community must embrace three steps (which loosely parallel apostolic teaching and fellowship, the liturgical breaking of bread, and almsgiving). First, humans must grow in scientific awareness as taught through the major scientific journals of the day; second, we must come to love the planet and attend regularly to the ways in which it is threatened; and third, we must concentrate upon global sustainable development, above all by consuming less and by having fewer children.

113 Consider, e.g., the apology offered by Richard Hays: "I remain among the wealthy of the world, and the churches in which I have participated for the last twenty years have made only fitful and tepid attempts to respond to the New Testament's imperatives concerning the sharing of possessions. I say 'for the last twenty years' because from 1971 to 1976 my wife and I participated in Metanoia Fellowship, a small church community in Massachusetts that practiced radical economic sharing through a common purse, seeking to have 'all things in common.' The ultimate demise of that particular communal-discipleship initiative in no way vitiates the legitimacy of its vision or excuses our subsequent failure to seek other communal expressions of the New Testament vision for sharing possessions" (*The Moral Vision of the New Testament: Community, Cross, New Creation: A Contemporary Introduction to New Testament Ethics* [New York: HarperCollins, 1996], 468).

114 Ratzinger, *Eschatology*, 117. Cf. Francis X. Durrwell, C.Ss.R., *The Resurrection: A Biblical Study*, trans. Rosemary Sheed (New York: Sheed & Ward, 1960), 270–71, although Durrwell is somewhat too negative toward historical, material existence per se.

115 Horsley and Silberman single out Colossians 3 as a sign of late first-century otherworldly deformation of the gospel (see *The Message and the Kingdom*, 225), but their interpretation of this text fails to perceive the relationship of our passage to Jesus' passage.

CHAPTER 5

1 The theological tradition emphasizes the glorious character of the reward. Commenting on Matthew 19:29, where Jesus promises that those who sacrifice earthly goods "for my name's sake, will receive a hundredfold, and inherit eternal life," Hilary of Poitiers speaks of "heavenly joy," Theodore of Heraclea of "spiritual joys far exceeding earthly ones," and Cyril of Alexandria of "paradise" and the "Jerusalem above." See *Matthew 14–28*, ed. Manlio Simonetti, Ancient Christian Commentary on Scripture, vol. 1b (Downers Grove, Ill.: InterVarsity, 2002), 104–5. Cf. Bauckham and Hart, *Hope against Hope*. Bauckham and Hart emphasize that Scripture's eschatological language should be read as symbolizing a reality far greater than can be imagined.

2 N. T. Wright, *Justification: God's Plan and Paul's Vision* (Downers Grove, Ill.: IVP Academic, 2009), 188.

3 Wright, *Justification*, 188.

4 Anderson, *Sin*, 135. The attempt to remove all "juridical" notions from the theology of salvation assumes that the conceptual framework of "debt" has no place for love. This faulty assumption shapes the approach of Francis X. Durrwell,

C.Ss.R., *Christ Our Passover: The Indispensable Role of Resurrection in Our Salvation,* trans. John F. Craghan (Liguori, Mo.: Liguori, 2004), 48–51, 55–59, 97–101. For Durrwell, the cross is significant solely as the path to resurrection. Cf. Durrwell, *The Resurrection,* 38, 54–55.

5 Anderson, *Sin,* 159–60. See also John Chrysostom's homily "Concerning Almsgiving and the Ten Virgins," in St. John Chrysostom, *On Repentance and Almsgiving,* trans. Gus George Christo (Washington, D.C.: Catholic University of America Press, 1998), 28–42, esp. 30–34. For discussion of private property, almsgiving, and merit in the patristic period, see Hengel, *Property and Riches in the Early Church,* chaps. 10 and 11, on Clement of Alexandria and Cyprian of Carthage, respectively.

6 See Anderson, *Sin,* 157.

7 Ben Witherington III seems to suggest that the answer is yes: "In Judaism, almsgiving was one of the three pillar virtues, but it presupposed one had assets from which to share. What Jesus says amounts to a rejection of conventional Jewish piety that said it was all right to be wealthy so long as one was also generous. Jesus is clearly enunciating a new Jewish ethic here, and it is not surprising that the young man is said to have gone away sad (v. 22). The bar had just been raised on what amounted to being a good or godly person, much less being a disciple of Jesus" (*Matthew* [Macon, Ga.: Smyth & Helwys, 2006], 370).

8 Anderson, *Sin,* 177.

9 Cf. Hengel, *Property and Riches in the Early Church,* 20–21.

10 Anderson, *Sin,* 180.

11 Anderson, *Sin,* 180.

12 Anderson, *Sin,* 187. See also Gorman, *Inhabiting the Cruciform God.*

13 Anderson, *Sin,* 188.

14 See I–II, q. 114, a. 2. On the disproportion between human actions and the glorious reward, see Reinhard Hütter, "*Desiderium Naturale Visionis Dei—Est autem duplex hominis beatitudo sive felicitas*: Some Observations about Lawrence Feingold's and John Milbank's Recent Interventions in the Debate over the Natural Desire to See God," *Nova et Vetera* 5 (2007): 117–18.

15 As can be seen in Michael Root, "Aquinas, Merit, and Reformation Theology after the *Joint Declaration on the Doctrine of Justification,*" *Modern Theology* 20 (2004): 5–22.

16 See III, q. 24, aa. 3–4. On Christ's merit see Joseph P. Wawrykow, *God's Grace and Human Action: "Merit" in the Theology of Thomas Aquinas* (Notre Dame: University of Notre Dame Press, 1995), 238–47, which emphasizes that God ordained or predestined Christ to be the Redeemer and therefore "Christ was given grace to such a degree that Christ's acts were meritorious not only for himself, but even meritorious condignly for others" (247). For the medieval context of Aquinas' views on Christ's merit, see Marschler, *Auferstehung und Himmelfahrt Christi,* 210–311. See also Romanus Cessario, O.P., "Aquinas on Christian Salvation," in Weinandy, Keating, and Yocum, *Aquinas on Doctrine,* 117–37.

17 Cited in III, q. 49, a. 6, *sed contra* and corpus. In his *The Epistle to the Philippians* (London: A. & C. Black, 1998), Markus Bockmuehl states that although this passage should not be thought of "in the sense of a reward," nonetheless it should be

seen as "the moral counterbalance to the acceptance of suffering. Theodicy requires that innocent suffering should be vindicated: only thus can it be meaningful, and only so can God be seen to be just. From the Christian perspective, suffering is never an end in itself. It always stands in a necessary relationship to God's justice" (140–41). This relationship to God's justice is what Aquinas has in view when he speaks of a reward. Joseph Ratzinger comments on Philippians 2:6-11: "Not the grasping audacity of Prometheus but the Son's obedience on the cross is the place where man's divinization is accomplished. Man can become God, not by making himself God, but by allowing himself to be made 'Son.' Here in this gesture of Jesus as the Son, and nowhere else, the Kingdom of God is realized. This is why the first are to be last, and the last first" (*Eschatology*, 64–65).

18 Cited in III, q. 49, a. 6. See also Bockmuehl, *The Epistle to the Philippians*, 141, as well as Wawrykow, *God's Grace and Human Action*, 278–84.

19 III, q. 49, a. 6.

20 See III, q. 47, a. 2. See also I–II, q. 114, a. 1, ad 1, where Aquinas takes up Luke 17:9-10; in this passage Jesus asks rhetorically, "Does he [the master] thank the servant because he did what was commanded? So you also, when you have done all that is commanded you, say, 'We are unworthy servants; we have only done what was our duty.'"

21 See III, q. 8, aa. 1 and 5; III, q. 48, a. 1; III, q. 48, a. 2, ad 1. For discussion see Romanus Cessario, O.P., *The Godly Image: Christ and Salvation in Catholic Thought from Anselm to Aquinas* (Petersham, Mass.: St. Bede's, 1990), 89–90, 160–66; William D. Lynn, S.J., *Christ's Redemptive Merit: The Nature of Its Causality According to St. Thomas* (Rome: Gregorian University Press, 1962), esp. 144–65.

22 III, q. 49, a. 1, ad 5.

23 See I–II, q. 114, a. 3, *sed contra*. See George T. Montague, S.M., *First and Second Timothy, Titus* (Grand Rapids: Baker Academic, 2008), 197–98: "The Greek word [for "crown"] is used for a deposit that waits to be retrieved or a treasure that is held in keeping, waiting to be claimed. As Paul has kept the faith, so the reward is kept for him. . . . The notion of reward implies merit on the part of the one rewarded. In this, Paul agrees with the first-century rabbis. But for the apostle it is the merit of a righteousness that has been attained by faith in Christ (Rom 3:22), a faith that in Paul's case has also been manifested by a total commitment even unto imminent martyrdom."

24 I–II, q. 114, a. 3.

25 I, q. 95, a. 4. Thus "the greater the charity whence our actions proceed, the more perfectly shall we enjoy God" (I, q. 95, a. 4; cf. I–II, q. 114, a. 4). Livio Melina argues that "it is precisely insofar as merit is ultimately rooted in charity, that is, in an interpersonal relationship of friendship with Christ, that the category is definitively freed not only from legalism but also from any suspicion of selfishness." *The Epiphany of Love: Toward a Theological Understanding of Christian Action*, trans. Susan Dawson Vasquez with Stephan Kampowski (Grand Rapids: Eerdmans, 2010), 141.

26 I–II, q. 114, a. 3. Congruent merit requires grace: see Wawrykow, *God's Grace and Human Action*, 198–99; Thomas M. Osborne Jr., "Unbelief and Sin in Thomas Aquinas and the Thomistic Tradition," *Nova et Vetera* 8 (2010): 620–23.

27 I–II, q. 114, a. 1; cf. I–II, q. 114, a. 3: "If it is considered as regards the substance of the work, and inasmuch as it springs from free will, there can be no condignity because of the very great inequality" between humans and God. Aquinas observes that "by all the good we do, we cannot make sufficient return to God, since yet more is his due" (I–II, q. 114, a. 1, obj. 1; cf. III, q. 49, a. 3, ad 2). He interprets Jesus' remark about "unworthy servants" (Luke 17:10) in this light.

28 This point is made by Pope Benedict XVI, *Spe Salvi* (Vatican City: Libreria Editrice Vaticana, 2007), §35: "Certainly we cannot 'build' the Kingdom of God by our own efforts—what we build will always be the kingdom of man with all the limitations proper to our human nature. The Kingdom of God is a gift, and precisely because of this, it is great and beautiful and constitutes the response to our hope. And we cannot—to use the classical expression—'merit' Heaven through our works. Heaven is always more than we could merit, just as being loved is never something 'merited', but always a gift. However, even when we are fully aware that Heaven far exceeds what we can merit, it will always be true that our behavior is not indifferent before God and therefore is not indifferent for the unfolding of history." Cf. *Catechism of the Catholic Church*, §2007.

29 I–II, q. 114, a. 3. Wawrykow explains that adoptive filiation "grants to the child new rights. The child now has the right to, or is owed (*debitur*), what belongs to the parent. The adopted child becomes the parent's heir. Thus, in terms of merit, God's free act of love by which the person is chosen to eternal life creates for the recipient of God's love new rights—rights, that is, to inherit the goal to which God has called him. What we have here, then, is a further instance of Thomas's reflections about the intimate relation which exists between justice and love in God's dealings with the world" (*God's Grace and Human Action*, 195–96n102; cf. 203–4). For the non-competitive character of divine and human action, with a focus on the doctrine of merit, see W. Matthews Grant, "Our Merits, God's Gifts," in *Reason and the Rule of Faith: Conversations in the Tradition with John Paul II*, ed. Christopher J. Thompson and Steven A. Long (New York: University Press of America, 2011), 167–75.

30 *Catechism of the Catholic Church*, §2011. As Wawrykow puts it, "grace elevates people to the Spirit's own level and orients them to the Spirit's own end, God. What belongs 'naturally' to the Spirit comes into the purview of those possessed and directed by the Spirit" (*God's Grace and Human Action*, 194).

31 I–II, q. 114, a. 3. Wawrykow notes that "the person makes an act of charity by which he intends that all he does will be referred to God and done for God's sake. As long as mortal sin does not intervene, this one act is enough to direct all subsequent acts to God, and so to merit" (*God's Grace and Human Action*, 201n110). For further discussion, in the context of ecumenical debate, see Christopher Malloy, *Engrafted into Christ: A Critique of the Joint Declaration* (New York: Peter Lang, 2005), 282–83, 289–93.

32 *Catechism of the Catholic Church*, §2008. The *Catechism* goes on to say, "Filial adoption, in making us partakers by grace in the divine nature, can bestow *true merit* on us as a result of God's gratuitous justice. This is our right by grace, the full right of love, making us 'co-heirs' with Christ and worthy of obtaining 'the promised inheritance of eternal life.' The merits of our good works are the gifts of divine goodness" (§2009; the internal quotation is from the Council of Trent).

33 Cited in I–II, q. 114, a. 8, obj. 3. The RSV changes this to "what has been entrusted to me," but adds a note that gives the literal translation: "what I have entrusted to him." As Wawrykow says, "Meriting, then, is a perfection. It illustrates the greater dignity and worth of the human being" (*God's Grace and Human Action*, 242). The reward of Paul's good works is eschatological rather than temporal; temporal goods have to do with merit only when they are given to help us on our way to eternal union with God: see I–II, q. 114, a. 10; cf. III, q. 69, a. 3. See also Wawrykow's comparison of I–II, q. 114, a. 10 to Aquinas' *Commentary on Job*: *God's Grace and Human Action*, 228–32.

34 For Aquinas on justification, see Keating, "Justification, Sanctification and Divinization in Thomas Aquinas."

35 III, q. 24, a. 4, ad 3. For the same point see the *Catechism of the Catholic Church*, §2010.

36 I, q. 114, a. 5, ad 2.

37 III, q. 48, a. 2; cf. III, q. 69, a. 2. Aquinas comments, "The head and members are as one mystic person; and therefore Christ's satisfaction belongs to all the faithful as being his members" (III, q. 48, a. 2, ad 1).

38 I–II, q. 114, a. 2, ad 1. For Aquinas, all merit flows from God's predestination of Jesus as "the cause of our salvation" (III, q. 24, a. 4, ad 3). He observes that "man's merit with God only exists on the presupposition of the divine ordination, so that man obtains from God, as a reward of his operation, what God gave him the power of operation for" (I–II, q. 114, a. 1). For discussion see Rudolph Schnackenburg, *The Epistle to the Ephesians: A Commentary*, trans. Helen Heron (Edinburgh: T&T Clark, 1991), 50–56; Wawrykow, *God's Grace and Human Action*, 266–76; Malloy, *Engrafted into Christ*, 305–6. Cf. Augustine, *On the Predestination of the Saints*, in Augustine, *Four Anti-Pelagian Writings*, trans. John A. Mourant and William J. Collinge (Washington, D.C.: Catholic University of America Press, 1992), 218–70.

39 See the *Catechism of the Catholic Church*, §2010.

40 Cited in I–II, q. 114, a. 8. Regarding this article, Wawrykow argues that Aquinas has esp. in view "the increase of *habitual* grace and of the habit of charity" (*God's Grace and Human Action*, 224). Wawrykow goes on to explain that "the use of the theological virtue does not directly effect the growth of the virtue, as is the case with acquired virtue. The act of the theological virtue does not create more of the virtue. As supernatural, it is caused and created only by God. Rather, under the influence of God the possessor of the virtue simply disposes himself for more of the virtue. The actual increase of the virtue, the granting of a more intense possession of it, remains the work of God" (225).

41 See II–II, q. 24, a. 6, ad 1. See Wawrykow, *God's Grace and Human Action*, 226, drawing on Lynn, *Christ's Redemptive Merit*, 54–60. See also Malloy, *Engrafted into Christ*, 285–89.

42 See I–II, q. 114, aa. 7, 9.

43 I–II, q. 114, a. 6.

44 I–II, q. 114, a. 6. See Wawrykow, *God's Grace and Human Action*, 216–19.

45 I–II, q. 114, a. 6, ad 3.

46 II–II, q. 32, a. 1, *sed contra*.

47 See II–II, q. 32, a. 1, ad 3. On the relationship of believers' acts of satisfaction to Christ's superabundant satisfaction, see Cessario, *The Godly Image*, 118–21, 197–200; O'Connor, *The Obligation of Almsgiving*, 86–87; François Daguet, *Théologie du dessein divin chez Thomas d'Aquin. Finis omnium Ecclesia* (Paris: J. Vrin, 2003), 504–6.

48 Cited in II–II, q. 32, a. 10, *sed contra*.

49 Cited in II–II, q. 32, a. 10, obj. 3.

50 Farrow, *Ascension and Ecclesia*, 164.

51 I–II, q. 114, a. 10.

52 See also Ratzinger, *Eschatology*, 98–101.

CHAPTER 6

1 Lewis Ayres, "The Soul and the Reading of Scripture: A Note on Henri De Lubac," *Scottish Journal of Theology* 61 (2008): 183n22. Ayres observes, "Deep engagement with notions of soul in Hellenised Judaism around or just before the time of Christ is demonstrated by texts such as 2 Macc. 6:20, 2 Enoch 23:5, Test. Job 20:3. Within the New Testament James 1:21 and 5:20 demonstrate the non-controversial use of such language (cf. 1 Pet. 1:22)" (177n9).

2 See Ayres, "The Soul and the Reading of Scripture," 186. See also Alfred J. Freddoso, "Good News, Your Soul Hasn't Died Quite Yet," *Proceedings of the American Catholic Philosophical Association* 75 (2001): 87.

3 See the *Catechism of the Catholic Church*, §§364–66. For background see Ratzinger, *Eschatology*, 140, 150. By contrast, Simon Tugwell, O.P., argues that "Christian belief does not require the ascription of immortality or even life to the soul on its own. Such dogmatic authority as has been given to the phrase 'the immortality of the soul' can be squared with the mainstream of christian tradition most simply by interpreting it as insisting on the immortality of the human person, and that can be taken as meaning essentially the belief that, by the act of God, there is something there even after death which can be judged by God and awarded either eternal life or everlasting damnation" (*Human Immortality and the Redemption of Death* [Springfield, Ill.: Templegate, 1990], 164; cf. 81–82). But if God must act to preserve "something" of the human person after death, what is this "something"? The attempt to claim that God makes "something" of the human person immortal after the death of the whole human person presents difficulties more serious than Tugwell grants, even if Tugwell is right to say that the fundamental point of controversy is "post mortem life of the person versus extinction of the person" (122, cf. 108, 113).

4 In Alasdair MacIntyre's words, Descartes provided "a picture of human nature according to which we are animals and in addition something else. . . . The force of the 'and' is to suggest that this second nature can, at least in the most important respects, only be accounted for in its own terms. Its relation to our given biological nature is thought of as external and contingent" (*Dependent Rational Animals: Why Human Beings Need the Virtues* [Chicago: Open Court, 1999], 49–50). For scholastic background to Descartes on the soul, see Roger Ariew, *Descartes and the Last Scholastics* (Ithaca: Cornell University Press, 1999). For his part, MacIntyre argues that "[t]he teleological directedness of the human body as a complex whole

engaged in understanding itself is not something derivable from or to be understood in terms of either its physical or its physiological composition" ("What Is a Human Body?," in MacIntyre, *The Tasks of Philosophy: Selected Essays*, vol. 1 [Cambridge: Cambridge University Press, 2006], 102).

5   See Joel B. Green, *Body, Soul, and Human Life: The Nature of Humanity in the Bible* (Grand Rapids: Baker Academic, 2008). For the opposing view, see esp. Cooper, *Body, Soul, and Life Everlasting.*

6   Nancey Murphy, *Bodies and Souls, or Spirited Bodies?* (Cambridge: Cambridge University Press, 2006), 15.

7   John Cooper distances the biblical doctrine of the spiritual soul more sharply from Greek philosophy than I think necessary to do, although my argument largely accords with his. Cooper writes, "A major charge is that dualism is an imposition of Greek philosophy and Hellenistic religion on Christian anthropology which distorts the biblical picture of human nature. Our defense has been that dualism is implicit in the biblical account of what happens at death, that the New Testament employs an anthropology already developed in Judaism and rooted in the Old Testament. This anthropology superficially resembles Hellenistic views in that it, too, affirms personal survival of death, but its functional holism and affirmation of bodily existence set it sharply against them. Affirming dualism does not commit one to endorsing Greek thought or claiming that the New Testament has been shaped by Hellenistic religion. It is maintaining something inherently biblical" (*Body, Soul, and Life Everlasting*, 179).

8   Murphy, *Bodies and Souls, or Spirited Bodies?*, ix. For my summary here, I use portions of my review of her book in *National Catholic Bioethics Quarterly* 7 (2007): 635–38.

9   Murphy, *Bodies and Souls, or Spirited Bodies?*, ix.

10 For the phrase "nonreductive physicalism," see Murphy, *Bodies and Souls, or Spirited Bodies?*, 69, 106–7. Along these lines, see also the essays in *Whatever Happened to the Soul? Scientific and Theological Portraits of Human Nature*, ed. Warren S. Brown, Nancey Murphy, and H. Newton Malony (Minneapolis: Fortress, 1998), as well as Segal, *Life after Death*, 341–44.

11 Murphy, *Bodies and Souls, or Spirited Bodies?*, 83.

12 Murphy, *Bodies and Souls, or Spirited Bodies?*, 65.

13 Murphy, *Bodies and Souls, or Spirited Bodies?*, 69.

14 Murphy, *Bodies and Souls, or Spirited Bodies?*, 66.

15 Murphy, *Bodies and Souls, or Spirited Bodies?*, 69.

16 Murphy, *Bodies and Souls, or Spirited Bodies?*, 69.

17 I, q. 76, a. 6, ad 1. For discussion of the soul as the form of the body (rather than as an angelic substance) see Stephen L. Brock, "The Physical Status of the Spiritual Soul in Thomas Aquinas," *Nova et Vetera* 3 (2005): 231–57. Ratzinger finds in Aquinas' position the union of the best insights of Plato and Aristotle: "The soul belongs to the body as 'form,' but that which is the form of the body is still spirit. It makes man a person and opens him to immortality. Compared with all the conceptions of the soul available in antiquity, this notion of the soul is quite novel. It is a product of Christian faith, and of the exigencies of faith for human thought" (Ratzinger, *Eschatology*, 149). See also John Goyette, "St. Thomas on the Unity of

Substantial Form," *Nova et Vetera* 7 (2009): 781–90. Goyette is responding esp. to Terence L. Nichols, "Aquinas's Concept of Substantial Form and Modern Science," *International Philosophical Quarterly* 36 (1996): 303–18.

18 I, q. 76, a. 1; cf. I, q. 77, a. 4. For discussion see Eleonore Stump, *Aquinas* (London: Routledge, 2003), 191–216.

19 See I, q. 79, a. 4, ad 4.

20 Edward Feser, *Aquinas: A Beginner's Guide* (Oxford: Oneworld, 2009), 144.

21 For a more thorough discussion, see Edward Feser, *The Last Superstition: A Refutation of the New Atheism* (South Bend, Ind.: St. Augustine's Press, 2008), 229–47.

22 W. Norris Clarke, S.J., "The Immediate Creation of the Human Soul by God and Some Contemporary Challenges," in Clarke, *The Creative Retrieval of St. Thomas Aquinas: Essays in Thomistic Philosophy, New and Old* (New York: Fordham University Press, 2009), 182; cf. 187 in response to Ernan McMullin. Although he does not discuss Murphy, see also Tobias Kläden's *Mit Leib und Seele . . . Die* mind-brain-*Debatte in der Philosophie des Geistes und die* anima-forma-corporis-*Lehre des Thomas von Aquin* (Regensburg: Verlag Friedrich Pustet, 2005). For historical background see Dominik Perler, "Alter und neuer Naturalismus. Eine historische Hinführung zur aktuellen Debatte über die Leib-Seele-Problematik," in *Naturalisierung des Geistes—Sprachlosigkeit der Theologie? Die Mind-Brain-Debatte und das christliche Menschenbild*, ed. Peter Neuner (Freiburg: Herder, 2003), 15–42.

23 Derek S. Jeffreys, "The Soul Is Alive and Well: Non-reductive Physicalism and Emergent Mental Properties," *Theology and Science* 2 (2004): 220. See also Edward Feser, *Philosophy of Mind*, rev. ed. (Oxford: Oneworld, 2006), 234. In her response to Jeffreys, which functions as a response to Clarke as well, Murphy emphasizes that modern science (and philosophy) can no longer accept Aristotelian-Thomistic metaphysics. This point, however, is exactly what is being contested. See Murphy, "Response to Derek Jeffreys," *Theology and Science* 2 (2004): 227–30.

24 Clarke, "The Immediate Creation of the Human Soul," 185. For discussion see also Stewart Goetz and Charles Taliaferro, *A Brief History of the Soul* (Oxford: Wiley-Blackwell, 2011), 156–81; Stump, *Aquinas*, 200–210; Feser, *The Last Superstition*, 208–9. On the cost of doing without formal causality in action theory, Clarke cites Alicia Juarrero, *Dynamics in Action: Intentional Behavior as a Complex System* (Cambridge, Mass.: MIT Press, 1999).

25 See Feser, *The Last Superstition*, 127–29.

26 I, q. 84, a. 7.

27 I, q. 89, a. 1, obj. 2.

28 I, q. 89, a. 1. See Gilles Emery, O.P., "The Unity of Man, Body and Soul, in St. Thomas Aquinas," in Emery, *Trinity, Church, and the Human Person: Thomistic Essays* (Naples, Fla.: Sapientia Press, 2007), 230–33. Peter Geach remarks, "I am of the mind of Aquinas about the survival of 'separated souls', when he says in his commentary on I Corinthians that my soul is not I, and if only my soul is saved then I am not saved nor is any man. Even if Christians believe there are 'separate souls', the Christian hope is the glorious resurrection of the body, not the survival of a 'separated soul'" (*God and the Soul*, 2nd ed. [South Bend, Ind.: St. Augustine's Press, 2000], 40).

29 See I, q. 89, a. 1, as well as Aquinas, *Summa contra gentiles* IV: Salvation, trans.

Charles J. O'Neil (Notre Dame: University of Notre Dame Press, 1975), chap. 79. For further discussion see Anton C. Pegis, "Between Immortality and Death: Some Further Reflections on the *Summa Contra Gentiles*," *Monist* 58 (1974): 1–15, esp. his concluding comments: "If we accept what St. Thomas is saying, then, on the same philosophical ground on which he established the unity of man, we must say that death is a spiritual event. The body dies within the same spiritual world of the soul in which it lived" (15). Cf. Randall S. Rosenberg, "Being-Toward-a-Death-Transformed: Aquinas on the Naturalness and Unnaturalness of Human Death," *Angelicum* 83 (2006): 747–66.

30 I, q. 89, a. 1. For discussion see Carl N. Still, "Do We Know All after Death? Thomas Aquinas on the Disembodied Soul's Knowledge," *Proceedings of the American Catholic Philosophical Association* 75 (2001): 107–19.

31 See I, q. 89, a. 1, ad 3. John Haldane describes the situation of separated souls by introducing the notion of "residual substances," by which he means "a something to which are transferred certain powers hitherto possessed and exercised by a more extensive and more potent substance." See Haldane, "The Examined Death," in Haldane, *Reasonable Faith* (London: Routledge, 2010), 158; see also in the same volume his "Philosophy, Death, and Immortality," 173–74. See also Feser, *Aquinas*, 157–61; Reginald Garrigou-Lagrange, O.P., *Life Everlasting and the Immensity of the Soul*, trans. Patrick Cummins, O.S.B. (Rockford, Ill.: Tan Books, 1991), 86–90.

32 See Murphy, *Bodies and Souls, or Spirited Bodies*, 19. For discussion see Ratzinger, *Eschatology*, 124–29. Ratzinger finds that like other Second-Temple Jews, the New Testament authors presume the existence of the intermediate state without specifying the "anthropological 'substrate'" that makes a conscious intermediate state possible (128).

33 Murphy, *Bodies and Souls, or Spirited Bodies*, 19.

34 Murphy, *Bodies and Souls, or Spirited Bodies*, 21.

35 Green, *Body, Soul, and Human Life*, 45.

36 See Green, *Body, Soul, and Human Life*, 34.

37 Green, *Body, Soul, and Human Life*, 164; for the diversity of Judaism in the Second-Temple period, see 51, 60. Murphy draws from an essay included in Green's book but previously published as Joel B. Green, "Eschatology and the Nature of Humans: A Reconsideration of Pertinent Biblical Evidence," *Science and Christian Belief* 14 (2002): 33–50. Jerry L. Walls raises concerns about Green's position that are similar to my own: see Walls, *Heaven*, 98–102.

38 E. P. Sanders, "Did Paul's Theology Develop?," in *The Word Leaps the Gap: Essays on Scripture and Theology in Honor of Richard B. Hays*, ed. J. Ross Wagner, C. Kavin Rowe, and A. Katherine Grieb (Grand Rapids: Eerdmans, 2008), 340. For the view that Paul rejects any form of body-soul dualism, see Hans Dieter Betz, "The Concept of the 'Inner Human Being' (*ho esō anthrōpos*) in the Anthropology of Paul," *New Testament Studies* 46 (2000): 315–41. For discussion of the vast array of early and mid-twentieth century exegesis on 2 Corinthians 5, much of it still valuable, see André Feuillet, "La Demeure céleste et la Destinée des chrétiens. Exégèse de *II Cor.*, v, 1-10 et contribution à l'étude des fondements de l'eschatologie paulinienne," *Recherches de science religieuse* 44 (1956): 161–92, 360–402. Indebted

to Feuillet, Hans Urs von Balthasar argues that the intermediate state unites the believer to "Christ's transfigured humanity" and thus is not purely spiritual (Balthasar, "Some Points of Eschatology," 262).

39 See James D. G. Dunn, *The Theology of Paul the Apostle* (Grand Rapids: Eerdmans, 1998), 489.

40 Lincoln, *Paradise Now and Not Yet*, 69. As we saw in chapter 1, N. T. Wright also affirms that Paul here has in view a conscious "intermediate state." See Wright, *The Resurrection of the Son of God*, 367, 369.

41 Green, *Body, Soul, and Human Life*, 177. He treats Philippians 1:23 only in a footnote. For similar approaches see two essays in Longenecker, *Life in the Face of Death*: Murray J. Harris, "Resurrection and Immortality in the Pauline Corpus," 164, and Richard Longenecker, "Is There Development in Paul's Resurrection Thought?," 194–97.

42 W. D. Davies and Dale C. Allison Jr., *Commentary on Matthew VIII–XVIII*, vol. 2 of *The Gospel According to Saint Matthew* (New York: T&T Clark, 1991), 206.

43 Rudolph Schnackenburg, *The Gospel of Matthew*, trans. Robert R. Barr (Grand Rapids: Eerdmans, 2002), 100.

44 See Stephen E. Fowl, *Philippians* (Grand Rapids: Eerdmans, 2005), 51.

45 Gordon D. Fee, *Philippians* (Downers Grove, Ill.: InterVarsity, 1999), 72.

46 Fee, *Philippians*, 72. See Ernest Best, *Second Corinthians* (Louisville, Ky.: John Knox Press, 1987), 48. The view that the dead are resurrected at the instant of death is advocated by Karl Rahner, S.J., in his "'The Intermediate State,'" in *Jesus, Man, and the Church*, trans. Margaret Kohl, vol. 17 of Rahner, *Theological Investigations* (New York: Crossroad, 1981), 114–24. For this view see also Gisbert Greshake, *Auferstehung der Toten: Ein Beitrag zur gegenwärtigen theologischen Diskussion über die Zukunft der Geschichte* (Essen: Ludgerus, 1969), 360–414; Gisbert Greshake and Jacob Kremer, *Resurrectio Mortuorum. Zum theologischen Verständnis der leiblichen Auferstehung* (Darmstadt: Wissenschaftliche Buchgesellschaft, 1986); Murray J. Harris, *Raised Immortal: Resurrection and Immortality in the New Testament* (Grand Rapids: Eerdmans, 1985); Bernard Prusak, "Bodily Resurrection in Catholic Perspectives," *Theological Studies* 61 (2000): 82–87, 92–99; Peter C. Phan, *Eternity in Time: A Study of Karl Rahner's Eschatology* (London: Associated University Presses, 1988), 116–34, 176–77; Phan, "Contemporary Context and Issues in Eschatology," *Theological Studies* 55 (1994): 520–27. For criticism of Greshake's and Rahner's position, see Bryan Kromholtz, O.P., "La résurrection au dernier jour selon saint Thomas d'Aquin," *Revue Thomiste* 109 (2009): 55–78; Ratzinger, *Eschatology*, 107–12; Wolfhart Pannenberg, *Systematic Theology*, vol. 3, trans. Geoffrey W. Bromiley (Grand Rapids: Eerdmans, 1998), 577–80; Cooper, *Body, Soul, and Life Everlasting*, 164–69. See also the concerns raised by the Congregation for the Doctrine of the Faith's *The Reality after Death*, published in *Acta Apostolicae Sedis* 71 (1979): 939–43; and by the International Theological Commission's "Some Current Questions in Eschatology," published in *Irish Theological Quarterly* 58 (1992): 209–43. For discussion of Rahner's and Ratzinger's positions in light of the work of Emmanuel Levinas, see Josef Wohlmuth, *Mysterium der Verwandlung. Eine Eschatologie aus katholischer Perspektive im Gespräch mit jüdischem Denken der Gegenwart* (Paderborn: Ferdinand Schöningh, 2005), 176–87.

47 Green, *Body, Soul, and Human Life*, 179.

48 Green, *Body, Soul, and Human Life*, 179. In response to this position, Norris Clarke remarks, "This is the second serious philosophical flaw in the nonreductive physicalists' position. . . . They admit that when we die, we die totally; there is nothing left of my original uniqueness, nothing but aggregates of more elementary material particles. What then about the Resurrection at the Last Day—an essential ingredient of any authentic Christian belief? Their answer is that God 'recreates' the original *me* again at the appropriate later time. But this is a metaphysical impossibility. The recreated entity might be a clone, *like* me in many ways, but not the *same* unique personal *me*, because the new unity, the self—the 'I'—organizing the similar body is not the same as me, for the simple reason that it never experienced the same personal life, the same *story* with all its challenges, successes and failures, that became an inseparable part of my identity before my death. That self is simply gone, and not even the omnipotence of God can do what is a metaphysical impossibility: recreate the identical being that existed before, with no bond of continuity on the personal level between the before and the after" ("The Immediate Creation of the Human Soul," 188). The same point is made by Ratzinger, *Eschatology*, 106.

49 Green, *Body, Soul, and Human Life*, 159.

50 Green, *Body, Soul, and Human Life*, 164.

51 In addition to Matthew 10:28, Philippians 1:21-23, and 2 Corinthians 5:6-8, Green should have treated Wisdom of Solomon 1:4, 2:2-3, 3:1-5. For the significance of Wisdom of Solomon's teachings, see Norman Russell, *The Doctrine of Deification in the Greek Patristic Tradition* (Oxford: Oxford University Press, 2004), 55–58; John J. Collins, *Jewish Wisdom in the Hellenistic Age* (Louisville, Ky.: Westminster John Knox, 1997), 178–95.

52 Murphy, *Bodies and Souls, or Spirited Bodies?*, 139–40; cf. her "The Resurrection Body and Personal Identity: Possibilities and Limits of Eschatological Knowledge," in Peters, Russell, and Welker, *Resurrection*, 202–18.

53 For contemporary interpretation of 2 Peter 1:4, see Bauckham, *Jude, 2 Peter*, 180–82. See also James Starr, "Does 2 Peter 1:4 Speak of Deification?," in *Partakers of the Divine Nature: The History and Development of Deification in the Christian Traditions*, ed. Michael J. Christensen and Jeffery A. Wittung (Grand Rapids: Baker Academic, 2007), 81–92; Finlan, "Second Peter's Notion of Divine Participation," 32–50. See also Witherington, *A Socio-Rhetorical Commentary on 1–2 Peter*, 304–5, as well as the treatment of Philo and of Jewish apocalyptic texts in Russell, *The Doctrine of Deification in the Greek Patristic Tradition*, 58–71.

54 Nichols, *Death and Afterlife*, 123. This point is elided in Jürgen Moltmann's attempt to revise the Platonic immortal soul, so that the soul describes not a "substance" but "a relationship of the whole person to the immortal God" (Moltmann, "Is There Life after Death?," 244).

55 Gregory of Nyssa, *On the Soul and the Resurrection*, 28.

56 Murphy, *Bodies and Souls, or Spirited Bodies?*, 21.

CHAPTER 7

1 Thiselton, *First Epistle to the Corinthians*, 1070.

2   Rudolph Schnackenburg, *The Johannine Epistles: Introduction and Commentary*, trans. Reginald and Ilse Fuller (New York: Crossroad, 1992), 160.

3   Schnackenburg, *The Johannine Epistles*; cf. Horst Balz, "Early Christian Faith as 'Hope against Hope,'" in Reventlow, *Eschatology in the Bible*, 31–48.

4   Wright, *Surprised by Hope*, 101. God will give our bodies an "incorruptible physicality," effected by "God's *pneuma*, God's breath of new life, the energizing power of God's new creation" (156).

5   Jürgen Moltmann, *In the End—the Beginning: The Life of Hope*, trans. Margaret Kohl (Minneapolis: Fortress, 2004), 139. Cf. Moltmann, *The Coming of God: Christian Eschatology*, trans. Margaret Kohl (Minneapolis: Fortress, 1996), 259–319, 336–39. Moltmann relies on biblical images of feasting and song to convey the glorious participation of the blessed in the eternal cosmic liturgy, "the heavenly praise and the uttered joy in existence of all other living things" in "the communication of his divine plenitude" (*The Coming of God*, 338–39). For the development of Moltmann's eschatology over the course of his career, see Schwarz, *Eschatology*, 146–51.

6   Ratzinger, *Eschatology*, 192.

7   Ratzinger, *Eschatology*, 192. For engagement with Ratzinger, see Josef Wohlmuth, *Mysterium der Verwandlung*, 164–72 and elsewhere.

8   Wright, *Surprised by Hope*, 278, 105.

9   Carlo Leget, "Eschatology," in *The Theology of Thomas Aquinas*, ed. Rik Van Nieuwenhove and Joseph Wawrykow (Notre Dame: University of Notre Dame Press, 2005), 381. See also Leget, *Living with God*, 245–46. Leget offers an instructive comparison of Aquinas' theology of creation with Aquinas' eschatology: Leget, *Living with God*, 210–12. I should mention here Paul O'Callaghan's *Christ Our Hope: An Introduction to Eschatology* (Washington, D.C.: Catholic University of America Press, 2011). Although O'Callaghan's masterful book appeared too late for me to integrate it into this study, a brief examination of his book suggests to me that my conclusions in this chapter (and in chap. 1) accord with his.

10   I–II, q. 3, a. 8. See Servais Pinckaers, O.P., *The Sources of Christian Ethics*, trans. Mary Thomas Noble, O.P. (Washington, D.C.: Catholic University of America Press, 1995), 182–90.

11   I–II, q. 2, a. 8. Christoph Schönborn notes, "According to some contemporary thinkers, the 'megalomania of the yearning' for deification is the cause of the threats that weigh down upon our world: the destruction of the world and the self-destruction of man. The solution, however, lies not (as is asserted) in extinguishing this yearning but in its correct orientation. It is not the greatness of the yearning but its perversion that threatens man. If this yearning is kept closed in on itself, it can only destroy man. If it is opened out onto its true goal, it can lead to receiving God's bliss, which is the only valid answer to human yearning" (*From Death to Life*, 62–63).

12   I–II, q. 2, a. 8, ad 1.

13   I–II, q. 4, a. 8. This distinction between what is "essential" to perfect happiness, and what pertains to happiness' *bene esse*, ensures that Aquinas' account of happiness remains God-centered. The risk, however, is that Aquinas' position could be misread as an individualistic account of happiness. See Garrigou-Lagrange, *Life*

Everlasting and the Immensity of the Soul, 229, 241–47; Ray C. Petry, "The Social Character of Heavenly Beatitude According to the Thought of St. Thomas Aquinas," *Thomist* 7 (1944): 65–79; Petry, *Christian Eschatology and Social Thought: A Historical Essay on the Social Implications of Some Selected Aspects in Christian Eschatology to A.D. 1500* (Nashville: Abingdon, 1956), 256–58, 359–61. See also Henri de Lubac, S.J., *Catholicism: A Study of Dogma in Relation to the Corporate Destiny of Mankind*, trans. Lancelot C. Sheppard (New York: Sheed & Ward, 1958), 52–53. For the reconciliation of individuals and society in the eschatological kingdom of God, see also Pannenberg, *Systematic Theology*, vol. 3, 580–86.

14 I, q. 12, a. 2. For discussion of I, q. 12, aa. 1–7, see Pierre-Yves Maillard, *La vision de Dieu chez Thomas d'Aquin. Une lecture de l'"In Ioannem" à la lumière de ses sources augustiniennes* (Paris: J. Vrin, 2001), 189–92, 196–97, 201–2. For the philosophical background to Aquinas' approach, see Christian Trottmann, *La vision béatifique. Des disputes scolastiques à sa définition par Benoît XII* (Rome: École française de Rome, 1995), 305–9. With remarkable thoroughness, Trottmann details the twelfth–fourteenth-century debates about the intellectual mode of the beatific vision. See also William J. Hoye, *Actualitas Omnium Actuum: Man's Beatific Vision of God as Apprehended by Thomas Aquinas* (Meisenheim am Glan: Verlag Anton Hain, 1975).

15 I, q. 12, a. 6, obj. 3. See the overview of John Saward, drawing esp. upon Aquinas and Denys the Carthusian: Saward, *Sweet and Blessed Country*, 27–35, 41–45.

16 I, q. 12, a. 6, obj. 3.

17 I, q. 12, a. 3, ad 1.

18 I, q. 12, a. 4, *sed contra*. See Maillard, *La vision de Dieu chez Thomas d'Aquin*, 87–88, 193.

19 See Leget, *Living with God*, 224: "God did not need to create for any goal. For the blessed the same is true: there is no further end apart from sharing in God's beatitude. Both motives flow together in the notion of eternal life: in giving eternal life, the triune God gives Himself, and giving oneself is a sign of great love. In eternal life man is assimilated to God's overflowing goodness (or love), sharing the same copious beatitude which is the origin of creation." For a theology of "glory," see Hans Urs von Balthasar, *Seeing the Form*, trans. Erasmo Leiva-Merikakis, vol. 1 of *The Glory of the Lord: A Theological Aesthetics* (San Francisco: Ignatius Press, 1987).

20 I, q. 12, a. 6.

21 I, q. 12, a. 6. Cf. Leget, *Living with God*, 222; Russell Hittinger, "When It Is More Excellent to Love Than to Know: The Other Side of Thomistic 'Realism,'" *Proceedings of the American Catholic Philosophical Association* 57 (1983): 171–79.

22 I, q. 12, a. 7, ad 1. Nothing could be further from Aquinas' approach than Caroline Walker Bynum's claim that "[t]he majority opinion among thirteenth- and fourteenth-century theologians stressed the afterlife as stasis, blessedness as the stilling of desire" (*The Resurrection of the Body*, 289). Richard Bauckham and Trevor Hart point out that "it is especially in the modern period that dissatisfaction with the 'static' image of eternal life as achieved perfection has grown. This must reflect the general ethos of the modern period in the West. Modern people do not want to come to rest and to enjoy the fruit of their labours, because it is the struggle to achieve and the vision of further progress that really give pleasure. . . . Christian

eschatology maintains that God himself is the goal for which we were created and which, once attained, will prove endlessly satisfying. If God is really God, it must be better to find God than eternally to seek God" (*Hope against Hope*, 157–58).

23 I, q. 12, a. 7, ad 1.

24 I, q. 12, a. 7, ad 2 and 3. God will cause himself to be wholly "seen" by the blessed, even though "not as perfectly as he is capable of being seen," because he is infinite. See Garrigou-Lagrange, *Life Everlasting and the Immensity of the Soul*, 216–30, 241–42.

25 Wright, *Surprised by Hope*, 105.

26 Bauckham and Hart, *Hope against Hope*, 159.

27 I, q. 12, a. 10; see also I, q. 10, a. 3. On this topic, treating an extraordinary range of scholastic theologians from Thomas Aquinas through John of St. Thomas, see Carl J. Peter, *Participated Eternity in the Vision of God: A Study of the Opinion of Thomas Aquinas and His Commentators on the Duration of the Acts of Glory* (Rome: Gregorian University Press, 1964). See also Leget, *Living with God*, 218–21, as well as the word study of *aeternitas* in Aquinas and other thirteenth-century thinkers, in Rory Fox, *Time and Eternity in Mid-Thirteenth-Century Thought* (Oxford: Oxford University Press, 2006), 282–308.

28 I, q. 10, a. 3, ad 2. Simon Tugwell makes a helpful observation here: "We also need to bear in mind the standard procedures of negative theology. To say that beatitude is eternal and therefore non-successive does not mean that all the richness of time is lost, it means that it is retained, but without the concomitant impoverishment which is inseparable from successiveness. . . . To say that beatitude is eternal and therefore not, in any ordinary sense, in time, is to claim for it all the intensity which we sometimes find in peculiarly rich moments of enjoyment, but in such a way that there is no longer any inevitable decline from that intensity, as there must always be in time. It is to suggest that, though such moments cannot in any way be prolonged—duration can only be the death of them—they can still be kept" (*Human Immortality and the Redemption of Death*, 153–54). The insistence that beatitude as a participation in divine eternity is thereby the negation, rather than the fulfillment, of history is commonplace but in my view mistaken: see Anselm K. Min, *Paths to the Triune God: An Encounter between Aquinas and Recent Theologies* (Notre Dame: University of Notre Dame Press, 2005), 164; Ted Peters, *God—The World's Future*, 2nd ed. (Minneapolis: Fortress, 2000), 332–34.

29 Plato, *Phaedrus* 247c, in Plato, *The Collected Dialogues*, 494.

30 I, q. 45, a. 6. For this theme in Aquinas' *Commentary on the Sentences*, see Gilles Emery, O.P., "Trinity and Creation: The Trinitarian Principle of the Creation in the Commentaries of Albert the Great, Bonaventure, and Thomas Aquinas on the *Sentences*," in Emery, *Trinity in Aquinas* (Ypsilanti, Mich.: Sapientia Press, 2003), 53–70; cf. Emery, *La Trinité créatrice: Trinité et creation dans les commentaires aux Sentences de Thomas d'Aquin et de ses précurseurs Albert le Grand et Bonaventure* (Paris: Vrin, 1995). See also Hans Urs von Balthasar, "Creation and Trinity," *Communio* 15 (1988): 285–93.

31 I, q. 45, a. 6; cf. ad 1. Cf. Emery, "The Personal Mode of Trinitarian Action in St. Thomas Aquinas," in Emery, *Trinity, Church, and the Human Person: Thomistic Essays* (Naples, Fla.: Sapientia Press, 2007), 115–53.

32 Miroslav Volf argues that "we should think of the time of the world to come not as the 'fullness of time,' but as 'reconciliation of times.' The difference lies precisely in the refusal of closure, which the term 'fullness' suggests. For joy to be complete, there is no need for the Boethian 'whole, simultaneous and complete possession' of life, as not only Moltmann but also Pannenberg and Jüngel maintain. Indeed, such total simultaneity and total possession would make joy impossible" ("Enter into Joy! Sin, Death, and the Life of the World to Come," in Polkinghorne and Welker, *The End of the World and the Ends of God*, 275). But intimate communion with God differs radically from intimate communion with another being, in which the polarity between openness and closure applies. Cf. Pannenberg, *Systematic Theology*, 601–7, as well as (for engagement with Moltmann on this point) Richard Bauckham, "Time and Eternity," in *God Will Be All in All: The Eschatology of Jürgen Moltmann*, ed. Richard Bauckham (Edinburgh: T&T Clark, 1999), 155–226. This latter volume contains an essay by Volf that, again in dialogue with Moltmann, argues for eschatological redemption as the key to eschatological "completion": see Volf, "After Moltmann: Reflections on the Future of Eschatology," 233–57, esp. 245–52. On the impossibility of losing beatitude, see Simon Francis Gaine, O.P., *Will There Be Free Will in Heaven? Freedom, Impeccability and Beatitude* (New York: T&T Clark, 2003), 103–36.

33 Matthew L. Lamb, *Eternity, Time, and the Life of Wisdom* (Naples, Fla.: Sapientia Press, 2007), 64. See also Ashley, O.P., *Theologies of the Body*, 602–3; Bauckham and Hart, *Hope against Hope*, 39–43. As Bauckham and Hart put it, "every present will find itself, redeemed and fulfilled, in the new creation" (43).

34 David Bentley Hart, *The Doors of the Sea: Where Was God in the Tsunami?* (Grand Rapids: Eerdmans, 2005), 102.

35 Hart, *The Doors of the Sea*, 102–3. See also de Lubac, *The Splendor of the Church*, 310; Durrwell, *The Resurrection*, 339–40.

36 See Wright, *Surprised by Hope*, 67, 184–86 and elsewhere. In opposition to oppressive structures, some theologians seek to replace "kingdom" with "kin-dom," but what is thereby lost is the reality of God's just reign and our participation in it. See Luis G. Pedraja, "Eschatology," in *Handbook of Latina/o Theologies*, ed. Edwin David Aponte and Miguel A. De La Torre (St. Louis: Chalice Press, 2006), 119.

37 For discussion of Isaiah 24–27, see Patrick D. Miller, "Judgment and Joy," in Polkinghorne and Welker, *The End of the World and the Ends of God*, 155–70; Dan G. Johnson, *From Chaos to Restoration: An Integrative Reading of Isaiah 24–27* (Sheffield: JSOT Press, 1988).

38 Leget comments that "with the resurrection of Christ the plenitude and abundance of the restored (or rather: glorified) life with God is revealed to humankind. Thus, interpreting the eschatological passages in Holy Scripture, the resurrection of Christ has an important hermeneutical function for Aquinas. . . . The relation between body and soul in the state of consummated life with God is one of overflowing expression. In *vita aeterna* human life is still material, corporal, but now radically 'redefined' proceeding from the completed relationship with God. In this 'redefinition' everything is consistently based upon the relationship with God" (*Living with God*, 215, 227).

39 I–II, q. 4, a. 5, ad 4; cf. Leget, *Living with God*, 225–27. For historical background

(concentrating on the fourteenth-century debates), see Bynum, *The Resurrection of the Body*, 283–89. For concerns regarding the role of the body in beatitude, see Philip Blond, "The Beatific Vision of St Thomas Aquinas," in *Encounter between Eastern Orthodoxy and Radical Orthodoxy: Transfiguring the World through the Word*, ed. Adrian Pabst and Christoph Schneider (Burlington, Vt.: Ashgate, 2009), 185–212.

40 Drawing upon Ratzinger's *Introduction to Christianity*, Bernard Prusak concludes that "[c]ontemporary theology does not understand the resurrection of the body in the manner of Aquinas who said that flesh, bones, and blood would be included. . . . A consensus has emerged, across a spectrum of theologians, that a physiological understanding of bodily resurrection is inadequate for conceptualizing the transformed mode of existence that is the risen life" ("Bodily Resurrection in Catholic Perspectives," 99). It seems to me, however, that bodiliness cannot be separated from flesh, bones, and blood, even if we cannot know what they will be like in the risen body. See also Silas Langley, "Aquinas, Resurrection, and Material Continuity," *Proceedings of the American Catholic Philosophical Association* 75 (2001): 135–47.

41 Cf. III, q. 45, a. 2.

42 I–II, q. 4, a. 6, citing *Gen. ad lit.* xii. 35. For a similar perspective, see Amy Plantinga Pauw, "'Heaven Is a World of Love': Edwards on Heaven and the Trinity," *Calvin Theological Journal* 30 (1995): 392–401. On Augustine's theology of the beatific vision (and its relation to Aquinas'), see Trottmann, *La vision béatifique*, 54–67; Maillard, *La vision de Dieu chez Thomas d'Aquin*. For Augustine's theology of resurrection and eternal life see also Tarmo Toom, "*Totus homo*: Augustine on Resurrection," in *Resurrection and Responsibility: Essays on Theology, Scripture, and Ethics in Honor of Thorwald Lorenzen*, ed. Keith D. Dyer and David J. Neville (Eugene, Ore.: Pickwick, 2009), 59–73; Gerald O'Collins, S.J., "Augustine on the Resurrection," in *Saint Augustine the Bishop: A Book of Essays*, ed. F. LeMoine and C. Kleinhenz (New York: Garland, 1994), 65–75; Robert Puchniak, "Augustine's Conception of Deification, Revisited," in Finlan and Kharlamov, *Theōsis*, 122–33; Mamerto Alfeche, O.S.A., "The Rising of the Dead in the Works of Augustine," *Augustiniana* 39 (1989): 54–98. For the argument (mistaken in my view) that Augustine deviates from St. Paul by insisting on the true corporeality of the spiritual body, see Paula Fredriksen, "Vile Bodies: Paul and Augustine on the Resurrection of the Flesh," in *Biblical Hermeneutics in Historical Perspective: Studies in Honor of Karlfried Froehlich on His Sixtieth Birthday*, ed. Mark S. Burrows and Paul Rorem (Grand Rapids: Eerdmans, 1991), 75–87.

43 Wright, *Surprised by Hope*, 117.

44 Wright, *Surprised by Hope*, 102.

45 For discussion see esp. Joseph L. Mangina, *Revelation* (Grand Rapids: Brazos Press, 2010).

46 Aquinas cites 2 Peter 3:12 in Suppl., q. 74, a. 2, *sed contra* and 2 Peter 3:10 in Suppl., q. 74, a. 3. For cautions regarding the use of the *Summa theologiae*'s "Supplement" (which presents material from Aquinas' *Commentary on the Sentences*), see Jean-Pierre Torrell, O.P., *Aquinas's Summa: Background, Structure, and Reception*, trans. Benedict M. Guevin, O.S.B. (Washington, D.C.: Catholic University of

America Press, 2005), 62. In his *Summa contra gentiles* IV, chaps. 79–97, Aquinas briefly treats the characteristics of the risen body (immortality, corporeal, perfect in age and beauty, no need for eating or procreation, and so forth) as well as the unchangeable will of the souls of the dead, the last judgment, and the cessation of the movements of the heavens. But the brevity of chapters 79–97 means that Aquinas focuses largely on technical philosophical points. Thomas S. Hibbs has helpfully summarized chapters 79–97 in his *Dialectic and Narrative in Aquinas: An Interpretation of the Summa Contra Gentiles* (Notre Dame: University of Notre Dame Press, 1995), 163–66.

47 See Suppl., q. 74, a. 2, ad 3. Aquinas' view undermines the critique of Bauckham and Hart, *Hope against Hope*, 129: "Medieval flight from nature was harmless compared with modern interference in nature. Nevertheless, the mildly Platonist other-worldliness of the Christian tradition, along with the anthropocentrism which was also a Greek inheritance of Christian theology, deprived Christianity of the will or the power to resist the modern project of technological subjugation of nature. If God's creation is ultimately only a throw-away world, destined to perish when its purpose as a vale of human soul-making is fulfilled, it may not seem to matter too much what we do with it." Even so, Bauckham and Hart are quite right to say that "the new creation of all things will be a taking, through transformation, into eternity, of all that has ever happened throughout the aeons of this world's time" (132).

48 Witherington, *A Socio-Rhetorical Commentary on 1–2 Peter*, 380, cf. 381–82.

49 Josef Pieper, *Hope and History: Five Salzburg Lectures*, trans. David Kipp (San Francisco: Ignatius Press, 1994), 102.

50 Ratzinger, *Eschatology*, 202–3. Regarding the eschatological images found in Scripture, see also the balanced perspective of Bauckham and Hart, *Hope against Hope*, 73–108; as well as Pannenberg, *Systematic Theology*, 621–22; Farrow, *Ascension Theology*, 132–39.

51 Suppl., q. 77, a. 4, ad 1. Cf. Carlo Leget's remark that for Aquinas "[b]oth the beginning and the consummation of creation do not take place within the coordinates of materiality and time, but concern the very beginning and consummation of these coordinates" (*Living with God*, 210).

52 Christian Link, "Points of Departure for a Christian Eschatology," in Reventlow, *Eschatology in the Bible*, 106–7. For Link it is axiomatic that theologians must abandon "the idea of a historical, and therefore chronologically calculable, 'return' of Christ; this would logically imply a former absence. The appearance ('arrival') of Christ, the 'Day of the Lord' (1 Thess. 5.2) is not something that will happen in time. That day is not to be seen as the final day in *our* succession of time, as a point at which there would be a sudden and violent break in our history. Rather, it has to be understood as a reality that lies so to speak at the vertical of every point of time here on earth" (108). If Christ's "return" is solely "at the vertical of every point of time here on earth," however, its specifically transitional character is lost: it would characterize all time rather than uniquely characterizing the mystery of the final transition. For Christ's Second Coming as the transcendent culmination of history see Bauckham and Hart, *Hope against Hope*, 117–22. For a far more nuanced version of Link's thesis, emphasizing that each moment of time

is marked by God's eternity (so that "eschatology" describes far more than the linear-historical end of time), see Barth, *The Resurrection of the Dead*, 101–7. The validity (against all utopias) of Christian expectation of "a catastrophic end within history" is defended by Josef Pieper, *The End of Time: A Meditation on the Philosophy of History*, trans. Michael Bullock (San Francisco: Ignatius Press, 1999), 148; by Bauckham and Hart, *Hope against Hope*, 110–17; and by Douglas Farrow, *Ascension Theology*, 96–113. See also Hughes, *Constructing Antichrist*, focusing on patristic and medieval interpretation of 2 Thessalonians.

53 Suppl., q. 74, a. 1; cf. Suppl., q. 75, a. 5.

54 Suppl., q. 74, a. 1.

55 Suppl., q. 74, a. 5, ad 3.

56 Aquinas notes that while the Fathers differ on the question of whether all will undergo death, "the safer and more common opinion is that all shall die and rise again from death" (Suppl., q. 78, a. 1).

57 Suppl., q. 74, a. 9, ad 1. Cf. Ted Peters' remark that "[w]e cannot separate human destiny from cosmic destiny. . . . What happens to persons depends on what happens to the cosmos. The resurrection to a spiritual body can occur only at the advent of the eschaton. If there is no cosmic transformation, then there is no resurrection" (*God—the World's Future*, 327).

58 See Suppl., q. 74, a. 8. The fire is the same fire that burns in hell: see Suppl., q. 74, a. 9, in which Aquinas cites John the Baptist's words that Jesus' "winnowing fork is in his hand, to clear his threshing floor, and to gather the wheat into his granary, but the chaff he will burn with unquenchable fire" (Luke 3:17).

59 Cf. John 5:28-29, cited in Suppl., q. 75, a. 2, *sed contra*.

60 Suppl., q. 75, a. 2, ad 3. Cf. III, q. 56, a. 1, ad 3, where Aquinas explains that Jesus' resurrection is "the efficient and exemplar cause of our resurrection."

61 Suppl., q. 76, a. 2.

62 Cf. Farrow, *Ascension Theology*, 141: "it is precisely this world and our humanity that will be confronted once again by God in *his* humanity."

63 III, q. 54, a. 3. For a "metacosmic" view of glorified bodiliness, see, e.g., Sergius Bulgakov, *The Holy Grail and the Eucharist*, trans. Boris Jakim (Hudson, N.Y.: Lindisfarne Books, 1997).

64 Suppl., q. 77, a. 1, ad 4. On this controverted topic, see Richard Bauckham, "Must Christian Eschatology Be Millenarian? A Response to Jürgen Moltmann," in Brower and Elliott, *Eschatology in Bible and Theology*, 263–77; Bauckham and Hart, *Hope against Hope*, 132–39; Miroslav Volf, in Bauckham, *God Will Be All in All*, 239–45, 257. See also the summary of positions, from the New Testament and the Fathers through Joachim of Fiore and modern Dispensationalism, in Schwarz, *Eschatology*, 332–37.

65 See Suppl., q. 77, a. 1, ad 2 and 3. Thus Farrow observes that "if Mary is the prototype of the church's free participation in Christ, then her end will be of the kind that is proper to the church, displaying in advance the principle that the members follow where the head leads" (*Ascension Theology*, 84).

66 Suppl., q. 77, a. 2. See also Ratzinger, *Eschatology*, 197–99.

67 III, q. 59, a. 5. See esp. Kromholtz, *On the Last Day*. For an overview of Aquinas' position, see Leo J. Elders, S.V.D., "Le jugement dernier dans la théologie de Saint

Thomas d'Aquin," in Elders, *Sur les traces de saint Thomas d'Aquin théologien. Étude de ses commentaires bibliques. Thèmes théologiques*, trans. Véronique Pommeret (Paris: Parole et Silence, 2009), 493–508. For the difficulty of reconciling the significance of the last judgment with the immediate judgment of the person after death (and for the history of theological debates on this matter), see Tugwell, *Human Immortality and the Redemption of Death*, 74–75, 118–19, 130–55.

68   III, q. 59, a. 4; cf. Tugwell, *Human Immortality and the Redemption of Death*, 147. Regarding the last judgment, Wright states, "Judgment—the sovereign declaration that *this* is good and to be upheld and vindicated, and *that* is evil and to be condemned—is the only alternative to chaos. . . . God is utterly committed to set the world right in the end" (*Surprised by Hope*, 178–79). See also Ted Peters' observation that the purpose of the last judgment is "to reveal the justice and sovereignty of God. Up until this time the truth of God's justice will have been hidden under the ambiguities of history" (*God—the World's Future*, 329–30). For further discussion see Pope Benedict XVI, *Spe Salvi* (Vatican City: Libreria Editrice Vaticana, 2007), §42.

69   III, q. 59, a. 4. Not all rational creatures share in beatitude, since the judgment of love excludes those who freely reject love.

70   Wright, *Surprised by Hope*, 288. Bauckham and Hart similarly comment that "in the new creation the creatures in their redeemed perfection will all reflect God precisely in being their own true reality. . . . Eternal life will be theocentric because the reality of creation is theocentric and will then be unambiguously and joyously so" (*Hope against Hope*, 172).

71   See Wright, *Surprised by Hope*, 44 and elsewhere.

72   Cited in Suppl., q. 82, a. 1.

73   See Suppl., q. 79, a. 2. Although he faults medieval piety, Wright recognizes that "medieval theologians like Thomas and Bernard insisted on the bodily resurrection. They, like the New Testament and the early church fathers, held a strong view of God's good creation. They knew that it must be reaffirmed, not abandoned" (Wright, *Surprised by Hope*, 158). Regarding the details of bodily resurrection, Aquinas is aware that "[t]he parts of matter are not permanent in the body but ebb and flow," so that not all the person's bodily matter will be included in the risen body (Suppl., q. 80, a. 5, *sed contra*). He states that "the whole of what is in man will rise again, if we speak of the totality of the species which is dependent on quantity, shape, position and order of parts, but the whole will not rise again if we speak of the totality of matter" (Suppl., q. 80, a. 5). Although all the Fathers and medievals were interested in questions regarding the material continuity of the risen body, Caroline Walker Bynum overemphasizes this dimension: see Bynum, *Fragmentation and Redemption: Essays on Gender and the Human Body in Medieval Religion* (New York: Zone Books, 1991), 240–44, 258–70.

74   Suppl., q. 82, a. 2. See Bynum, *The Resurrection of the Body*, 242–43.

75   Suppl., q. 82, a. 4, ad 1.

76   Suppl., q. 83, a. 1. For succinct discussion of the "gifts" or qualities of the resurrected and glorified body (impassibility, subtlety, agility, clarity), see Leget, *Living with God*, 228–29; for medieval background, see Nikolaus Wicki, *Die Lehre von*

der himmlischen Seligkeit in der mittelalterlichen Scholastik von Petrus Lombardus bis Thomas von Aquin (Freiburg: Universitätsverlag, 1954), 202–12.

77 Suppl., q. 84, a. 1.

78 See Suppl., q. 84, a. 2, including ad 2. Tugwell notes that this is the only exception that Aquinas makes to the immobility of the new creation: see Tugwell, *Human Immortality and the Redemption of Death*, 153. Aquinas holds that when the blessed see the whole, they will see the damned as God sees them: see Suppl., q. 94, a. 1, ad 2; q. 94, a. 3, ad 2.

79 Suppl., q. 85, a. 1, ad 3.

80 Suppl., q. 88, a. 1, q. 90, a. 2. Cf. the discussion of the "last judgment" in Bauckham and Hart, *Hope against Hope*, 139–47.

81 Suppl., q. 87, a. 2, ad 3.

82 Suppl., q. 91, a. 1.

83 See Suppl., q. 93, a. 3. This contravenes any supposition that eternal life promotes otherworldliness, rather than active charity, in the present life. On this point see Bauckham and Hart, *Hope against Hope*, 182: "[P]art of what it means to be Christian, a follower of Christ, is to be committed to living history differently, pursuing the characteristic marks of the kingdom of God as Jesus describes and embodies these (truth, goodness, justice, peace, holiness, etc.) *in* this world even though God's kingdom is not *of* this world"; cf. 193–203. Although Bauckham and Hart reject the notion of meritorious action, they arrive at a similar notion by emphasizing "participation in Christ through the power of God's Spirit of holiness. . . . Wherever the forces of sin and death are resisted or overcome the Spirit of Life (who is none other than the Living God made known in Jesus Christ) may be identified at work constantly renewing creation" (183; cf. 193).

84 Wright, *Surprised by Hope*, 161.

85 Suppl., q. 96, a. 1.

86 See Suppl., q. 95, a. 5.

87 Suppl., q. 96, a. 1, obj. 1 and *sed contra*.

88 Suppl., q. 96, a. 1, *sed contra*.

89 Suppl., q. 96, a. 2.

90 Suppl., q. 96, a. 5.

91 Suppl., q. 96, a. 6. For discussion of why Jesus, at the right hand of the Father, wills that the Church live by way of martyrdom, see Farrow, *Ascension Theology*, 92–98.

92 Suppl., q. 96, a. 7, obj. 3.

93 Suppl., q. 96, a. 7, obj. 3.

94 Suppl., q. 96, a. 7, ad 3.

95 See Wright, *Surprised by Hope*, 245.

96 Wright, *Surprised by Hope*, 248.

97 Wright, *Surprised by Hope*, 261.

98 Suppl., q. 96, a. 11.

99 Wright, *Surprised by Hope*, 161.

100 Suppl., q. 85, a. 1. Although they exhibit different degrees of glory, the blessed all enjoy a fullness of glory that is unmarked by defect. John Thiel is mistaken, in my view, when he claims that although the blessed cannot sin, "the transformation that makes the blessed dead who they most are is real and meaningful only

to the extent that its gracefulness neither annuls the effects of sin nor reduces the redeemed to a less than personal existence. . . . For the blessed dead to be themselves, though, they must continue to be persons shaped by the history of sin. For the blessed dead to be most fully themselves, they must continue to act in the afterlife in imitation of Jesus' own resurrected life in ways that defeat the burden of sin that they both made and suffered" ("For What May We Hope? Thoughts on the Eschatological Imagination," *Theological Studies* 67 [2006]: 540–41). As Revelation 21–22 suggests (among other biblical passages), it is not possible both to share supremely in the life of the Trinity, who is infinite holiness, and to continue to need to "defeat the burden of sin." What is needed here is a deeper sense of the meaning of the last judgment (and the consummation of God's providential order). Along these lines see Pannenberg, *Systematic Theology*, 611.

101 Suppl., q. 85, a. 1, ad 4.
102 Wright, *Surprised by Hope*, 262.
103 Wright, *Surprised by Hope*, 269.
104 Wright, *Surprised by Hope*, 269.
105 See Suppl., q. 91, aa. 2 and 5.
106 See the similar perspective of Walls, *Heaven*, 110–12.

CONCLUSION

1 This crisis has been exacerbated by the denial that the existence of God is philosophically knowable. For responses to this denial, see Feser, *The Last Superstition*; Thomas Joseph White, O.P., *Wisdom in the Face of Modernity: A Study in Thomistic Natural Theology* (Ave Maria, Fla.: Sapientia Press, 2009); and Francesca Aran Murphy, *God Is Not a Story: Realism Revisited* (Oxford: Oxford University Press, 2007). I should also note the recent claim that quantum fluctuation and inflation can be the creative source of the cosmos: see Stephen Hawking and Leonard Mlodinow, *The Grand Design* (New York: Bantam Books, 2010). Even if this theory worked philosophically, which it does not because it supposes that utter nothingness includes active causality, John Polkinghorne rightly observes that "the best that this point of view could achieve . . . would be an everlasting randomness, an eternal lottery in which occasional, but transient, prizes might be won. One is back with a picture of possible islands of meaningfulness within an engulfing ocean of absurdity" ("Eschatology: Some Questions and Some Insights from Science," in Polkinghorne and Welker, *The End of the World and the Ends of God*, 33–34). Cf. John Haldane, "Philosophy Lives," *First Things*, no. 209 (2011): 43–46.

2 Thus, with regard to the existential impoverishment brought about by contemporary Western secularism, Carlos Eire pungently observes, "I don't know about you, but I'm outraged by a universe that exists eternally, but only allows me a tiny scrap of time" (Eire, *A Very Brief History of Eternity*, 217). For recent attempts to preserve life's meaning despite the expectation of personal annihilation, see Mark Johnston, *Surviving Death* (Princeton: Princeton University Press, 2010); Annie Dillard, *For the Time Being* (New York: Alfred A. Knopf, 1999); Michael Fishbane, *Sacred Attunement: A Jewish Theology* (Chicago: University of Chicago Press, 2008). See my review of Fishbane's book in *Nova et Vetera* 8 (2010): 711–16.

3 Edmund N. Carpenter, II, "Before I Die . . . ," *Wall Street Journal*, February 6–7,

2010, A13. See also Plato, *Apology*, trans. Hugh Tredennick, 40c and 42a, in Plato, *The Collected Dialogues*, 25–26; Sukie Miller (with Suzanne Lipsett), *After Death: Mapping the Journey* (New York: Simon & Schuster, 1997), 166. Miller's syncretism appears in more scholarly form in John Hick, *Death and Eternal Life* (New York: Harper and Row, 1976); for the problems with syncretism see J. A. Di Noia, O.P., *The Diversity of Religions: A Christian Perspective* (Washington, D.C.: Catholic University of America Press, 1992).

4   Rahner, "Hidden Victory," 154; see also Rahner's "The Hermeneutics of Eschatological Assertions" and "The Life of the Dead" in *Theological Investigations*, vol. 4, trans. Kevin Smyth (Baltimore: Helicon, 1966), 323–46 and 347–54, respectively. For an appreciative account of Rahner's theology of death, tracing its development over his career, see David Albert Jones, *Approaching the End: A Theological Exploration of Death and Dying* (Oxford: Oxford University Press, 2007), 146–86. For concerns regarding Rahner's theology of resurrection (Christ's and ours), see Paul D. Molnar, *Incarnation and Resurrection: Toward a Contemporary Understanding* (Grand Rapids: Eerdmans, 2007), 57–68.

5   Farrow, *Ascension Theology*, 85–86.

6   Gregory of Nyssa, *On the Soul and the Resurrection*, trans. Catharine P. Roth (Crestwood, N.Y.: St. Vladimir's Seminary Press, 2002), 88.

7   Gregory of Nyssa, *On the Soul and the Resurrection*. See Balthasar, *Presence and Thought*, 47; cf. Brian E. Daley, S.J., "Balthasar's Reading of the Church Fathers," in Oakes and Moss, *The Cambridge Companion to Hans Urs von Balthasar*, 195–97.

8   Gregory of Nyssa, *On the Soul and the Resurrection*, 88. We can agree with Gregory and Macrina here, without accepting all their proposals about the nature of the resurrected body.

9   See Garrigou-Lagrange, O.P., *Life Everlasting and the Immensity of the Soul*, vii–viii, 212–17.

10   Dawkins, *The God Delusion*, 357. See also Richard Rorty's proposal that "because of human beings' gradual success in making their lives, and their world, less wretched," humans now no longer need to find meaning by looking "beyond nature to the supernatural, and beyond life to an afterlife, but only beyond the human past to the human future" ("Religious Faith, Intellectual Responsibility and Romance," in Rorty, *Philosophy and Social Hope* [New York: Penguin, 1999], 162). Rorty grants that this is the case "only in those lucky parts of the world where wealth, leisure, literacy and democracy have worked together to prolong our lives and fill our libraries" (162). For similar views see John Stuart Mill, "Utility of Religion," in Mill, *Three Essays on Religion* (Amherst, N.Y.: Prometheus Books, 1998), 122; and Gianni Vattimo, *After Christianity*, trans. Luca D'Isanto (New York: Columbia University Press, 2002), 54. Cf. Thomas G. Guarino's excellent response to Vattimo: Guarino, *Vattimo and Theology* (New York: T&T Clark, 2009), esp. 144 and 157.

11   On this point, and on divine generosity, see Walls, *Heaven*, 163–97. See also Bernard Schumacher's observation that the "question as to whether death is an evil (for the dead person himself), which I have discussed here on the theoretical level, seems to me to be of paramount importance for the current ethical debate about death. . . . If Epicurus was right in asserting that someone's death cannot be considered as an evil for him, how could we maintain that an evil has befallen

the person who has been killed?" (*Death and Mortality in Contemporary Philosophy*, trans. Michael J. Miller [Cambridge: Cambridge University Press, 2011], 219). On Christian eschatology as the alternative to postmodern nihilism, see Bauckham and Hart, *Hope against Hope*, 20–43, 59–71.

12   See Augustine, *Homilies on the First Epistle of John*, trans. Boniface Ramsey (Hyde Park, N.Y.: New City Press, 2008); Søren Kierkegaard, *Works of Love: Some Christian Reflections in the Form of Discourses*, trans. Howard and Edna Hong (New York: Harper & Row, 1962). See also Pope Benedict XVI, *Deus Caritas Est* (Vatican City: Libreria Editrice Vaticana, 2005); Jésus Luzarraga, "Eternal Life in the Johannine Writings," *Communio* 18 (1991): 24–34.

13   Plato, *Timaeus* 29e, 1162. See also Archbishop Demetrios, "Hellenism and Orthodoxy: A Linguistic and Spiritual Journey," *St. Vladimir's Theological Quarterly* 54 (2010): 267–80.

14   Plato, *Phaedrus* 249e, trans. R. Hackforth, in Plato, *The Collected Dialogues*, 496. Nonetheless, Plato imagined that eternal life will consist in blessed souls' dwelling on their appointed star, and he supposed that the godlike universe contemplates itself, so as to need "no other friendship or acquaintance," not even a friendship with God. See Plato, *Timaeus* 34b and 42b, 1165, 1171. The problems with Platonic (and Aristotelian and Plotinian) eschatology are well described in Florovsky, "Eschatology in the Patristic Age," 240–49. For a defense of Plato's eschatology, see Josef Pieper, *The Platonic Myths*, trans. Dan Farrelly (South Bend, Ind.: St. Augustine's Press, 2011).

15   Plato, *Phaedrus* 250c, 497.

16   See Søren Kierkegaard, *Fear and Trembling*, trans. Walter Lowrie, in Kierkegaard, *Fear and Trembling and The Sickness unto Death* (Princeton: Princeton University Press, 1954), 51. For evidence of Kierkegaard's point, see David Benatar, *Better Never to Have Been: The Harm of Coming into Existence* (Oxford: Clarendon Press, 2006). Benatar's book was brought to my attention by G. J. McAleer's essay "'I Am Awaited by This Love, and So My Life Is Good': Children and Hope," *Nova et Vetera* 6 (2008): 829–36. Cf. G. J. McAleer, *To Kill Another: Homicide and Natural Law* (New Brunswick, N.J.: Transaction Publishers, 2011); Aurel Kolnai, "The Humanitarian versus the Religious Attitude," *Thomist* 7 (1944): 429–57.

17   Cf. Hans Urs von Balthasar, "Eternal Life and the Human Condition," trans. Josephine Koeppel, *Communio* 18 (1991): 4–23.

Works Cited

ᴄᴏ

Aaron, David H. *Biblical Ambiguities: Metaphor, Semantics, and Divine Imagery.* Leiden: Brill, 2002.

Alfeche, Mamerto, O.S.A. "The Rising of the Dead in the Works of Augustine." *Augustiniana* 39 (1989): 54–98.

Alfeyev, Hilarion (Metropolitan). *Christ the Conqueror of Hell: The Descent into Hades from an Orthodox Perspective.* Crestwood, N.Y.: St. Vladimir's Seminary Press, 2009.

Allison, Dale C., Jr. *The Historical Christ and the Theological Jesus.* Grand Rapids: Eerdmans, 2009.

———. *Resurrecting Jesus: The Earliest Christian Tradition and Its Interpreters.* New York: T&T Clark, 2005.

Anderson, Gary A. *Sin: A History.* New Haven: Yale University Press, 2009.

Apostolopoulos, Charalambos. *Phaedo Christianus: Studien zur Verbindung und Abwägung des Verhältnisses zwischen dem platonischen "Phaidon" und dem Dialog Gregors von Nyssa "Über die Seele und die Auferstehung."* Frankfurt: Lang, 1986.

Aquinas, Thomas. *Commentary on the Epistle to the Hebrews.* Trans. Chrysostom Baer, O. Praem. South Bend, Ind.: St. Augustine's Press, 2006.

———. *De potentia.* Trans. The English Dominican Fathers. Eugene, Ore.: Wipf & Stock, 2004.

————. *Summa contra gentiles. Book IV: Salvation*. Trans. Charles J. O'Neil. Notre Dame: University of Notre Dame Press, 1975.

————. *Summa theologiae*. Trans. The English Dominican Fathers. Westminster, Md.: Christian Classics, 1981.

Ariew, Roger. *Descartes and the Last Scholastics*. Ithaca: Cornell University Press, 1999.

Ashley, Benedict, O.P. *Theologies of the Body: Humanist and Christian*. Braintree, Mass.: Pope John Center, 1985.

Athanasius. *Athanasius: Select Works and Letters*. Ed. Archibald Robertson. Trans. John Henry Newman. Nicene and Post-Nicene Fathers, vol. 4. Peabody, Mass.: Hendrickson, 1994.

————. *Discourse IV Against the Arians*. In *Athanasius: Select Works and Letters*.

————. *Letter LIX, To Epictetus*. In *Athanasius: Select Works and Letters*.

Augustine. *Four Anti-Pelagian Writings*. Trans. John A. Mourant and William J. Collinge. Washington, D.C.: Catholic University of America Press, 1992.

————. *Homilies on the First Epistle of John*. Trans. Boniface Ramsey. Hyde Park, N.Y.: New City Press, 2008.

————. *Letter 164*. In *The Confessions and Letters of Augustine*, trans. J. G. Cunningham. Nicene and Post-Nicene Fathers, vol. 1. Peabody, Mass.: Hendrickson, 1994.

————. *On the Psalms*. Trans. Scholastica Hebgin and Felicitas Corrigan. Westminster, Md.: Newman Press, 1960.

Ayres, Lewis. "The Soul and the Reading of Scripture: A Note on Henri De Lubac." *Scottish Journal of Theology* 61 (2008): 173–90.

Balthasar, Hans Urs von. *The Action*. Trans. Graham Harrison. Vol. 4 of *Theo-Drama: Theological Dramatic Theory*. San Francisco: Ignatius Press, 1994.

————. *The Christian State of Life*. Trans. Sr. Mary Frances McCarthy. San Francisco: Ignatius Press, 1983.

————. "Creation and Trinity." *Communio* 15 (1988): 285–93.

————. "The Descent into Hell." In Balthasar, *Spirit and Institution*, trans. Edward T. Oakes, S.J., 401–14. Vol. 4 of *Explorations in Theology*. San Francisco: Ignatius Press, 1995.

————. "Eternal Life and the Human Condition." Trans. Josephine Koeppel. *Communio* 18 (1991): 4–23.

————. "The Fathers, the Scholastics, and Ourselves." Trans. Edward T. Oakes, S.J. *Communio* 24 (1997): 347–96.

————. *The Last Act*. Trans. Graham Harrison. Vol. 5 of *Theo-Drama: Theological Dramatic Theory*. San Francisco: Ignatius Press, 1998.

————. *Mary for Today*. Trans. Robert Nowell. San Francisco: Ignatius Press, 1988.

———. *Mysterium Paschale: The Mystery of Easter.* Trans. Aidan Nichols, O.P. Grand Rapids: Eerdmans, 1993.

———. *Paul Struggles with His Congregation: The Pastoral Message of the Letters to the Corinthians.* Trans. Brigitte L. Bojarska. San Francisco: Ignatius Press, 1992.

———. *Presence and Thought: An Essay on the Religious Philosophy of Gregory of Nyssa.* Trans. Mark Sebanc. San Francisco: Ignatius Press, 1995.

———. *Seeing the Form.* Trans. Erasmo Leiva-Merikakis. Vol. 1 of *The Glory of the Lord: A Theological Aesthetics.* San Francisco: Ignatius Press, 1987.

———. "Some Points of Eschatology." In Balthasar, *The Word Made Flesh,* trans. A. V. Littledale with Alexander Dru, 255–77. Vol. 1 of *Explorations in Theology.* San Francisco: Ignatius Press, 1989.

Balz, Horst. "Early Christian Faith as 'Hope against Hope.'" In Reventlow, *Eschatology in the Bible and in Jewish and Christian Tradition,* 31–48.

Barr, James. *Biblical Faith and Natural Theology.* Oxford: Oxford University Press, 1993.

———. *The Garden of Eden and the Hope of Immortality.* London: SCM Press, 1992.

Barth, Karl. *The Resurrection of the Dead.* Trans. H. J. Stenning. Eugene, Ore.: Wipf & Stock, 2003.

Bauckham, Richard. *The Fate of the Dead: Studies on the Jewish and Christian Apocalypses.* Leiden: Brill, 1998.

———, ed. *God Will Be All in All: The Eschatology of Jürgen Moltmann.* Edinburgh: T&T Clark, 1999.

———. *Jesus and the God of Israel: God Crucified and Other Studies on the New Testament's Christology of Divine Identity.* Grand Rapids: Eerdmans, 2009.

———. *Jude, 2 Peter.* Nashville: Thomas Nelson, 1996.

———. "Life, Death, and the Afterlife in Second Temple Judaism." In Bauckham, *The Jewish World around the New Testament,* 245–56. Grand Rapids: Baker Academic, 2010.

———. "Must Christian Eschatology Be Millenarian? A Response to Jürgen Moltmann." In Brower and Elliott, *Eschatology in Bible and Theology,* 263–77.

———. "Time and Eternity." In Bauckham, *God Will Be All in All,* 155–226.

Bauckham, Richard, and Trevor Hart. *Hope against Hope: Christian Eschatology at the Turn of the Millennium.* Grand Rapids: Eerdmans, 1999.

Beale, Greg K. "The Eschatological Conception of New Testament Theology." In Brower and Elliott, *Eschatology in Bible and Theology,* 11–52.

Benatar, David. *Better Never to Have Been: The Harm of Coming into Existence.* Oxford: Clarendon, 2006.

Benedict XVI (pope; see also Ratzinger, Joseph). *Deus Caritas Est.* Vatican City: Libreria Editrice Vaticana, 2005.

————. "Intervention at the Fourteenth General Congregation of the Synod (14 October 2008)." *Insegnamenti* 4, no. 2 (2008): 493–94.

————. "On the Encyclical *God Is Love.*" In Cordes, *Where Are the Helpers?*, 9–13.

————. *Sacramentum Caritatis.* Vatican City: Libreria Editrice Vaticana, 2007.

————. *Spe Salvi.* Vatican City: Libreria Editrice Vaticana, 2007.

————. *Verbum Domini.* Vatican City: Libreria Editrice Vaticana, 2010.

Benoit, Pierre. *Jesus and the Gospel.* Vol. 1. Trans. Benet Weatherhead. New York: Herder & Herder, 1973.

Best, Ernest. *Second Corinthians.* Louisville, Ky.: John Knox, 1987.

Betz, Hans Dieter. "The Concept of the 'Inner Human Being' (*ho esō anthrōpos*) in the Anthropology of Paul." *New Testament Studies* 46 (2000): 315–41.

Bird, Michael F. *Are You the One Who Is to Come? The Historical Jesus and the Messianic Question.* Grand Rapids: Baker Academic, 2009.

Blackwell, Ben C. "Immortal Glory and the Problem of Death in Romans 3.23." *Journal for the Study of the New Testament* 32 (2010): 285–308.

Blankenhorn, Bernhard, O.P. "The Instrumental Causality of the Sacraments: Thomas Aquinas and Louis-Marie Chauvet." *Nova et Vetera* 4 (2006): 255–93.

Blond, Philip. "The Beatific Vision of St Thomas Aquinas." In *Encounter between Eastern Orthodoxy and Radical Orthodoxy: Transfiguring the World through the Word*, ed. Adrian Pabst and Christoph Schneider, 185–212. Burlington, Vt.: Ashgate, 2009.

Bock, Darrell L. *Acts.* Grand Rapids: Baker Academic, 2007.

Bockmuehl, Markus. "Compleat History of the Resurrection: A Dialogue with N. T. Wright." *Journal for the Study of the New Testament* 26 (2004): 489–504.

————. "Did St. Paul Go to Heaven When He Died?" In *Jesus, Paul and the People of God: A Theological Dialogue with N. T. Wright*, ed. Nicholas Perrin and Richard B. Hays, 211–31. Downers Grove, Ill.: InterVarsity, 2011.

————. *The Epistle to the Philippians.* London: A. & C. Black, 1998.

————. "Resistance and Redemption in the Jesus Tradition." In *Redemption and Resistance: The Messianic Hopes of Jews and Christians in Antiquity*, ed. Markus Bockmuehl and James Carleton Paget, 65–77. New York: T&T Clark, 2007.

————. "Resurrection." In *The Cambridge Companion to Jesus*, ed. Markus Bockmuehl, 102–18. Cambridge: Cambridge University Press, 2001.

Borg, Marcus J. "An Appreciative Disagreement." In Newman, *Jesus and the Restoration of Israel*, 227–43.

Brink, Gijsbert van den. "How to Speak with Intellectual and Theological Decency on the Resurrection of Christ? A Comparison of Swinburne and Wright." *Scottish Journal of Theology* 61 (2008): 408–19.

Brock, Stephen L. "The Physical Status of the Spiritual Soul in Thomas Aquinas." *Nova et Vetera* 3 (2005): 231–57.

Brodeur, Scott. *The Holy Spirit's Agency in the Resurrection of the Dead: An Exegetico-Theological Study of 1 Corinthians 15,44b-49 and Romans 8,9-13.* Rome: Editrice Pontificia Università Gregoriana, 1996.

Brower, Kent E., and Mark W. Elliott, eds. *Eschatology in Bible and Theology: Evangelical Essays at the Dawn of a New Millennium.* Downers Grove, Ill.: InterVarsity, 1997.

Brown, Raymond E., S.S. *The Death of the Messiah.* Vol. 2. New York: Doubleday, 1994.

———. *The Virginal Conception and Bodily Resurrection of Jesus.* New York: Paulist Press, 1973.

Brown, Warren S., Nancey Murphy, and H. Newton Malony, eds. *Whatever Happened to the Soul? Scientific and Theological Portraits of Human Nature.* Minneapolis: Fortress, 1998.

Brueggemann, Walter. "Always in the Shadow of the Empire." In *The Church as Counterculture*, ed. Michael L. Budde and Robert W. Brimlow, 39–58. Albany: State University of New York Press, 2000.

———. "Faith at the *Nullpunkt.*" In Polkinghorne and Welker, *The End of the World and the Ends of God*, 143–54.

Bryan, Steven M. *Jesus and Israel's Traditions of Judgement and Restoration.* Cambridge: Cambridge University Press, 2002.

Buccellati, Giorgio. "Ascension, Parousia, and the Sacred Heart: Structural Correlations." *Communio* 25 (1998): 69–103.

Bulgakov, Sergius. *The Holy Grail and the Eucharist.* Trans. Boris Jakim. Hudson, N.Y.: Lindisfarne Books, 1997.

———. *The Lamb of God.* Trans. Boris Jakim. Grand Rapids: Eerdmans, 2008.

Bynum, Carolyn Walker. *Fragmentation and Redemption: Essays on Gender and the Human Body in Medieval Religion.* New York: Zone Books, 1991.

———. *The Resurrection of the Body in Western Christianity, 200–1336.* New York: Columbia University Press, 1995.

Cadbury, Henry J. "Intimations of Immortality in the Thought of Jesus." In *Immortality and Resurrection*, ed. Krister Stendahl, 115–49. New York: Macmillan, 1965.

Caird, G. B. "The Christological Basis of Christian Hope." In Caird et al., *The Christian Hope*, 9–24. London: SPCK, 1970.

Calvin, John. *Institutes of the Christian Religion*. Trans. Henry Beveridge. Grand Rapids: Eerdmans, 1989.

Cantalamessa, Raniero, O.F.M. Cap. *Easter: Meditations on the Resurrection*. Trans. Demetrio S. Yocum. Collegeville, Minn.: Liturgical Press, 2006.

Carnley, Peter F. "Response." In Davis, Kendall, and O'Collins, *The Resurrection*, 29–40.

———. *The Structure of Resurrection Belief*. Oxford: Oxford University Press, 1987.

Carozzi, Claude. *Le voyage de l'âme dans l'au-delà d'après le littérature latine (Ve–XIIIe siècle)*. Palais Farnèse: École Français de Rome, 1994.

Carpenter, Edmund N., II. "Before I Die . . ." *Wall Street Journal*, February 6–7, 2010, A13.

Catechism of the Catholic Church. 2nd ed. Vatican City: Libreria Editrice Vaticana, 1997.

Cessario, Romanus, O.P. "Aquinas on Christian Salvation." In Weinandy, Keating, and Yocum, *Aquinas on Doctrine*, 117–37.

———. *Christian Faith and the Theological Life*. Washington, D.C.: Catholic University of America Press, 1996.

———. *The Godly Image: Christ and Salvation in Catholic Thought from Anselm to Aquinas*. Petersham, Mass.: St. Bede's, 1990.

Charry, Ellen. *God and the Art of Happiness*. Grand Rapids: Eerdmans, 2010.

The Church's Confession of Faith: A Catholic Catechism for Adults. German Catholic Bishops' Conference. San Francisco: Ignatius Press, 1987.

Clarke, W. Norris, S.J. "The Immediate Creation of the Human Soul by God and Some Contemporary Challenges." In Clarke, *The Creative Retrieval of St. Thomas Aquinas: Essays in Thomistic Philosophy, New and Old*, 173–90. New York: Fordham University Press, 2009.

Clement of Alexandria. *The Stromata, or Miscellanies*. In *Fathers of the Second Century*, ed. A. Cleveland Coxe. *Ante-Nicene Fathers*, vol. 2. Peabody, Mass.: Hendrickson, 1994.

Coakley, Sarah. "Is the Resurrection a 'Historical' Event? Some Muddles and Mysteries." In *The Resurrection of Jesus Christ*, ed. Paul Avis, 85–115. London: Darton, Longman & Todd, 1993.

Cohen, Shaye J. D. "Hellenism in Unexpected Places." In *Hellenism in the Land of Israel*, ed. John J. Collins and Gregory E. Sterling, 216–43. Notre Dame: University of Notre Dame Press, 2001.

Collins, John J. *Jewish Wisdom in the Hellenistic Age*. Louisville, Ky.: Westminster John Knox, 1997.

Colón-Emeric, Edgardo A. *Wesley, Aquinas and Christian Perfection: An Ecumenical Dialogue*. Waco, Tex.: Baylor University Press, 2009.

Congar, Yves, O.P. *Jesus Christ*. Trans. Luke O'Neill. New York: Herder & Herder, 1966.

———. "Le moment 'économique' et le moment 'ontologique' dans la Sacra Doctrina (Révélation, Théologie, Somme théologique)." In *Mélanges offerts à M.-D. Chenu*, 135–87. Paris, 1967.

Congregation for the Doctrine of the Faith. *The Reality after Death. Acta Apostolicae Sedis* 71 (1979): 939–43.

Connell, Martin F. "*Descensus Christi ad Inferos:* Christ's Descent to the Dead." *Theological Studies* 62 (2001): 262–82.

Cooper, Alan. "Ps 24:7-10: Mythology and Exegesis." *Journal of Biblical Literature* 102 (1983): 37–60.

Cooper, John W. *Body, Soul, and Life Everlasting: Biblical Anthropology and the Monism-Dualism Debate*. 2nd ed. Grand Rapids: Eerdmans, 2000.

Cordes, Paul Joseph Cardinal, ed. *Where Are the Helpers? Charity and Spirituality*. Trans. Anthony J. Figueiredo with James D. Mixson. Notre Dame: University of Notre Dame Press, 2010.

Crenshaw, James L. "Love Is Stronger Than Death: Intimations of Life beyond the Grave." In *Resurrection: The Origin and Future of a Biblical Doctrine*, ed. James H. Charlesworth et al., 53–78. New York: T&T Clark, 2006.

Crotty, Nicholas, C.P. "The Redemptive Role of Christ's Resurrection." *Thomist* 25 (1962): 54–106.

Cullmann, Oscar. *The Earliest Christian Confessions*. Trans. J. K. S. Reid. London: Lutterworth Press, 1949.

———. *Immortality of the Soul or Resurrection of the Dead? The Witness of the New Testament*. New York: Macmillan, 1958.

———. *Peter: Disciple, Apostle, Martyr*. Waco, Tex.: Baylor University Press, 2011.

Cyril of Alexandria. *On the Unity of Christ*. Trans. John Anthony McGuckin. Crestwood, N.Y.: St. Vladimir's Seminary Press, 1995.

Cyril of Jerusalem. *Lectures on the Christian Sacraments*. Trans. R. W. Church. Ed. F. L. Cross Crestwood, N.Y.: St. Vladimir's Seminary Press, 1977.

Daguet, François. *Théologie du dessein divin chez Thomas d'Aquin. Finis omnium Ecclesia*. Paris: J. Vrin, 2003.

Daley, Brian, S.J. "Balthasar's Reading of the Church Fathers." In Oakes and Moss, *The Cambridge Companion to Hans Urs von Balthasar*, 187–206.

———. "A Hope for Worms: Early Christian Hope." In Peters, Russell, and Welker, *Resurrection*, 136–64.

———. *The Hope of the Early Church: A Handbook of Patristic Eschatology*. Cambridge: Cambridge University Press, 1991.

Daniélou, Jean, S.J. *Études d'exégèse judéo-chrétienne*. Paris: Beauchesne et Ses Fils, 1966.

————. *The Lord of History: Reflections on the Inner Meaning of History*. Trans. Nigel Abercrombie. London: Longmans, Green, 1958.

————. *The Theology of Jewish Christianity*. Trans. and ed. J. A. Baker. London: Darton, Longman, & Todd, 1964.

Dauphinais, Michael, and Matthew Levering, eds. *Reading John with St. Thomas Aquinas: Theological Exegesis and Speculative Theology*. Washington, D.C.: Catholic University of America Press, 2005.

Davies, W. D., and Dale C. Allison, Jr. *Commentary on Matthew VIII–XVIII*. Vol. 2 of *A Critical and Exegetical Commentary on the Gospel According to Saint Matthew*. New York: T&T Clark, 1991.

————. *Commentary on Matthew XIX–XXVIII*. Vol. 3 of *A Critical and Exegetical Commentary on the Gospel According to Saint Matthew*. New York: T&T Clark, 1997.

Davis, Stephen T., Daniel Kendall, S.J., and Gerald O'Collins, eds. *The Resurrection: An Interdisciplinary Symposium on the Resurrection of Jesus*. Oxford: Oxford University Press, 1997.

Dawkins, Richard. *The God Delusion*. Boston: Houghton Mifflin, 2006.

Day, John. "The Development of Belief in Life after Death in Ancient Israel." In *After the Exile: Essays in Honour of Rex Mason*, ed. John Barton and David J. Reimer, 231–57. Macon, Ga.: Mercer University Press, 1996.

Demetrios (Archbishop). "Hellenism and Orthodoxy: A Linguistic and Spiritual Journey." *St. Vladimir's Theological Quarterly* 54 (2010): 267–80.

Dever, William G. *Did God Have a Wife? Archaeology and Folk Religion in Ancient Israel*. Grand Rapids: Eerdmans, 2005.

Dillard, Annie. *For the Time Being*. New York: Alfred A. Knopf, 1999.

Di Noia, J. A., O.P. *The Diversity of Religions: A Christian Perspective*. Washington, D.C.: Catholic University of America Press, 1992.

Dulles, Avery, S.J. "Who Can Be Saved?" In Dulles, *Church and Society: The Laurence J. McGinley Lectures, 1988–2007*, 522–34. New York: Fordham University Press, 2008.

Dunn, James D. G. *Did the First Christians Worship Jesus? The New Testament Evidence*. Louisville, Ky.: Westminster John Knox, 2010.

————. *Jesus Remembered*. Vol. 1 of *Christianity in the Making*. Grand Rapids: Eerdmans, 2003.

————. *The Theology of Paul the Apostle*. Grand Rapids: Eerdmans, 1998.

Durrwell, Francis X., C.Ss.R. *Christ Our Passover: The Indispensable Role of Resurrection in Our Salvation*. Trans. John F. Craghan. Liguori, Mo.: Liguori, 2004.

————. *The Resurrection: A Biblical Study*. Trans. Rosemary Sheed. New York: Sheed & Ward, 1960.

Eire, Carlos. *A Very Brief History of Eternity*. Princeton: Princeton University Press, 2010.

Eitel, Adam. "The Resurrection of Jesus Christ: Karl Barth and the Historicization of God's Being." *International Journal of Systematic Theology* 10 (2008): 36–53.

Elders, Leo J., S.V.D. "Le jugement dernier dans la théologie de Saint Thomas d'Aquin." In Elders, *Sur les traces de saint Thomas d'Aquin théologien. Étude de ses commentaires bibliques. Thèmes théologiques*, trans. Véronique Pommeret, 493–508. Paris: Parole et Silence, 2009.

———. "La Résurrection du Christ dans la théologie de saint Thomas d'Aquin," *Nova et Vetera* (French ed.) 74 (1999): 21–31.

Emery, Gilles, O.P. "Missions invisibles et missions visibles: le Christ et son Esprit." *Revue Thomiste* 106 (2006): 51–99.

———. "The Personal Mode of Trinitarian Action in St. Thomas Aquinas." In Emery, *Trinity, Church, and the Human Person: Thomistic Essays*, 115–53. Naples, Fla.: Sapientia Press, 2007.

———. *The Trinitarian Theology of St. Thomas Aquinas*. Trans. Francesca Aran Murphy. Oxford: Oxford University Press, 2007.

———. *La Trinité créatrice: Trinité et creation dans les commentaires aux Sentences de Thomas d'Aquin et de ses précurseurs Albert le Grand et Bonaventure*. Paris: Vrin, 1995.

———. "Trinity and Creation: The Trinitarian Principle of the Creation in the Commentaries of Albert the Great, Bonaventure, and Thomas Aquinas on the *Sentences*." In Emery, *Trinity in Aquinas*, 33–70. Ypsilanti, Mich.: Sapientia Press, 2003.

———. "The Unity of Man, Body and Soul, in St. Thomas Aquinas." In Emery, *Trinity, Church, and the Human Person: Thomistic Essays*. Naples, Fla.: Sapientia Press, 2007: 209–35.

Evans, C. Stephen. "Methodological Naturalism in Historical Biblical Scholarship." In Newman, *Jesus and the Restoration of Israel*, 180–205.

Evans, Craig A. "In Appreciation of the Dominical and Thomistic Traditions: The Contribution of J. D. Crossan and N. T. Wright to Jesus Research." In *The Resurrection of Jesus: John Dominic Crossan and N. T. Wright in Dialogue*, ed. Robert B. Stewart, 48–57. Minneapolis: Fortress, 2006.

———. "Jesus and the Continuing Exile of Israel." In Newman, *Jesus and the Restoration of Israel*, 77–100.

Farrow, Douglas. *Ascension and Ecclesia: On the Significance of the Doctrine of the Ascension for Ecclesiology and Christian Cosmology*. Grand Rapids: Eerdmans, 1999.

———. *Ascension Theology*. New York: T&T Clark, 2011.

————. "Eucharist, Eschatology and Ethics." In Fergusson and Sarot, *The Future as God's Gift*, 199–215.

————. "Melchizedek and Modernity." In *The Epistle to the Hebrews and Christian Theology*, ed. Richard Bauckham et al., 281–301. Grand Rapids: Eerdmans, 2009.

Fee, Gordon D. *Philippians*. Downers Grove, Ill.: InterVarsity, 1999.

Fergusson, David. "Interpreting the Resurrection." *Scottish Journal of Theology* 38 (1985): 287–305.

Fergusson, David, and Marcel Sarot, eds. *The Future as God's Gift*. Edinburgh: T&T Clark, 2000.

Feser, Edward. *Aquinas: A Beginner's Guide*. Oxford: Oneworld, 2009.

————. *The Last Superstition: A Refutation of the New Atheism*. South Bend, Ind.: St. Augustine's Press, 2008.

————. *Philosophy of Mind*. Rev. ed. Oxford: Oneworld, 2006.

Feuillet, André. "La Demeure céleste et la Destinée des chrétiens. Exégèse de *II Cor.*, v, 1-10 et contribution à l'étude des fondements de l'eschatologie paulinienne." *Recherches de science religieuse* 44 (1956): 161–92.

Finlan, Stephen. "Second Peter's Notion of Divine Participation." In Finlan and Kharlamov, *Theōsis: Deification in Christian Theology*, 32–50.

Finlan, Stephen, and Vladimir Kharlamov, eds. *Theōsis: Deification in Christian Theology*. Eugene, Ore.: Pickwick, 2006.

Fishbane, Michael. *Sacred Attunement: A Jewish Theology*. Chicago: University of Chicago Press, 2008.

Fitzmyer, Joseph A., S.J. *The Gospel According to Luke (X-XXIV)*. Garden City, N.Y.: Doubleday, 1985.

Fletcher-Louis, Crispin H. T. "The Destruction of the Temple and the Relativization of the Old Covenant: Mark 13:31 and Matthew 5:18." In Brower and Elliott, *Eschatology in Bible and Theology*, 145–69.

Florovsky, Georges. "Eschatology in the Patristic Age: An Introduction." *Studia Patristica* 2 (1957): 235–50.

Fowl, Stephen E. *Philippians*. Grand Rapids: Eerdmans, 2005.

Fox, Rory. *Time and Eternity in Mid-Thirteenth-Century Thought*. Oxford: Oxford University Press, 2006.

Francis of Assisi. "Second Version of the Letter to the Faithful." In *Francis and Clare: The Complete Works*, trans. Regis J. Armstrong, O.F.M. Cap. and Ignatius C. Brady, O.F.M., 67–73. New York: Paulist Press, 1982.

Franks, Christopher A. *He Became Poor: The Poverty of Christ and Aquinas's Economic Teachings*. Grand Rapids: Eerdmans, 2009.

Freddoso, Alfred J. "Good News, Your Soul Hasn't Died Quite Yet." *Proceedings of the American Catholic Philosophical Association* 75 (2001): 79–96.

Fredriksen, Paula. "Vile Bodies: Paul and Augustine on the Resurrection of the Flesh." In *Biblical Hermeneutics in Historical Perspective: Studies in Honor of Karlfried Froehlich on His Sixtieth Birthday*, ed. Mark S. Burrows and Paul Rorem, 75–87. Grand Rapids: Eerdmans, 1991.

Froehlich, Karlfried. *Biblical Interpretation from the Church Fathers to the Reformation*. Burlington, Vt.: Ashgate, 2010.

Gaine, Simon Francis, O.P. *Will There Be Free Will in Heaven? Freedom, Impeccability and Beatitude*. New York: T&T Clark, 2003.

Garrigou-Lagrange, Reginald, O.P. *Life Everlasting and the Immensity of the Soul*. Trans. Patrick Cummins, O.S.B. Rockford, Ill.: Tan Books, 1991.

Gavrilyuk, Paul L. "Harnack's Hellenized Christianity or Florovsky's 'Sacred Hellenism': Questioning Two Metanarratives of Early Christian Engagement with Late Antique Culture." *St. Vladimir's Theological Quarterly* 54 (2010): 323–44.

———. *The Suffering of the Impassible God: The Dialectics of Patristic Thought*. Oxford: Oxford University Press, 2004.

Geach, Peter. *God and the Soul*. 2nd ed. South Bend, Ind.: St. Augustine's Press, 2000.

Gilbert, Maurice. "Immortalité? Résurrection? Faut-il choisir? Témoignage du judaïsme ancient." In *Le judaïsme à l'aube de l'ère chrétienne*, ed. Philippe Abadie and Jean-Pierre Lemonon, 271–97. Paris: Cerf, 2001.

Gillespie, Justin Edward. *The Development of Belief in the Resurrection within the Old Testament: A Critical Confrontation of Past and Present Proposals*. Rome: Pontificia Universitas Sanctae Crucis, 2009.

Godzieba, Anthony. "Bodies and Persons, Resurrected and Postmodern: Towards a Relational Eschatology." In *Theology and Conversation: Towards a Relational Theology*, ed. J. Haers and P. De Mey, 211–25. Leuven: Leuven University Press, 2003.

Goetz, Stewart and Charles Taliaferro. *A Brief History of the Soul*. Oxford: Wiley-Blackwell, 2011.

Gorman, Michael J. *Inhabiting the Cruciform God: Kenosis, Justification, and Theosis in Paul's Narrative Soteriology*. Grand Rapids: Eerdmans, 2009.

Goulder, Michael. "Did Jesus of Nazareth Rise from the Dead?" In *Resurrection: Essays in Honour of Leslie Houlden*, ed. Stephen Barton and Graham Stanton, 58–68. London: SPCK, 1994.

Gounelle, Rémi. *La descente du Christ aux Enfers: Institutionnalisation d'une croyance*. Paris: Institut d'Études augustiennes, 2000.

Gowan, Donald E. *Eschatology in the Old Testament*. 2nd ed. New York: T&T Clark, 2000.

Goyette, John. "St. Thomas on the Unity of Substantial Form." *Nova et Vetera* 7 (2009): 781–90.

Grant, W. Matthews. "Our Merits, God's Gifts." In *Reason and the Rule of Faith: Conversations in the Tradition with John Paul II*, ed. Christopher J. Thompson and Steven A. Long, 167–75. New York: University Press of America, 2011.

Gray, Timothy C. *The Temple in the Gospel of Mark: A Study in Its Narrative Role*. Tübingen: Mohr Siebeck, 2008.

Green, Garrett. "Imagining the Future." In Fergusson and Sarot, *The Future as God's Gift*, 73–87.

Green, Joel B. *Body, Soul, and Human Life: The Nature of Humanity in the Bible*. Grand Rapids: Baker Academic, 2008.

———. "Eschatology and the Nature of Humans: A Reconsideration of Pertinent Biblical Evidence." *Science and Christian Belief* 14 (2002): 33–50.

———. *1 Peter*. Grand Rapids: Eerdmans, 2007.

———. "'Witnesses of His Resurrection': Resurrection, Salvation, Discipleship, and Mission in the Acts of the Apostles." In Longenecker, *Life in the Face of Death*, 227–46.

Gregory of Nyssa, *On the Soul and the Resurrection*. Trans. Catharine P. Roth. Crestwood, N.Y.: St. Vladimir's Seminary Press, 2002.

Greshake, Gisbert. *Auferstehung der Toten: Ein Beitrag zur gegenwärtigen theologischen Diskussion über die Zukunft der Geschichte*. Essen: Ludgerus, 1969.

Greshake, Gisbert, and Jacob Kremer, *Resurrectio Mortuorum. Zum theologischen Verständnis der leiblichen Auferstehung*. Darmstadt: Wissenschaftliche Buchgesellschaft, 1986.

Grudem, Wayne. "He Did Not Descend into Hell: A Plea for Following Scripture Instead of the Apostles' Creed." *Journal of the Evangelical Theological Society* 34 (1991): 103–13.

Guardini, Romano. *The Death of Socrates: An Interpretation of the Platonic Dialogues: Euthyphro, Apology, Crito and Phaedo*. Trans. Basil Wrighton. New York: Meridian Books, 1962.

Guarino, Thomas G. *Vattimo and Theology*. New York: T&T Clark, 2009.

Guitmund of Aversa. *Of the Truth of the Body and Blood of Christ in the Eucharist*. Trans. Mark G. Vaillancourt. Washington, D.C.: Catholic University of America Press, 2009.

Gundry, Robert H. "The Essential Physicality of Jesus' Resurrection According to the New Testament." In *Jesus of Nazareth: Lord and Christ*, ed. Joel B. Green and Michael Turner, 204–19. Grand Rapids: Eerdmans, 1994.

———. "Trimming the Debate." In *Jesus' Resurrection: Fact or Figment? A Debate between William Lane Craig and Gerd Lüdemann*, ed. Paul Copan and Ronald K. Tacelli, 104–23. Downers Grove, Ill.: InterVarsity, 2000.

Hahn, Ferdinand. *The Titles of Jesus in Christology*. Trans. H. Knight and G. Ogg. Cleveland: World, 1969.

Haldane, John. "Philosophy Lives." *First Things*, no. 209 (2011): 43–46.

———. *Reasonable Faith*. London: Routledge, 2010.

Hansen, G. Walter. "Resurrection and the Christian Life in Paul's Letters." In Longenecker, *Life in the Face of Death*, 203–24.

Harris, Murray J. *Raised Immortal: Resurrection and Immortality in the New Testament*. Grand Rapids: Eerdmans, 1985.

———. "Resurrection and Immortality in the Pauline Corpus." In Longenecker, *Life in the Face of Death*, 147–70.

Hart, David Bentley. *The Beauty of the Infinite: The Aesthetics of Christian Truth*. Grand Rapids: Eerdmans, 2003.

———. *The Doors of the Sea: Where Was God in the Tsunami?* Grand Rapids: Eerdmans, 2005.

Harvey, Barry. *Can These Bones Live? A Catholic Baptist Engagement with Ecclesiology, Hermeneutics, and Social Theory*. Grand Rapids: Brazos Press, 2008.

Hauerwas, Stanley. *Against the Nations: War and Survival in a Liberal Society*. Notre Dame: University of Notre Dame Press, 1992.

Hawking, Stephen, and Leonard Mlodinow. *The Grand Design*. New York: Bantam Books, 2010.

Hay, David M. *Glory at the Right Hand: Psalm 110 in Early Christianity*. Nashville: Abingdon, 1973.

Hays, Richard B. *The Conversion of the Imagination: Paul as Interpreter of Israel's Scripture*. Grand Rapids: Eerdmans, 2005.

———. *First Corinthians*. Louisville, Ky.: John Knox, 1997.

———. *The Moral Vision of the New Testament: Community, Cross, New Creation: A Contemporary Introduction to New Testament Ethics*. New York: HarperCollins, 1996.

———. "Reading Scripture in Light of the Resurrection." In *The Art of Reading Scripture*, ed. Ellen F. Davis and Richard B. Hays, 216–38. Grand Rapids: Eerdmans, 2003.

———. "'Why Do You Stand Looking Up toward Heaven?' New Testament Eschatology at the Turn of the Millennium." *Modern Theology* 16 (2000): 115–35.

Heidegger, Martin. "Einleitung in die Phaenomenologie der Religion." In Heidegger, *Phänomenologie des religiösen Lebens*. Frankfurt: Klostermann, 1995.

Hengel, Martin. *Judaism and Hellenism: Studies in Their Encounter in Palestine during the Early Hellenistic Period*. Eugene, Ore.: Wipf & Stock, 2003.

———. *Property and Riches in the Early Church: Aspects of a Social History of Early Christianity*. Trans. John Bowden. Philadelphia: Fortress, 1974.

———. "'Sit at My Right Hand!' The Enthronement of Christ at the Right

Hand of God and Psalm 110:1." In Hengel, *Studies in Early Christology*, 119–225. Edinburgh: T&T Clark, 1995.

Hester, David. "The Eschatology of the Sermons of Symeon the Younger the Stylite." *St. Vladimir's Theological Quarterly* 34 (1990): 329–42.

Hibbs, Thomas S. *Dialectic and Narrative in Aquinas: An Interpretation of the Summa Contra Gentiles*. Notre Dame: University of Notre Dame Press, 1995.

Hick, John. *Death and Eternal Life*. New York: Harper & Row, 1976.

———. *The Metaphor of God Incarnate*. London: SCM Press, 1993.

Hittinger, Russell. "When It Is More Excellent to Love Than to Know: The Other Side of Thomistic 'Realism.'" *Proceedings of the American Catholic Philosophical Association* 57 (1983): 171–79.

Hofer, Andrew, O.P. "Balthasar's Eschatology on the Intermediate State: The Question of Knowability." *Logos* 12 (2009): 148–72.

Hooker, Morna D. *The Gospel According to Saint* Mark. London: A. & C. Black, 1991.

———. "Raised for Our Acquittal (Rom 4:25)." In *Resurrection in the New Testament*, ed. R. Bieringer, V. Koperski, and B. Lataire, 323–41. Leuven: Leuven University Press, 2002.

Horsley, Richard A. *Covenant Economics: A Biblical Vision of Justice for All*. Louisville, Ky.: Westminster John Knox, 2009.

Horsley, Richard A., and Neil Asher Silberman. *The Message and the Kingdom: How Jesus and Paul Ignited a Revolution and Transformed the Ancient World*. Minneapolis: Fortress, 2002.

Hoye, William J. *Actualitas Omnium Actuum: Man's Beatific Vision of God as Apprehended by Thomas Aquinas*. Meisenheim am Glan: Verlag Anton Hain, 1975.

Hughes, Kevin L. *Constructing Antichrist: Paul, Biblical Commentary, and the Development of Doctrine in the Middle Ages*. Washington, D.C.: Catholic University of America Press, 2005.

Hunsinger, George. "The Daybreak of the New Creation: Christ's Resurrection in Recent Theology." *Scottish Journal of Theology* 57 (2004): 163–80.

Hurtado, Larry W. *At the Origins of Christian Worship: The Context and Character of Earliest Christian Devotion*. Grand Rapids: Eerdmans, 1999.

———. *Lord Jesus Christ: Devotion to Jesus in Earliest Christianity*. Grand Rapids: Eerdmans, 2003.

Hütter, Reinhard. "*Desiderium Naturale Visionis Dei—Est autem duplex hominis beatitudo sive felicitas*: Some Observations about Lawrence Feingold's and John Milbank's Recent Interventions in the Debate over the Natural Desire to See God." *Nova et Vetera* 5 (2007): 81–131.

International Theological Commission. "Some Current Questions in Eschatology." *Irish Theological Quarterly* 58 (1992): 209–43.

Irenaeus. *Against Heresies*. In *The Apostolic Fathers with Justin Martyr and Irenaeus*, ed. Alexander Roberts and James Donaldson, with A. Cleveland
Coxe. *Ante-Nicene Fathers*, vol. 1. Peabody, Mass.: Hendrickson, 1994.

Jantzen, Grace M. "Do We Need Immortality?" *Modern Theology* 1 (1984):
25–44.

Janzen, J. Gerald. *Job*. Atlanta: John Knox, 1985.

———. "Resurrection and Hermeneutics: On Exodus 3:6 in Mark 12:26."
Journal for the Study of the New Testament 23 (1985): 43–58.

Jeffreys, Derek S. "The Soul Is Alive and Well: Non-reductive Physicalism
and Emergent Mental Properties." *Theology and Science* 2 (2004): 205–25.

John Chrysostom. *On Repentance and Almsgiving*. Trans. Gus George Christo.
Washington, D.C.: Catholic University of America Press, 1998.

John of Damascus, *The Orthodox Faith*. Trans. Frederic H. Chase Jr. In *John of
Damascus, Writings*. Washington, D.C.: Catholic University of America
Press, 1958.

Johnson, Dan G. *From Chaos to Restoration: An Integrative Reading of Isaiah
24–27*. Sheffield: JSOT Press, 1988.

Johnson, Luke Timothy. *The Acts of the Apostles*. Collegeville, Minn.: Liturgical
Press, 1992.

———. *Among the Gentiles: Greco-Roman Religion and Christianity*. New
Haven: Yale University Press, 2009.

———. *Hebrews: A Commentary*. Louisville, Ky.: Westminster John Knox,
2006.

———. "A Historiographical Response to Wright's Jesus." In Newman, *Jesus
and the Restoration of Israel*, 206-24.

———. *Sharing Possessions: Mandate and Symbol of Faith*. Philadelphia: Fortress, 1981.

Johnson, Mark. Introduction to Thomas Aquinas, *St. Thomas Aquinas and the
Mendicant Controversies: Three Translations*, vii–xxxiv. Leesburg, Va.: Alethes Press, 2007.

Johnston, Mark. *Surviving Death*. Princeton: Princeton University Press, 2010.

Johnston, Philip S. *Shades of Sheol: Death and Afterlife in the Old Testament*.
Downers Grove, Ill.: InterVarsity, 2002.

Johnstone, Brian V. "The Debate on the Structure of the *Summa theologiae* of
St. Thomas Aquinas from Chenu (1939) to Metz (1998)." In *Aquinas as
Authority*, ed. Paul van Geest, Harm Goris, and Carlo Leget, 187–200.
Leuven: Peeters, 2002.

Jones, Beth Felker. *Marks of His Wounds: Gender Politics and Bodily Resurrection*. Oxford: Oxford University Press, 2007.

Jones, David Albert. *Approaching the End: A Theological Exploration of Death and Dying.* Oxford: Oxford University Press, 2007.

Juarrero, Alicia. *Dynamics in Action: Intentional Behavior as a Complex System.* Cambridge, Mass.: MIT Press, 1999.

Juel, Donald. *Messianic Exegesis: Christological Interpretation of the Old Testament in Early Christianity.* Philadelphia: Fortress, 1988.

Kaufmann, Yehezkel. *The Religion of Israel: From Its Beginnings to the Babylonian Exile.* Trans. and abridged by Moshe Greenberg. Chicago: University of Chicago Press, 1960.

Keating, Daniel A. "Justification, Sanctification and Divinization in Thomas Aquinas." In Weinandy, Keating, and Yocum, *Aquinas on Doctrine,* 139–58.

Keck, Leaner E., ed. *The New Interpreter's Bible,* vol. 10. Nashville: Abingdon, 2002.

Kelly, Anthony J. *The Resurrection Effect: Transforming Christian Life and Thought.* Maryknoll, N.Y.: Orbis Books, 2008.

Kierkegaard, Søren. *Fear and Trembling.* Trans. Walter Lowrie. In *Fear and Trembling and The Sickness unto Death.* Princeton: Princeton University Press, 1954.

———. *Works of Love: Some Christian Reflections in the Form of Discourses.* Trans. Howard and Edna Hong. New York: Harper & Row, 1962.

Kirk, J. R. Daniel. *Unlocking Romans: Resurrection and the Justification of God.* Grand Rapids: Eerdmans, 2008.

Kläden, Tobias. *Mit Leib und Seele . . . Die* mind-brain-*Debatte in der Philosophie des Geistes und die* anima-forma-corporis-*Lehre des Thomas von Aquin.* Regensburg: Verlag Friedrich Pustet, 2005.

Kodell, Jerome, O.S.B. *The Eucharist in the New Testament.* Collegeville, Minn.: Liturgical Press, 1988.

Kolnai, Aurel. "The Humanitarian versus the Religious Attitude." *Thomist* 7 (1944): 429–57.

Köstenberger, Andreas J., and Scott R. Swain. *Father, Son and Spirit: The Trinity in John's Gospel.* Downers Grove, Ill.: InterVarsity, 2008.

Kovacs, Judith, trans. and ed. *1 Corinthians: Interpreted by Early Christian Commentators.* Grand Rapids: Eerdmans, 2005.

Kovacs, Judith, and Christopher Rowland. *Revelation: The Apocalypse of Jesus Christ.* Oxford: Blackwell, 2004.

Kromholtz, Bryan, O.P. *On the Last Day: The Time of the Resurrection of the Dead According to Thomas Aquinas.* Fribourg: Fribourg University Press, 2010.

———. "La résurrection au dernier jour selon saint Thomas d'Aquin." *Revue Thomiste* 109 (2009): 55–78.

Kugel, James L. *How to Read the Bible: A Guide to Scripture, Then and Now.* New York: Free Press, 2007.

Lafontaine, René. "'Arrivés a Jésus, ils le trouvèrent mort' (Jo. xix, 39): Hans Urs von Balthasar, théologien du samedi saint." *Revue Thomiste* 86 (1986): 635–43.

Lamb, Matthew L. *Eternity, Time, and the Life of Wisdom.* Naples, Fla.: Sapientia Press, 2007.

Lambrecht, Jan, S.J. *Second Corinthians.* Collegeville, Minn.: Liturgical Press, 1999.

Langley, Silas. "Aquinas, Resurrection, and Material Continuity." *Proceedings of the American Catholic Philosophical Association* 75 (2001): 135–47.

Lauber, David Edward. "Towards a Theology of Holy Saturday: Karl Barth and Hans Urs von Balthasar on the *descensus ad inferna.*" Ph.D. diss., Princeton Theological Seminary, 1999.

Legaspi, Michael. *The Death of Scripture and the Rise of Biblical Studies.* Oxford: Oxford University Press, 2010.

Leget, Carlo. "Eschatology." In *The Theology of Thomas Aquinas,* ed. Rik Van Nieuwenhove and Joseph Wawrykow, 365–85. Notre Dame, Ind.: University of Notre Dame Press, 2005.

———. *Living with God: Thomas Aquinas on the Relation between Life on Earth and "Life" after Death.* Leuven: Peeters, 1997.

Leithart, Peter J. *Defending Constantine: The Twilight of an Empire and the Dawn of Christendom.* Downers Grove, Ill.: IVP Academic, 2010.

———. *1 & 2 Kings.* Grand Rapids: Brazos Press, 2006.

Levenson, Jon D. *The Death and Resurrection of the Beloved Son: The Transformation of Child Sacrifice in Judaism and Christianity.* New Haven: Yale University Press, 1993.

———. *Resurrection and the Restoration of Israel: The Ultimate Victory of the God of Life.* New Haven: Yale University Press, 2006.

———. *Sinai and Zion: An Entry into the Jewish Bible.* San Francisco: Harper & Row, 1985.

Levering, Matthew. *Christ and the Catholic Priesthood: Ecclesial Hierarchy and the Pattern of the Trinity.* Chicago: Hillenbrand Books, 2010.

———. *Christ's Fulfillment of Torah and Temple: Salvation According to Thomas Aquinas.* Notre Dame: University of Notre Dame Press, 2002.

———. "God and Greek Philosophy in Contemporary Biblical Scholarship." *Journal of Theological Interpretation* 4 (2010): 169–85.

———. *Predestination: Biblical and Theological Paths.* Oxford: Oxford University Press, 2011.

———. Review of Michael Fishbane's *Sacred Attunement.* In *Nova et Vetera* 8 (2010): 711–16.

————. Review of Nancey Murphy's *Bodies and Souls, or Spirited Bodies?* In *National Catholic Bioethics Quarterly* 7 (2007): 635–38.

————. *Sacrifice and Community: Jewish Offering and Christian Eucharist.* Oxford: Blackwell, 2005.

Licona, Michael R. *The Resurrection of Jesus: A New Historiographical Approach.* Downers Grove, Ill.: IVP Academic, 2010.

Lincoln, Andrew T. *Paradise Now and Not Yet: Studies in the Role of the Heavenly Dimension in Paul's Thought with Special Reference to His Eschatology.* Cambridge: Cambridge University Press, 1981.

Link, Christian. "Points of Departure for a Christian Eschatology." In Reventlow, *Eschatology in the Bible and in Jewish and Christian Tradition*, 98–110.

Litwa, M. David. "2 Corinthians 3:18 and Its Implications for *Theosis*." *Journal of Theological Interpretation* 2 (2008): 117–33.

Lohfink, Gerhard. *Die Himmelfahrt Jesu: Untersuchungen zu den Himmelfahrts- und Erhöhungstexten bei Lukas.* Munich: Kösel-Verlag, 1971.

Longenecker, Richard. "Is There Development in Paul's Resurrection Thought?" In Longenecker, *Life in the Face of Death*, 171–202.

Longenecker, Richard N., ed. *Life in the Face of Death.* Grand Rapids: Eerdmans, 1998.

Lubac, Henri de, S.J. *Catholicism: A Study of Dogma in Relation to the Corporate Destiny of Mankind.* Trans. Lancelot C. Sheppard. New York: Sheed & Ward, 1958.

————. *De Joachim à Schelling.* Vol. 1 of *La postérité spirituelle de Joachim de Flore.* Paris: Éditions Lethielleux, 1979.

————. *The Motherhood of the Church.* Trans. Sergia Englund, OCD. San Francisco: Ignatius Press, 1982.

————. *The Splendor of the Church.* Trans. Michael Mason. San Francisco: Ignatius Press, 1986.

Lüdemann, Gerd. *The Resurrection of Jesus: History, Experience, Theology.* Trans. John Bowden. Minneapolis: Fortress, 1994.

Lütz, Manfred. "The Church, Love, and Power." In Cordes, *Where Are the Helpers?*, 139–62.

Luzarraga, Jésus. "Eternal Life in the Johannine Writings." *Communio* 18 (1991): 24–34.

Lynn, William D., S.J. *Christ's Redemptive Merit: The Nature of Its Causality According to St. Thomas.* Rome: Gregorian University Press, 1962.

Mach, Michael. "Concepts of Jewish Monotheism during the Hellenistic Period." In Newman, Davila, and Lewis, *The Jewish Roots of Christological Monotheism*, 21–42.

MacIntyre, Alasdair. *Dependent Rational Animals: Why Human Beings Need the Virtues.* Chicago: Open Court, 1999.

————. "Natural Law as Subversive: The Case of Aquinas." In MacIntyre, *Ethics and Politics: Selected Essays*, vol. 2, 41–63. Cambridge: Cambridge University Press, 2006.

————. "What Is a Human Body?" In MacIntyre, *The Tasks of Philosophy: Selected Essays*, vol. 1, 86–103. Cambridge: Cambridge University Press, 2006.

Madigan, Kevin J., and Jon D. Levenson. *Resurrection: The Power of God for Christians and Jews*. New Haven: Yale University Press, 2008.

Maillard, Pierre-Yves. *La vision de Dieu chez Thomas d'Aquin. Une lecture de l'"In Ioannem" à la lumière de ses sources augustiniennes*. Paris: J. Vrin, 2001.

Malloy, Christopher. *Engrafted into Christ: A Critique of the Joint Declaration*. New York: Peter Lang, 2005.

Mangina, Joseph L. *Revelation*. Grand Rapids: Brazos Press, 2010.

Mansini, Guy, OSB. "Mercy 'Twice Blest.'" In *John Paul II and St. Thomas Aquinas*, ed. Michael Dauphinais and Matthew Levering, 75–100. Naples, Fla.: Sapientia Press, 2006.

Marcus, Ralph. "Divine Names and Attributes in Hellenistic Jewish Literature." *Proceedings of the American Academy for Jewish Research* 3 (1931–32): 43–120.

Markschies, Christopher. "'Sessio ad dexteram.' Bemerkungen zu einem altchristlichen Bekenntnismotiv in der christologischen Diskussion altkirchlicher Theologen." In *Le Trône de Dieu*, ed. M. Philonenko. Tübingen, 1993.

Marschler, Thomas. *Auferstehung und Himmelfahrt Christi in der Scholastichen Theologie bis zu Thomas von Aquin*. Münster: Aschendorff, 2003.

Martin, Regis. *The Suffering of Love: Christ's Descent into the Hell of Human Hopelessness*. Petersham, Mass.: St. Bede's, 1995.

Marxsen, Willi. "The Resurrection of Jesus as a Historical and Theological Problem." In *The Significance of the Message of the Resurrection for Faith in Jesus Christ*, ed. C. F. D. Moule, 15–50. London: SCM Press, 1968.

Matera, Frank J. *II Corinthians: A Commentary*. Louisville, Ky.: Westminster John Knox, 2003.

McAleer, G. J. "'I Am Awaited by this Love, and So My Life Is Good': Children and Hope." *Nova et Vetera* 6 (2008): 829–36.

————. *To Kill Another: Homicide and Natural Law*. New Brunswick, N.J.: Transaction Publishers, 2011.

McGuckin, Terence. "The Eschatology of the Cross." *New Blackfriars* 75 (1994): 364–77.

Meeks, Wayne. "Judaism, Hellenism and the Birth of Christianity." In *Paul Beyond the Judaism/Hellenism Divide*, ed. Troels Engberg-Pedersen, 17–28. Louisville, Ky.: Westminster John Knox, 2001.

Melina, Livio. *The Epiphany of Love: Toward a Theological Understanding of Christian Action*. Trans. Susan Dawson Vasquez with Stephan Kampowski. Grand Rapids: Eerdmans, 2010.

Mettinger, Tryggve N. D. *No Graven Image? Israelite Aniconism in Its Ancient Near Eastern Context*. Stockholm: Almqvist & Wiksell, 1995.

Meyers, Carol. *Exodus*. Cambridge: Cambridge University Press, 2005.

Michalson, G. E., Jr. "Pannenberg on the Resurrection and Historical Method." *Scottish Journal of Theology* 33 (1980): 345–59.

Mill, John Stuart. "Utility of Religion." In Mill, *Three Essays on Religion*, 69–122 Amherst, N.Y.: Prometheus Books, 1998.

Miller, Patrick D. "Judgment and Joy." In Polkinghorne and Welker, *The End of the World and the Ends of God*, 155–70.

Miller, Sukie, with Suzanne Lipsett. *After Death: Mapping the Journey*. New York: Simon & Schuster, 1997.

Min, Anselm K. *Paths to the Triune God: An Encounter between Aquinas and Recent Theologies*. Notre Dame: University of Notre Dame Press, 2005.

Molnar, Paul D. *Incarnation and Resurrection: Toward a Contemporary Understanding*. Grand Rapids: Eerdmans, 2007.

Moltmann, Jürgen. *The Coming of God: Christian Eschatology*. Trans. Margaret Kohl. Minneapolis: Fortress, 1996.

———. *History and the Triune God: Contributions to Trinitarian Theology*. Trans. John Bowden. New York: Crossroad, 1991.

———. *In the End—the Beginning: The Life of Hope*. Trans. Margaret Kohl. Minneapolis: Fortress, 2004.

———. "Is There Life after Death?" In Polkinghorne and Welker, *The End of the World and the Ends of God*, 238–55.

Montague, George T. *First and Second Timothy, Titus*. Grand Rapids: Baker Academic, 2008.

Moreira, Isabel. *Heaven's Purge: Purgatory in Late Antiquity*. Oxford: Oxford University Press, 2010.

Morris, Leon. *The Gospel According to John*. Rev. ed. Grand Rapids: Eerdmans, 1995.

Mulholland, M. Robert, Jr. *Revelation: Holy Living in an Unholy World*. Grand Rapids: Zondervan, 1990.

Murphy, Francesca Aran. *God Is Not a Story: Realism Revisited*. Oxford: Oxford University Press, 2007.

Murphy, Nancey. *Bodies and Souls, or Spirited Bodies?* Cambridge: Cambridge University Press, 2006.

———. "Response to Derek Jeffreys." *Theology and Science* 2 (2004): 227–30.

———. "The Resurrection Body and Personal Identity: Possibilities and

Limits of Eschatological Knowledge." In Peters, Russell, and Welker, *Resurrection: Theological and Scientific Assessments*, 202–18.

Neusner, Jacob. *Rabbinic Judaism: The Theological System*. Boston: Brill Academic, 2002.

Newman, Carey C., ed. *Jesus and the Restoration of Israel: A Critical Assessment of N. T. Wright's "Jesus and the Victory of God."* Downers Grove, Ill: Inter-Varsity, 1999.

———. *Paul's Glory-Christology: Tradition and Rhetoric*. Leiden: Brill, 1991.

———. "Resurrection as Glory: Divine Presence and Christian Origins." In Davis, Kendall, and O'Collins, *The Resurrection*, 59–89.

Newman, Carey C., James R. Davila, and Gladys S. Lewis, eds. *The Jewish Roots of Christological Monotheism*. Leiden: Brill, 1999.

Nichols, Aidan, O.P. *No Bloodless Myth: A Guide through Balthasar's Dramatics*. Washington, D.C.: Catholic University of America Press, 2000.

Nichols, Terence L. "Aquinas's Concept of Substantial Form and Modern Science." *International Philosophical Quarterly* 36 (1996): 303–18.

———. *Death and Afterlife: A Theological Introduction*. Grand Rapids: Brazos Press, 2010.

Nickelsburg, George W. E. *1 Enoch: A Commentary on the Book of 1 Enoch*. Minneapolis: Fortress, 2001.

———. *Resurrection, Immortality, and Eternal Life in Intertestamental Judaism*. Cambridge, Mass.: Harvard University Press, 1972.

———. *Resurrection, Immortality, and Eternal Life in Intertestamental Judaism and Early Christianity*. 2nd ed. Cambridge, Mass.: Harvard University Press, 2006.

Norman, David J., O.F.M. "Doubt and the Resurrection of Jesus." *Theological Studies* 69 (2008): 786–811.

Novak, David. "Law and Eschatology: A Jewish-Christian Intersection." In *The Last Things: Biblical and Theological Perspectives on Eschatology*, ed. Carl E. Braaten and Robert W. Jenson, 90–112. Grand Rapids: Eerdmans, 2002.

Ntedika, Konde. *L'évolution de la doctrine du purgatoire chez Saint Augustin*. Paris: Études Augustiniennes, 1966.

Oakes, Edward T., S.J. *Pattern of Redemption: The Theology of Hans Urs von Balthasar*. New York: Continuum, 1994.

Oakes, Edward T., S.J., and David Moss, eds. *The Cambridge Companion to Hans Urs von Balthasar*. Cambridge: Cambridge University Press, 2004.

O'Callaghan, Paul. *Christ Our Hope: An Introduction to Eschatology*. Washington, D.C.: Catholic University of America Press, 2011.

O'Collins, Gerald, S.J. "Augustine on the Resurrection." In *Saint Augustine the Bishop: A Book of Essays*, ed. F. LeMoine and C. Kleinhenz, 65–75. New York: Garland, 1994.

————. "Christ's Resurrection as Mystery of Love." *Heythrop Journal* 25 (1984): 39–50.

————. *Interpreting the Resurrection*. Mahwah, N.J.: Paulist Press, 1988.

————. *Jesus: A Portrait*. London: Darton, Longman & Todd, 2008.

————. *Jesus Risen: An Historical, Fundamental, and Systematic Examination of Christ's Resurrection*. New York: Paulist Press, 1987.

————. "The Resurrection: The State of the Questions." In Davis, Kendall, and O'Collins, *The Resurrection*, 5–28.

O'Connor, Terence M. *The Obligation of Almsgiving in Common Necessity According to St. Thomas*. Lake Bluff, Ill.: Pontifical Institutum "Angelicum" de Urbe, 1959.

O'Donovan, Oliver. *Resurrection and Moral Order: An Outline for Evangelical Ethics*. 2nd ed. Grand Rapids: Eerdmans, 1994.

Osborne, Thomas M., Jr. "Unbelief and Sin in Thomas Aquinas and the Thomistic Tradition." *Nova et Vetera* 8 (2010): 613–26.

Osiek, Carolyn. "The Women at the Tomb: What Were They Doing There?" *Ex Auditu* 9 (1993): 97–107.

Pannenberg, Wolfhart. "Constructive and Critical Functions of Christian Eschatology." *Harvard Theological Review* 77 (1984): 119–39.

————. *Jesus: God and Man*. Trans. L. L. Wilkins and D. A. Priebe. London: SCM Press, 1968.

————. *Systematic Theology*, vol. 3. Trans. Geoffrey W. Bromiley. Grand Rapids: Eerdmans, 1998.

Pauw, Amy Plantinga. "'Heaven Is a World of Love': Edwards on Heaven and the Trinity." *Calvin Theological Journal* 30 (1995): 392–401.

Pedersen, Johannes. *Israel: Its Life and Culture*. Atlanta: Scholars Press, 1991.

Pedraja, Luis G. "Eschatology." In *Handbook of Latina/o Theologies*, ed. Edwin David Aponte and Miguel A. De La Torre, 114–20. St. Louis, Mo.: Chalice Press, 2006.

Pegis, Anton C. "Between Immortality and Death: Some Further Reflections on the *Summa Contra Gentiles*." *Monist* 58 (1974): 1–15.

Pelikan, Jaroslav. *Christianity and Classical Culture: The Metamorphosis of Natural Theology in the Christian Encounter with Hellenism*. New Haven: Yale University Press, 1993.

Perham, Michael. *The Communion of Saints: An Examination of the Place of the Christian Dead in the Belief, Worship, and Calendars of the Church*. London: SPCK, 1980.

Perler, Dominik. "Alter und neuer Naturalismus. Eine historische Hinführung zur aktuellen Debatte über die Leib-Seele-Problematik." In *Naturalisierung des Geistes—Sprachlosigkeit der Theologie? Die Mind-Brain-Debatte und das christliche Menschenbild*, ed. Peter Neuner, 15–42. Freiburg: Herder, 2003.

Pesch, Otto Hermann. *Thomas von Aquin: Grenze und Größe mittelalterlicher Theologie.* Mainz: Matthias-Grünewald-Verlag, 1988.

Peter, Carl J. *Participated Eternity in the Vision of God: A Study of the Opinion of Thomas Aquinas and His Commentators on the Duration of the Acts of Glory.* Rome: Gregorian University Press, 1964.

Peters, Ted. *God—The World's Future.* 2nd ed. Minneapolis: Fortress, 2000.

Peters, Ted, Robert John Russell, and Michael Welker, eds. *Resurrection: Theological and Scientific Assessments.* Grand Rapids: Eerdmans, 2002.

Petry, Ray C. *Christian Eschatology and Social Thought: A Historical Essay on the Social Implications of Some Selected Aspects in Christian Eschatology to A.D. 1500.* Nashville: Abingdon, 1956.

———. "The Social Character of Heavenly Beatitude According to the Thought of St. Thomas Aquinas." *Thomist* 7 (1944): 65–79.

Phan, Peter C. "Contemporary Context and Issues in Eschatology." *Theological Studies* 55 (1994): 507–36.

———. "Eschatology." In *The Cambridge Companion to Karl Rahner*, ed. Declan Marmion and Mary E. Hines, 174–92. Cambridge: Cambridge University Press, 2005.

———. *Eternity in Time: A Study of Karl Rahner's Eschatology.* London: Associated University Presses, 1988.

Pieper, Josef. *Death and Immortality.* Trans. Richard and Clara Winston. South Bend, Ind.: St. Augustine's Press, 1999.

———. *The End of Time: A Meditation on the Philosophy of History.* Trans. Michael Bullock. San Francisco: Ignatius Press, 1999.

———. *Hope and History: Five Salzburg Lectures.* Trans. David Kipp. San Francisco: Ignatius Press, 1994.

———. *The Platonic Myths.* Trans. Dan Farrelly. South Bend, Ind.: St. Augustine's Press, 2011.

Pinckaers, Servais, O.P. *The Pursuit of Happiness—God's Way: Living the Beatitudes.* Trans. Mary Thomas Noble. New York: Alba House, 1998.

———. *The Sources of Christian Ethics.* Trans. Mary Thomas Noble. Washington, D.C.: Catholic University Press, 1995.

Pitstick, Alyssa Lyra. *Light in Darkness: Hans Urs von Balthasar and the Catholic Doctrine of Christ's Descent into Hell.* Grand Rapids: Eerdmans, 2007.

Plato. *The Collected Dialogues.* Ed. Edith Hamilton and Huntington Cairns. Princeton: Princeton University Press, 1961.

Polkinghorne, John. "Eschatology: Some Questions and Some Insights from Science." In Polkinghorne and Welker, *The End of the World and the Ends of God*, 29–41.

Polkinghorne, John, and Michael Welker, eds. *The End of the World and the*

Ends of God: Science and Theology on Eschatology. Harrisburg, Pa.: Trinity Press International, 2000.

Powers, Daniel G. *Salvation through Participation: An Examination of the Notion of the Believers' Corporate Unity with Christ in Early Christian Soteriology.* Leuven: Peeters, 2001.

Prusak, Bernard P. "Bodily Resurrection in Catholic Perspectives." *Theological Studies* 61 (2000): 64–105.

Puchniak, Robert. "Augustine's Conception of Deification, Revisited." In Finlan and Kharlamov, *Theōsis*, 122–33.

Rahner, Karl. "The Hermeneutics of Eschatological Assertions." In Rahner, *Theological Investigations*, vol. 4, trans. Kevin Smyth, 323–46. Baltimore: Helicon, 1966.

———. "Hidden Victory." In Rahner, *Theological Investigations*, vol. 7, trans. David Bourke, 151–58. New York: Herder, 1971.

———. "'The Intermediate State.'" In Rahner, *Theological Investigations*, vol. 17, trans. Margaret Kohl, 114–24. New York: Crossroad, 1981.

———. "The Life of the Dead." In Rahner, *Theological Investigations*, vol. 4, trans. Kevin Smyth, 347–54. Baltimore: Helicon, 1966.

Ratzinger, Joseph (see also Benedict XVI [pope]). *Eschatology: Death and Eternal Life.* Trans. Michael Waldstein and Aidan Nichols, O.P. 2nd ed. Washington, D.C.: Catholic University of America Press, 2007.

———. *Faith and the Future.* San Francisco: Ignatius Press, 2009.

———. "Faith, Reason and the University: Memories and Reflections (The Regensburg Lecture)." Appendix 1 in James V. Schall, S.J., *The Regensburg Lecture.* South Bend, Ind.: St. Augustine's Press, 2007.

———. *Introduction to Christianity.* Trans. J. R. Foster. San Francisco: Ignatius Press, 2004.

———. *Jesus of Nazareth: From the Baptism in the Jordan to the Transfiguration.* Trans. Adrian J. Walker. New York: Doubleday, 2007.

———. *Light of the World: The Pope, the Church, and the Signs of the Times: A Conversation with Peter Seewald.* Trans. Michael J. Miller and Adrian J. Walker. San Francisco: Ignatius Press, 2010.

———. "The Sign of the Woman: An Introduction to the Encyclical 'Redemptoris Mater.'" In *Mary: God's Yes to Man*, 9–40. San Francisco: Ignatius Press, 1988.

Rauschenbusch, Walter. *Christianity and the Social Crisis.* Ed. Paul B. Raushenbush. New York: HarperCollins, 2007.

Reno, R. R. *Genesis.* Grand Rapids: Brazos Press, 2010.

Reventlow, Henning Graf, ed. *Eschatology in the Bible and in Jewish and Christian Tradition.* Sheffield: Sheffield Academic Press, 1997.

Root, Michael. "Aquinas, Merit, and Reformation Theology after the *Joint Declaration on the Doctrine of Justification.*" *Modern Theology* 20 (2004): 5–22.

Rorty, Richard. *Philosophy and Social Hope.* New York: Penguin, 1999.

Rose, Seraphim. *The Soul after Death: Contemporary "After-Death" Experiences in Light of the Orthodox Teaching on the Afterlife.* Platina, Calif.: St. Herman of Alaska Brotherhood, 2009.

Rosenberg, Randall S. "Being-Toward-a-Death-Transformed: Aquinas on the Naturalness and Unnaturalness of Human Death." *Angelicum* 83 (2006): 747–66.

Rowe, C. Kavin. *Early Narrative Christology: The Lord in the Gospel of Luke.* New York: Walter de Gruyter, 2006.

———. *World Upside Down: Reading Acts in the Graeco-Roman Age.* Oxford: Oxford University Press, 2009.

Ruello, Francis. "'La resurrection des corps sera l'oeuvre du Christ': Raison et foi au Moyen Âge." *Les Quatre Fleuves* 15–16 (1982): 93–112.

Russell, Norman. *The Doctrine of Deification in the Greek Patristic Tradition.* Oxford: Oxford University Press, 2004.

Salkeld, Brett. *Can Catholics and Evangelicals Agree about Purgatory and the Last Judgment?* Mahwah, N.J.: Paulist Press, 2011.

Sanders, E. P. "Did Paul's Theology Develop?" In *The Word Leaps the Gap: Essays on Scripture and Theology in Honor of Richard B. Hays*, ed. J. Ross Wagner, C. Kavin Rowe, and A. Katherine Grieb, 325–50. Grand Rapids: Eerdmans, 2008.

Savage, Timothy B. *Power through Weakness: Paul's Understanding of the Christian Ministry in 2 Corinthians.* Cambridge: Cambridge University Press, 1996.

Saward, John. *Sweet and Blessed Country: The Christian Hope for Heaven.* Oxford: Oxford University Press, 2005.

Schenk, Richard, O.P. "*And Jesus Wept*: Notes towards a Theology of Mourning." In Dauphinais and Levering, *Reading John with St. Thomas Aquinas*, 212–37.

Schmemann, Alexander. *For the Life of the World: Sacraments and Orthodoxy.* 2nd ed. Crestwood, N.Y.: St. Vladimir's Seminary Press, 1973.

———. *Great Lent: Journey to Pascha.* Rev. ed. Crestwood, New York: St. Vladimir's Seminary Press, 1974.

Schnackenburg, Rudolph. *The Epistle to the Ephesians: A Commentary.* Trans. Helen Heron. Edinburgh: T&T Clark, 1991.

———. *The Gospel of Matthew.* Trans. Robert R. Barr. Grand Rapids: Eerdmans, 2002.

————. *The Johannine Epistles: Introduction and Commentary.* Trans. Reginald and Ilse Fuller. New York: Crossroad, 1992.

Schneemelcher, W., ed. *New Testament Apocrypha*, vol. 1. Philadelphia: Westminster, 1963.

Schönborn, Christoph, O.P. *From Death to Life: The Christian Journey.* Trans. Brian McNeil, C.R.V. San Francisco: Ignatius Press, 1995.

Schumacher, Bernard. *Death and Mortality in Contemporary Philosophy.* Trans. Michael J. Miller. Cambridge: Cambridge University Press, 2011.

Schwarz, Hans. *Eschatology.* Grand Rapids: Eerdmans, 2000.

Schwöbel, Christoph. "Last Things First? The Century of Eschatology in Retrospect." In Fergusson and Sarot, *The Future as God's Gift*, 217–40.

Scola, Angelo. "Jesus Christ, Our Resurrection and Life: On the Question of Eschatology." Trans. Margaret Harper McCarthy. *Communio* 24 (1997): 311–25.

Scott, James M., ed. *Exile: Old Testament, Jewish and Christian Conceptions.* Leiden: Brill, 1997.

Segal, Alan. *Life after Death: A History of Afterlife in the Religions of the West.* New York: Doubleday, 2004.

Seitz, Christopher R. "'In Accordance with the Scriptures': Creed, Scripture, and 'Historical Jesus.'" In Seitz, *Word without End: The Old Testament as Abiding Theological Witness*, 51–60. Grand Rapids: Eerdmans, 1998.

Setzer, Claudia. *Resurrection of the Body in Early Judaism and Early Christianity: Doctrine, Community, and Self-Definition.* Leiden: Brill, 2004.

Shavit, Yaacov. *Athens in Jerusalem: Classical Antiquity and Hellenism in the Making of the Modern Secular Jew.* Trans. Chaya Naor and Niki Werner. London: Littman Library of Jewish Civilization, 1997.

Sheehan, Jonathan. *The Enlightenment Bible: Translation, Scholarship, Culture.* Princeton: Princeton University Press, 2005.

Simonetti, Manlio, ed. *Matthew 14-28.* Ancient Christian Commentary on Scripture, vol. 1b. Downers Grove, Ill.: InterVarsity, 2002.

Smith, Jane Idleman, and Yvonne Yazbeck Haddad. *The Islamic Understanding of Death and Resurrection.* Oxford: Oxford University Press, 2002.

Smith, Janet E. "Come and See.'" In Dauphinais and Levering, *Reading John with St. Thomas Aquinas*, 194–211.

Smith, Mark S. *The Early History of God: Yahweh and the Other Deities in Ancient Israel.* 2nd ed. Grand Rapids: Eerdmans, 2002.

————. *The Origins of Biblical Monotheism.* Oxford: Oxford University Press, 2003.

Sommer, Benjamin D. *The Bodies of God and the World of Ancient Israel.* Cambridge: Cambridge University Press, 2009.

Speyr, Adrienne von. *The Birth of the Church.* Vol. 4 of *Johannes.* San Francisco: Ignatius Press, 1994.

———. *The Mystery of Death.* Trans. Graham Harrison. San Francisco: Ignatius Press, 1988.

Spong, John Shelby. *Eternal Life: A New Vision: Beyond Religion, beyond Theism, beyond Heaven and Hell.* New York: HarperCollins, 2009.

Starr, James. "Does 2 Peter 1:4 Speak of Deification?" In *Partakers of the Divine Nature: The History and Development of Deification in the Christian Traditions,* ed. Michael J. Christensen and Jeffery A. Wittung, 81–92. Grand Rapids: Baker Academic, 2007.

Still, Carl N. "Do We Know All after Death? Thomas Aquinas on the Disembodied Soul's Knowledge." *Proceedings of the American Catholic Philosophical Association* 75 (2001): 107–19.

Strauss, David Friedrich. *The Life of Jesus Critically Examined.* Trans. George Eliot. Philadelphia: Fortress, 1972.

Strousma, Guy G. *The End of Sacrifice: Religious Transformations in Late Antiquity.* Trans. Susan Emanuel. Chicago: University of Chicago, 2009.

Stump, Eleonore. *Aquinas.* London: Routledge, 2003.

Taliaferro, Charles. "Why We Need Immortality." *Modern Theology* 6 (1990): 367–77.

Tertullian. "The Prescription against Heretics." Trans. Peter Holmes. In *Latin Christianity: Its Founder, Tertullian,* ed. A. Cleveland Coxe. *Ante-Nicene Fathers,* vol. 3. Peabody, Mass.: Hendrickson, 1994.

Thiel, John. "For What May We Hope? Thoughts on the Eschatological Imagination." *Theological Studies* 67 (2006): 517–41.

Thiselton, Anthony C. *The First Epistle to the Corinthians: A Commentary on the Greek Text.* Grand Rapids: Eerdmans, 2000.

Thompson, Marianne Meye. *Colossians and Philemon.* Grand Rapids: Eerdmans, 2005.

Toom, Tarmo. "*Totus homo*: Augustine on Resurrection." In *Resurrection and Responsibility: Essays on Theology, Scripture, and Ethics in Honor of Thorwald Lorenzen,* ed. Keith D. Dyer and David J. Neville, 59–73. Eugene, Ore.: Pickwick, 2009.

Torrell, Jean-Pierre, O.P. *Aquinas's Summa: Background, Structure, and Reception.* Trans. Benedict M. Guevin, O.S.B. Washington, D.C.: Catholic University of America Press, 2005.

———. "La causalité salvifique de la resurrection du Christ selon saint Thomas." *Revue Thomiste* 96 (1996): 179–208.

———. "Le sacerdoce du Christ dans la *Somme de théologie.*" *Revue Thomiste* 99 (1999): 75–100.

218 • Jesus and the Demise of Death

————. *Spiritual Master*. Vol. 2 of *Saint Thomas Aquinas*. Trans. Robert Royal. Washington, D.C.: Catholic University of America Press, 2003.

Trick, Bradley R. "Death, Covenants, and the Proof of Resurrection in Mark 12:18-27." *Novum Testamentum* 49 (2007): 232–56.

Trottmann, Christian. *La vision béatifique. Des disputes scolastiques à sa définition par Benoît XII*. Rome: École française de Rome, 1995.

Tucker, J. Brian. *You Belong to Christ: Paul and the Formation of Social Identity in 1 Corinthians 1–4*. Eugene, Ore.: Pickwick, 2010.

Tugwell, Simon, O.P. *Human Immortality and the Redemption of Death*. Springfield, Ill.: Templegate, 1990.

Turner, Ralph V. "*Descendit ad inferos*: Medieval Views on Christ's Descent into Hell and the Salvation of the Ancient Just." *Journal of the History of Ideas* 27 (1966): 173–94.

Valkenberg, Pim. "Aquinas and Christ's Resurrection: The Influence of the *Lectura super Ioannem* 20-21 on the *Summa theologiae*." In Dauphinais and Levering, *Reading John with St. Thomas Aquinas*, 277–89.

Vatican Council II: The Conciliar and Post Conciliar Documents. Vol. 1. New rev. ed. Ed. Austin Flannery, O.P. Northport, N.Y.: Costello, 1998.

Vattimo, Gianni. *After Christianity*. Trans. Luca D'Isanto. New York: Columbia University Press, 2002.

Verhey, Allen. *The Great Reversal: Ethics and the New Testament*. Grand Rapids: Eerdmans, 1984.

Vermes, Geza. *The Resurrection: History and Myth*. New York: Doubleday, 2008.

Vinzent, Markus. *Pseudo-Athanasius, Contra Arianos IV. Eine Schrift gegen Asterius von Kappadokien, Eusebius von Cäsarea, Markell von Ankyra und Photin von Sirmium*. Leiden: Brill, 1996.

Viviano, Benedict T., O.P. *The Kingdom of God in History*. Eugene, Ore.: Wipf & Stock, 2002.

Volf, Miroslav. "After Moltmann: Reflections on the Future of Eschatology." In Bauckham, *God Will Be All in All*, 233–57.

————. "Enter into Joy! Sin, Death, and the Life of the World to Come." In Polkinghorne and Welker, *The End of the World and the Ends of God*, 256–78.

Vonier, Anscar, O.S.B. *A Key to the Doctrine of the Eucharist*. Bethesda, Md.: Zaccheus Press, 2003.

Wainwright, Geoffrey. "Eschatology." In Oakes and Moss, *The Cambridge Companion to Hans Urs von Balthasar*, 113–30.

————. *Eucharist and Eschatology*. Peterborough: Epworth Press, 2003.

Wall, Robert W. *The Acts of the Apostles: Introduction, Commentary, and Reflections*. In Keck, *The New Interpreter's Bible*, vol. 10.

Walls, Jerry L. *Heaven: The Logic of Eternal Joy.* Oxford: Oxford University Press, 2002.

Ware, Kallistos. *The Orthodox Way.* Rev. ed. Crestwood, N.Y.: St. Vladimir's Seminary Press, 2002.

Wawrykow, Joseph P. *God's Grace and Human Action: "Merit" in the Theology of Thomas Aquinas.* Notre Dame: University of Notre Dame Press, 1995.

Weber, Hermann J. *Die Lehre von der Auferstehung der Toten in den Haupttraktaten der scholastischen Theologie von Alexander von Hales zu Duns Skotus.* Freiburg: Herder, 1973.

Weinandy, Thomas G., O.F.M. Cap. "The Human Acts of Christ and the Acts That Are the Sacraments." In *Ressourcement Thomism: Sacred Doctrine, the Sacraments, and the Moral Life,* ed. Reinhard Hütter and Matthew Levering, 150–68. Washington, D.C.: Catholic University of America Press, 2010.

Weinandy, Thomas G., O.F.M. Cap., Daniel A. Keating, and John P. Yocum, eds. *Aquinas on Doctrine: A Critical Introduction.* New York: T&T Clark, 2004.

Welker, Michael. "Resurrection and Eternal Life: The Canonic Memory of the Resurrected Christ, His Reality, and His Glory." In Polkinghorne and Welker, *The End of the World and the Ends of God,* 279–90.

———. "Wright on the Resurrection." *Scottish Journal of Theology* 60 (2007): 458–75.

Werner, Martin. *Die Entstehung des christlichen Dogmas.* Bern: P. Haupt, 1941.

White, Thomas Joseph, O.P. *Wisdom in the Face of Modernity: A Study in Thomistic Natural Theology.* Ave Maria, Fla.: Sapientia Press, 2009.

Wicki, Nikolaus. *Die Lehre von der himmlischen Seligkeit in der mittelalterlichen Scholastik von Petrus Lombardus bis Thomas von Aquin.* Freiburg: Universitätsverlag, 1954.

Williams, A. N. *The Ground of Union: Deification in Aquinas and Palamas.* Oxford: Oxford University Press, 1999.

Williams, Stephen. "Thirty Years of Hope: A Generation of Writing on Eschatology." In Brower and Elliott, *Eschatology in Bible and Theology,* 243–62.

Witherington, Ben, III. *Jesus, Paul, and the End of the World: A Comparative Study in New Testament Eschatology.* Downers Grove, Ill.: InterVarsity, 1992.

———. *Jesus the Sage: The Pilgrimage of Wisdom.* Minneapolis: Fortress, 2000.

———. *John's Wisdom: A Commentary on the Fourth Gospel.* Louisville, Ky.: Westminster John Knox, 1995.

———. *Matthew.* Macon, Ga.: Smyth & Helwys, 2006.

———. *Revelation.* Cambridge: Cambridge University Press, 2003.

————. *A Socio-Rhetorical Commentary on 1–2 Peter*. Vol. 2 of *Letters and Homilies for Hellenized Christians*. Downers Grove, Ill.: IVP Academic, 2007.

Witherington, Ben, III and Laura M. Ice. *The Shadow of the Almighty: Father, Son, and Spirit in Biblical Perspective*. Grand Rapids: Eerdmans, 2002.

Wohlmuth, Josef. *Mysterium der Verwandlung. Eine Eschatologie aus katholischer Perspektive im Gespräch mit jüdischem Denken der Gegenwart*. Paderborn: Ferdinand Schöningh, 2005.

Wright, N. T. *The Challenge of Jesus: Rediscovering Who Jesus Was and Is*. Downers Grove, Ill.: InterVarsity, 1999.

————. "An Incompleat (but Grateful) Response to the Review by Markus Bockmuehl of *The Resurrection of the Son of God*." *Journal for the Study of the New Testament* 26 (2004): 505–10.

————. *Jesus and the Victory of God*. Minneapolis: Fortress, 1996.

————. *Justification: God's Plan and Paul's Vision*. Downers Grove, Ill.: IVP Academic, 2009.

————. *The Letter to the Romans: Introduction, Commentary, and Reflections*. In Keck, *The New Interpreter's Bible*, vol. 10.

————. *The New Testament and the People of God*. Minneapolis: Fortress, 1992.

————. "Reflected Glory: 2 Corinthians 3.18." In *The Climax of the Covenant: Christ and the Law in Pauline Theology*, 175–92. Minneapolis: Fortress, 1992.

————. "Response to Markus Bockmuehl." In *Jesus, Paul and the People of God: A Theological Dialogue with N. T. Wright*, ed. Nicholas Perrin and Richard B. Hays, 231–34. Downers Grove, Ill.: InterVarsity, 2011.

————. *The Resurrection of the Son of God*. Minneapolis: Fortress, 2003.

————. *Surprised by Hope: Rethinking Heaven, the Resurrection, and the Mission of the Church*. New York: HarperCollins, 2008.

Yoder, John Howard. "The Restitution of the Church: An Alternative Perspective on Christian History." In Yoder, *The Jewish-Christian Schism Revisited*, ed. Michael G. Cartwright and Peter Ochs, 133–44. Grand Rapids: Eerdmans, 2003.

Index

Aaron, David H., 154n15

Acts, Book of, 3, 5–6, 18, 38, 40, 43–44, 49, 50, 59, 63–67, 69, 72, 82, 151n42, 161n17

adoption, 5, 54, 89–92, 94, 112, 144n1, 171n29

Alfeyev, Hilarion, 21, 24, 26

alienation, 19, 141n26, 166n89

Allison, Dale, 2, 28, 33, 59, 104

almsgiving, 3, 65, 68, 73, 77–83, 85–89, 93–94, 110, 119, 159n5, 161n17, 168n112, 169n7

Ambrose, 81–82

Anderson, Gary, 86–89, 93–94, 168n4

angels, 5, 20, 39–42, 45–46, 54, 78, 102, 118, 125, 133n11

apocalyptic, 1, 33, 34, 116, 145n12, 159n6, 161n18, 178n53

Apostles' Creed, 2, 4–5, 11, 142n38

Aquinas, Thomas, 1–3, 8, 11, 16, 22–26, 28, 34–42, 44, 47–60, 65, 73–83, 86, 89–94, 98–102, 107, 110–22, 124, 132n5, 135n27, 142nn43, 44, 143nn47, 50, 144n57, 150nn40, 41, 151n52, 155n33, 157nn73, 85, 158n105, 164nn46, 47, 50, 165n55, 167n90, 170nn17, 20, 171nn27, 29, 172nn34, 37, 38, 40, 174n17, 175nn28, 29, 176n29, 179n13, 180n22, 182n38, 183n40, 184nn46, 47, n51, 185nn56, 58, 60, 186n73, 187n78

Aristotle, 7, 50, 174n17

Athanasius, 21

Augustine, 5, 22, 50–51, 53, 75, 78, 87, 114, 116, 118, 128, 135n27, 142n43, 143n50, 157n82, 158n96

Ayres, Lewis, 97, 173n1

baptism, 22, 38, 64–65, 75

Barth, Karl, 8, 141n30

Bauckham, Richard, 3, 9, 46, 52, 83, 112, 133n15, 145n13, 155n22, n23,

221